LONDON
HIDDEN INTERIORS

ENGLISH HERITAGE

LONDON
HIDDEN INTERIORS

Philip Davies

Photography by
Derek Kendall

ATLANTIC PUBLISHING

To all those in the London Region of English Heritage,
and its predecessor, the GLC Historic Buildings Division,
without whose dedication and skill many of the
buildings illustrated here would no longer exist.
London owes them a great debt.

Atlantic Publishing
First published in 2012
Reprinted 2014

Atlantic Publishing
38 Copthorne Road, Croxley Green
Hertfordshire, WD3 4AQ, UK

© Atlantic Publishing 2012
Text © Philip Davies
Photographs from English Heritage — see page 447

A catalogue record is available for this book
from the British Library

ISBN 978-0-9568642-4-6

Also available in the USA from Welcome Rain:
ISBN 978-1-5664-9976-7

Printed and bound in China

Contents

Introduction

I love thee, London! …
Thou art the greatest thing on the earth's face
That man hath made; thou art what man can do.
Let the world worship God! ye cities, bow!
And last and lowest, thou, proud London, thou!

Philip James Bailey (1816-1902)

The decades between 1900 and 1940, wrote the historian Harold Clunn, "witnessed the greatest amount of rebuilding all over the metropolis that has ever taken place within so short a period of time since the Great Fire of London".

Lost London 1870-1945 and *Panoramas of Lost London* looked at the buildings and places which were swept away in this process as London was transformed from an essentially domestic-scaled city of 18th and 19th century terraces into a great world metropolis. In the early part of the 20th century, as older buildings and districts were levelled to make way for a new city, some of London's most important historic buildings and their interiors were demolished – down came the mediaeval coaching inns of Southwark and Holborn, down came the great aristocratic houses of Mayfair and the West End, down came the Adelphi, the Foundling Hospital and Nash's Regent Street; and in the City of London, down came Smirke's General Post Office, Christ's Hospital and Newgate Prison, along with countless other vernacular buildings, pubs, shops and houses that had stood for centuries across the capital.

Many believed that little of London's rich and ancient architectural heritage would survive such a sustained onslaught. "London cares nothing for its past," lamented the writer H J Massingham in 1933, but increasingly it did. Public reaction added real momentum to the growth of the conservation movement as it developed into an articulate and influential force in the 1930s. By 1939 London had been reconstructed

St Pancras Renaissance Hotel: The grand staircase is one of London's most glorious Gothic interiors. Although not original, the blood red walls and fleur de lys decoration were restored at the insistence of the author to maintain its dramatic spatial quality.

to become the world's largest and greatest city, but it was also one that stood on the brink of catastrophe.

Almost exactly a year after the outbreak of the Second World War, on Black Saturday, 7 September 1940, an armada of 1,000 German planes appeared over the city in a formation so vast it spread over 800 square miles and blocked out the sun. When they departed, large areas of the docks and the East End lay ablaze, and over 2,000 Londoners lay dead or seriously injured in the smouldering ruins below.

"London can take it" was the watchword of the day, and it did too; but it paid a shocking price. It would never be the same again. After five more years of total war, 29,890 Londoners were killed and over 50,000 were seriously injured, many of whom never fully recovered.

The level of devastation was immense – on a scale not seen since the Great Fire of London in 1666. Acres of London were laid waste. One in six of its buildings was damaged or destroyed, and many of its most treasured historic buildings and landmarks lay in ruins. In the City of London over one-third of the structures were levelled. Twenty of the City's 47 churches were gutted, along with 17 historic livery company halls. Six more were badly damaged, although miraculously the Apothecaries, Ironmongers and Vintners escaped. The ancient halls and libraries of Inner Temple and Gray's Inn were destroyed, and Middle Temple Hall and Staple Inn bombed. London's historic docks were devastated, and the Guildhall, the Palace of Westminster, Lambeth Palace and the British Museum all severely damaged. Great gaps were rent in the familiar backcloth of London's elegant Georgian squares as the fabric of entire terraces was torn apart by bombing. West London generally escaped more lightly, but Chelsea Old Church was lost and the great Jacobean mansion Holland House gutted by fire. In the historic inner London districts of Holborn, Shoreditch and Finsbury, 19 per cent of the entire built-up area was lost; in Southwark and Bermondsey, 15 per cent.

Given the remorseless pace of change from 1870 onwards, and the catastrophic damage inflicted during the Second World War, one might be forgiven for thinking that much of London's architectural heritage had been obliterated, and that what survived was given the *coup de grace* by insensitive post-war planning and architecture. But this is not the case.

Many historic buildings, of course, survived intact, if somewhat battered and frayed, and after the war many of those which had been ravaged by bombing were restored – quietly, painstakingly and with great sensitivity; not least the Palace of Westminster, Buckingham Palace, the Guildhall and a dozen or so Wren churches. But it was not just the famous set pieces that benefited; elsewhere, at a time of great national shortages, bold decisions were taken to reinstate many other historic buildings and their priceless interiors with skill and craftsmanship as a very visible symbol of national resurgence. As a consequence, in spite of the scale of change over the previous 75 years and the extent of wartime damage, a wealth of treasures can still be found hidden behind London's inscrutable façades about which the public knows little, or of which it is only dimly aware.

Having been responsible for managing change to London's historic structures and places for over 40 years, I have been fortunate to have had access to a whole range of buildings, from the great offices of state and government to the citadels of industry and commerce. The purpose of this book is for the first time to give the general public an opportunity to share this experience, using privileged access to the buildings to acquire 1,700 superb colour photographs, most of which have been taken specifically for this publication by the gifted photographer Derek Kendall, who has devoted his career to capturing the intangible character of historic buildings and places across the country with consummate skill and understanding.

In contrast to the perceived lack of concern at the loss of so much of London's heritage in the first part of the 20th century, today there is unprecedented public interest in its history and buildings and, not least, what lies behind closed doors inside the offices, institutions,

Pollock's Toy Museum: A house of wonders and a gateway into the timeless world of childhood.

clubs and private houses that so many pass unwittingly every day; from the discreet grandeur of Whitehall and clubland to the fascinating subterranean spaces that lie beneath the capital. The hugely popular annual Open House London event has created access to over 750 buildings and places normally closed to the public and now attracts over a quarter of a million visitors.

London: Hidden Interiors covers 180 examples, which have been selected from a complete range of building types to convey the richness and diversity of London's architectural heritage, and the secrets that lie within. Nothing on this scale has ever been attempted before, and the size and complexity of the project means that it is unlikely ever to be repeated. Each has had to earn its place, and many deserve much greater coverage than can be accorded here. Almost every building type has been the subject of entire books or thematic studies. For those interested in exploring more, there is an extended bibliography of further reading. Many of the buildings are private and not open to the public. Where limited or full public access is possible, details can be found on the website at www.londonhiddeninteriors.co.uk.

The selection is an entirely personal one. It concentrates generally on the buildings and interiors that are lesser known and to which the public are not normally allowed – the hidden and the unusual, the quirky and the eccentric – although there is space too for some of the better known, like the Soane Museum (p160) and Eltham Palace (p354). A number celebrate unsung conservation successes of recent years, which deserve greater recognition.

Many of London's finest interiors are well known, or readily accessible to the public or the inquisitive observer, and for that reason much of the familiar has been excluded. London has a rich legacy of museums commemorating dozens of individuals from Dickens, Keats, Handel, Carlyle and Hogarth to William Morris, Francisco di Miranda, Alexander Fleming and Benjamin Franklin, and a host of specialist subjects from the Ragged School to musical instruments, cinema, canals, tea, fans and even packaging and advertising. Generally the popular visitor attractions run by English Heritage and the National Trust have been eschewed here in favour of London's more offbeat and unusual museums, like the Ophthalmic Museum in Craven Street (p174) with its extraordinary collection of glass eyes, the Pathology Museum at St Bartholomew's Hospital (p200) with its unparalleled collection of medical specimens, the enchanting Pollock's Toy Museum (p131) and the obscure Petrie and Grant collections at University College, London (p132 & p134). Alas, room could not be found for many other fascinating and eccentric collections, such as the medical museum at the Royal London Hospital, with its skeleton of the Elephant Man, or the wonderful TV and Wireless Museum run from a private house in Norwood, with its serried ranks of early valve radios and televisions in streamlined walnut cabinets. Each month the Model Railway Club, founded in 1910, meets in the unprepossessing surroundings of Keen House in Calshot Street to re-enact the wonders of the railway age in miniature, a stone's throw from King's Cross and St Pancras Stations – the most important complex of railway buildings in Britain.

Interiors are particularly vulnerable to the whims of their owners and the vicissitudes of fashion. Some of the buildings illustrated owe their existence to enlightened patronage, private endeavour, public lobbying, individual enthusiasm or sheer accident, but the principal reason why so many survive is statutory protection.

Architectural conservation is one of the great cultural success stories of the past century. What started off as a *cri de coeur* from amateur enthusiasts and social reformers at the end of the 19th century grew steadily in to a mass movement linked to progressive ideas of town planning and social change. Effective action took a long time to achieve in the face of fierce opposition from vested interests, but it was the scale of wartime losses that helped to prompt decisive action.

In 1947 a national system for the listing of buildings was introduced. Twenty years later the concept of extending similar considerations to whole places through the designation of conservation areas was pioneered by Duncan Sandys. As the chair of a wartime cabinet committee on VI flying bombs and V2 rockets, Sandys had seen first hand the extent of damage to the national heritage. As a passionate enthusiast, he vowed to protect what remained from comprehensive redevelopment in favour of a much more discriminating approach, starting with an understanding of the value of what already exists. In 1968 this sea change in government attitudes paved the way for the introduction of a coherent system of statutory protection, and the need for prior listed building consent for any works which affect the character or appearance of listed buildings, irrespective of their grade, externally or internally. By recognising them as complete entities, for over 40 years this highly flexible process has saved countless buildings and their interiors from demolition or uninformed alterations. The system has ensured that those areas which contribute to the total significance of a building are protected properly, while facilitating well-informed change to those parts of lesser importance. As a result Britain leads the world in the management of its historic environment.

✱✱✱✱✱✱✱✱✱✱✱✱✱✱✱✱✱✱✱✱✱✱✱✱✱✱✱✱✱✱✱✱✱✱✱✱✱✱

For many the reticent urbane façades of clubland and St James's are an abiding source of mystery and fascination, a private world of intrigue and espionage haunted by the spectres of intrepid young chaps off to save the Empire from dastardly deeds in far-flung places. "The talk was that strange, slight talk which governs the British Empire, which governs it in secret, and yet would scarcely enlighten an ordinary Englishman even if he could hear it". This is the arcane world of John Buchan and Dornford Yates, but also one lampooned mercilessly by P G Wodehouse and others. For Bertie Wooster a good club was somewhere raucous, where "if you want to attract a fellow's attention, you heave a bit of bread at him", although his butler Jeeves preferred a more refined atmosphere at his own club for gentlemen's gentlemen, the fictional Junior Ganymede.

The earliest clubs of St James's started life as coffee or chocolate houses, where groups of gentlemen began to pay fees to the

Sanderson Hotel: Conservation can involve the creative adaptation of old buildings to new uses unlocking their hidden potential and providing exciting new perspectives as with these fine modern stained glass windows by John Piper and Patrick Reyntiens.

proprietor for certain privileges such as dinner, gaming and overnight accommodation. In 1764 Allmack's split in to Boodles and Brooks's, the former catering for country gentlemen and the latter for Whigs. Nearby, Robert Arthur converted White's Chocolate House in to the grandest club of all – White's – as a refuge for Tories. As coffee lost its exclusivity and became a popular drink for all, so clubs replaced coffee houses as a relaxed urban rendezvous for well-heeled gentlemen. Clubs were a refuge from the stifling formality of balls, soirées and dinner parties, where a gentleman could come and go as he pleased and have "the command of regular servants without having to pay or manage them … and have whatever meal or refreshment he wants, at all hours … served up as in his own house". By 1900 London had around 200 clubs, housed in a diverse array of buildings and catering for everyone from army and naval officers to old India hands and fly-fishers.

Some of the best clubhouses have been included here – the Reform (p76), from where Phileas Fogg set off on his adventures in *Around the World in 80 Days*; the Oxford and Cambridge (p86), with its magnificent staircase and replica bronze sculpture of Donatello's David; and the RAC (p80), with its sybaritic Byzantine swimming pool coruscated with mosaics. Magnificent though they are, the Georgian elegance of Boodles, Brooks's and White's have yielded their place to the lustrous

Park Lane Hotel: The jaw-dropping Silver Gallery forms part of the swankiest sequence of Art Deco interiors in London.

delights of the National Liberal Club (p62) with its magnificent array of tiled rooms, and the eccentricities of the Beefsteak (p170), a gentlemen's dining club approached through a discreet door in Irving Street in the distinctly unfashionable milieu of Leicester Square. The high point of any visit to the exclusive City of London Club in Old Broad Street is a trip to its superb set of marble and tiled lavatories tucked away in the basement, an aesthetic experience exceeded only by those lying hidden in spiritual serenity beneath John Wesley's house one mile to the north in City Road (p224).

People like to congregate with those with whom they share common interests and pursuits, so alongside traditional gentlemen's clubs are countless private members' clubs, from the grand to the distinctly questionable. The current vogue for more informal clubs has proved the salvation of many historic buildings. Home House in Portman Square, for instance (p108), with its palatial interiors by Robert Adam, was once one of London's most conspicuous historic buildings at risk, but is now amongst its most stylish private clubs.

Of the great gaming salons, the Clermont Club (p104) is widely regarded as the finest terrace house in London, built in 1742-6 for Lady Isabella Fitch by William Kent, and the legendary haunt of the 7th Lord Lucan prior to his mysterious disappearance in November 1974 following the murderous attack on his children's nanny. To have excluded it would be unthinkable. Nearby at 30 Curzon Street,

Crockford's now occupies a pair of houses united by Robert Adam in 1771-2 with typical panache, with a dining room approached through a shell-headed apse and a first floor drawing room with a splendid barrel-vaulted ceiling.

Nightclubs appealing to the affluent middle classes have formed an inextricable part of the allure of the West End since the early 20th century. With a tradition for decorative excess that puts even the most flamboyant cinema interiors to shame, they tend to be subject to shifting trends in popular fashion and therefore transient.

From 1910 onwards Soho was the centre of London's racy nightlife, with a strong dose of sex thrown in for good measure. At The Morgue in Ham Yard the receptionist was dressed as a nun, though "far from virtuous", we are told, the tables were coffins lit by pendant skeleton lamps, and the waiters were dressed as devils with eyes made up to glow like balls of fire; but some interiors were decorated by the leading artists of the day. The Cave of the Golden Calf in Soho, run by the wife of the morose Swedish playwright August Strindberg, was kitted out in 1913 by Jacob Epstein and Wyndham Lewis. For the annual Chelsea Arts Ball, famous artists such as Frank Brangwyn were employed to create wildly romantic themes from Noah's Ark, the Arabian Nights or Ancient Egypt and, most racily of all, The Naked Truth, which offered ample opportunity for nudity. The last period survivor from these bohemian days, the Colony Club in Dean Street, frequented by Lucian Freud, Peter O'Toole and Francis Bacon, finally closed in 2008, its bright bilious-green interior deemed too ephemeral to merit listing.

But this tradition continues in new guises. The Groucho Club caters for the world of the arts, entertainment and media, while opposite, in a superb, panelled early 18th century town house, Black's is a riotous reinvention of a Georgian supper club from the age of Joshua Reynolds and Samuel Johnson, with oak benches, faded sofas and blazing log fires. At Sketch in Conduit Street, Mayfair, an elegant house of 1779 by James Wyatt has been transformed into an achingly fashionable restaurant, lecture room, arts and music venue with bizarre installations of contemporary art and lighting which rival the wildest excesses of the 1930s. Skin-coloured chairs merge surreally into the walls, innovative lighting confers a louche atmosphere, and black and red resin oozes down the stairs at the head of which is *The Precious One* by Mauro Peruchetti, a sexy, seated mannequin covered in reflective crystals. It is all reversible, but likely to induce apoplexy amongst the more faint-hearted architectural purists.

Of the hotels included, two – the Sanderson (p126) in Berners Street and the former Regent Palace behind Piccadilly Circus (p114) – are exemplars of outstanding conservation work, and a third, the former Great Eastern Hotel at Liverpool Street (p230), retains its mystical Masonic temple, although the suggestion that it was once hidden behind a false wall and only discovered during refurbishment work is a popular urban myth.

The Sanderson, the former showrooms and offices of the Sanderson Wallpaper and Paint Co, with its fine stained-glass window by John Piper, has been converted and enhanced with flair, imagination and humour into one of London's most intriguing and quirky hotel interiors, styled by Philippe Starck and the architects Denton Corker Marshall.

Conversely, the dowdy old 1,000-room Regent Palace Hotel has been radically overhauled into a new complex of offices and shops as part of a wider development strategy for the entire area by the Crown Estate. The unique Art Deco interiors of the old hotel have been lovingly restored, whilst the old Titanic Bar has been dismantled, relocated, re-erected and restored within the reconfigured building in a bold and ambitious conservation exercise. New coloured faience façades have been inserted between the original retained corner prows in a masterly scheme by Jeremy Dixon & Partners with Donald Insall & Partners responsible for the conservation of the flamboyant interiors.

Elsewhere, some of London's finest hotel interiors are now tourist attractions in their own right – for instance, the superb Promenade, Grill Room and Oliver Messel Suite in the Dorchester, the theatrical Art Deco entrance hall and tea room at Claridge's by Basil Ionides and Oswald Milne, and the grandiloquent Ritz with its flamboyant French interiors by Mewès and Davis. St Pancras, with its soaring Gothic staircase, once the highlight of any tour of hidden, neglected London, has now been restored to its former glory in one of the most spectacular conservation projects of recent times.

Far less well known than Claridges or the Dorchester is the Park Lane Hotel (p100), misleadingly located in Piccadilly, where the rather understated exterior conceals a whole sequence of the swankiest Art Deco interiors imaginable, with a glitzy staircase resplendent with stylish murals, geometric handrails and cylindrical lights culminating in a huge basement ballroom. By way of complete contrast, a short distance away in Inverness Terrace, Bayswater, is the Grand Royale London Hyde Park Hotel (p412) in a house reputed to have been the love-nest of King Edward VII, when Prince of Wales, and Lillie Langtry, complete with robust neo-Jacobean oak staircase and reception room and a rare private theatre.

At Marylebone, the former Great Central Hotel boasts a fine staircase and armorial stained glass depicting the arms of the old Great Central Railway, but its central courtyard, converted to an internal atrium in 1989-91, leaves much to be desired. Elsewhere, the Waldorf in Aldwych and the inestimable Savoy have also been compromised by discordant contemporary interventions that have eroded rather than enhanced their period character, while the nearby Strand Palace is crying out for the sort of imaginative reinstatement that the Regent Palace has enjoyed. Its basement still retains the original stepped, illuminated Art Deco staircase and period washrooms. The original Jazz Moderne entrance hall, lifts and fittings designed by Oliver Bernard were all removed as part of a misguided refurbishment project in 1967-70. Even at the time much of this was recognised as being of outstanding importance, and salvaged by the Victoria & Albert Museum, where unfortunately it has languished in storage ever since.

Dorchester Hotel: Oliver Messel, the theatre designer and friend of Noel Coward, created stage sets for Diaghilev. In 1953, with characteristic bravura, he applied his theatrical flair to the design of a luxury suite on the seventh floor of the Dorchester Hotel.

What greater attraction could there be for any hotel than to bring the original interiors back to the place for which they were designed?

London has over 140 theatres, 50 of which lie within the two square miles of the West End in a breathtaking array of architectural styles spanning over two centuries. The oldest, the Theatre Royal, Drury Lane (1811-12), founded in 1663, is actually the fourth building on the site. Other early examples are the Theatre Royal, Haymarket (1821), by John Nash, which replaced an older building of 1726, and the Royal Opera House (1887-8) by E M Barry, the third on its site since 1732; but the boom period for the construction of new theatres was between 1885 and 1916, when 19 were erected across the West End, many in a virtually continuous phalanx along the new streets carved out by the Metropolitan Board of Works and its successor, the London County Council: Shaftesbury Avenue, Charing Cross Road, the Strand and Aldwych.

London's West End theatres and their lavish interiors have been the subject of many excellent publications. They are the focus of continuous monitoring by the Theatres Trust, which was founded in 1978 as the National Advisory Body for Theatres to promote theatre buildings and to act as a champion for their future. The post-war period was particularly challenging, as many faced closure or were vulnerable to intense development pressures. One of my earliest tasks as a young conservation officer was to serve a statutory notice to prevent the demolition of the unlisted Shaftesbury Theatre over one weekend in 1973, after its ceiling collapsed following a particularly energetic performance of the rock musical Hair.

Theatre was regarded as therapeutic, and private theatres and multi-purpose entertainment halls were built in institutions and hospitals across the country, such as at Normansfield Hospital, Teddington, (p393), which has recently been beautifully restored, as well as in private houses such as Inverness Terrace (p412). Few would guess that lost in the vast halls of Alexandra Palace (p332) are the ghostly remains of a full working theatre, a stone's throw from the simple unadorned studio from where the world's first high definition TV service was broadcast on 2 November 1936. Mothballed with the aid of grants from English Heritage, it is hoped that one day the theatre will reopen as part of a new multi-purpose leisure complex within the palace.

West End theatre offered entertainment for those that could afford it, but for those with only a few coppers to spare the raucous informality of the music hall provided a ready alternative. No story of the London theatre would be complete without highlighting Wilton's Music Hall (p306), the oldest surviving music hall in the world, concealed behind an unremarkable domestic façade in Grace's Alley, Stepney. Another early surviving example with an intact interior, Hoxton Hall, opened in 1863. It enjoyed a brief life as a music hall before it became a Temperance hall in 1879, and later the Bedford Quaker Institute.

In 1909 a Cinematograph Act was passed which controlled film licensing, Sunday opening and the design of cinema premises, giving birth to a whole new type of building – a separate fire-resistant projection box connected to the auditorium by shuttered projection

London Palladium: The legendary variety theatre was designed by Frank Matcham in 1910 behind the older retained facade of the 1868 Corinthian Bazaar. Below is a view from one of the boxes of the auditorium dressed for a performance.

portholes with its own emergency exit, plus the provision of fire exits and lavatories for the paying public.

With the arrival of films the cinema rapidly supplanted the music hall as the main source of cheap entertainment for the masses, opening up a dreamworld of fantasy and escapism far removed from the bleak realities of everyday life. For the poor it offered a parallel universe of unimaginable luxury, with plush furnishings in exotic magical surroundings, but in a relaxed and informal setting where women could go alone and feel quite safe.

Some of the earliest cinemas were just insalubrious sheds with wooden benches. These were closed immediately with the introduction of the new Act, while many erstwhile theatres were converted into full-time cinemas. The Coronet, Notting Hill, built as an opera house in 1902, became a cinema in 1916. The Electric Palace (now the Gate) in Notting Hill was converted from a restaurant to a cinema in 1911, retaining its encrusted plasterwork ceiling. The nearby Electric Cinema in Portobello Road, opened in March 1911, is perhaps the archetypal cinema interior of the period, with plaster panels and gas secondary lighting, although the Picturehouse (now Phoenix) in East Finchley with its simple barrel vault (1909) is regarded as one of the earliest surviving purpose-built cinemas in its original use, now handsomely restored with the benefit of a grant from the Heritage Lottery Fund.

In 1911 there were 94 cinemas in the capital. Ten years later there were 266, as ever larger and more lavish venues were built for mass entertainment in an ever more exotic mixture of styles – Venetian, Italian Renaissance, Jazz Moderne, Art Deco, Egyptian, Moorish and even Chinese. The Grange, Kilburn (1914), boasted 1,300 seats. The Trocadero, a supercinema at Elephant and Castle (built in 1930 and demolished in 1964), was a veritable monster with 3,394 seats dwarfed within a vast auditorium. The New Victoria, opened in 1930, was compared with a mermaid's palace with walls of back-lit plaster shells, but some of the largest and most fabulous interiors were built in inner London and the suburbs.

Variety shows were offered alongside cinema at the Astoria, Brixton (1929), and the Astoria, Finsbury Park (1930), both designed by the architect Edward Stone, the former (now the Brixton Academy) resembling a Renaissance garden while the latter (now the Universal Church of the Kingdom of God) has an exotic foyer in the form of a souk in an Arabian village beneath a romantic sky of twinkling stars. But by far the most fabulous of all in an age which revelled in escapist fantasy was the Granada, Tooting (p378), described as a "doge's palace" in a jaw-dropping combination of Moorish and Gothic design by the Russian prince and theatre designer Theodore Komisarjevsky; it is the only cinema in Britain to be listed Grade I.

The Grosvenor (1936), later Ace, in Rayners Lane (p438), with its great stylised elephant's trunk over the entrance, is one of the best of the cinemas that became the architectural and social focus of the new outer London suburbs. It is another conservation success story, having been converted with immense sensitivity into a Zoroastrian temple, enhancing its streamlined interior with an entirely appropriate spiritual

Astoria, Finsbury Park: Pure escapist fantasy with an entrance foyer designed as an Arabian souk, now sensitively converted to ecclesiastical use.

use. Finally, in south-east London the Rivoli Ballroom, Lewisham, once a cinema, is now the only intact 1950s ballroom in London, "a wonderland of plush red velvet gold-framed walls, Austrian crystal chandeliers and oversized chaise longues" evoking the post-war age of jazz, swing and rock and roll.

Other than swimming pools, which by their very nature necessitated large clear-span roofs, few of the great sporting venues have produced interiors of real note. One exception was Die Turnhalle, the German gymnasium at King's Cross, the first of its type to be erected in Britain. It was designed by Edward Gruning in 1864-5 for the German Gymnastics Society as a spacious hall beneath an impressive laminated timber roof structure, with cast-iron hooks for ropes, and large clear spaces for gymnastics as well as more hazardous pursuits such as broadsword practice and Indian club swinging. It is of considerable historical significance as it was the venue for the indoor events of the first National Olympic Games of the modern era, held in 1866.

Another Olympic exception is Zaha Hadid's aerodynamic Aquatics Centre (p342) for the London 2012 Olympics, a bravura piece of architecture and engineering which has bequeathed a building of real architectural quality as part of the much-hyped "legacy".

Alongside traditional sports like football, cricket, rugby, tennis and horse racing, the 1930s witnessed new forms of spectator sport including greyhound and motorcycle racing. The famous dog track at Walthamstow, its iconic neon sign a listed London landmark, only closed in August 2008 for redevelopment for housing in the face of intense local protest.

The best of the cricket grounds is the historic Pavilion at Lord's designed by Thomas Verity with its famous Long Room, and the MCC Museum where the original Ashes are displayed. The museum is

German Gymnasium, King's Cross: In areas undergoing great change, historic buildings have a vital role to play in placemaking. Once hidden behind a terrace of mid-19th-century buildings, the German Gymnasium, built for the first National Olympic Games in 1866, is now one of the highlights of the area's regeneration.

packed with wonderful cricketing memorabilia, including the stuffed sparrow bowled out for all eternity by Jahangir Khan for Cambridge University during a match with the MCC on 3 July 1936, and the battered copy of Wisden that sustained the commentator E W Swanton during his brutal captivity in a Japanese prisoner of war camp.

Of the football stadia, only two in London are listed – Fulham, whose 1905 stand designed by Archibald Leitch is the oldest in the Football League, and the famous Marble Halls at Highbury (p328), the former home of Arsenal FC. Since the relocation of Arsenal to the new Emirates Stadium, the old listed East Stand (1936) has been converted ingeniously into stylish new flats by Allies & Morrison, whilst retaining the historic 1930s interiors. New blocks around the perimeter of the old pitch enclose one of London's newest private squares.

London has over 6,000 restaurants, 3,400 pubs, 80 markets and more than 40,000 shops, many of which have succumbed to the pressures of globalisation as large conglomerates and corporate chains increasingly dominate the high street with clone shops and anodyne brands that have eroded local distinctiveness. The great West End department stores and emporia, such as the splendid Art Nouveau Food Hall at Harrods executed by the architect/ceramicist W J Neatby in 1902, and the kitsch neo-Egyptian interventions made by its former owner Mohamed Al-Fayed, are among some of London's most famous retail delights. Far less well known are the small shops and businesses which continue to flourish against all the odds in different parts of the capital – Martyn's in Muswell Hill (p330), a completely intact grocer's shop which has stood virtually unchanged for nearly a century; the Algerian Coffee Stores in Old Compton Street (p118), permeated with the exotic aroma of coffees from all over the world; Smith's tobacconists in

Charing Cross Road (p163) inexplicably still unlisted, and Bluston's in Kentish Town Road (p326) with its stainless-steel and Vitrolite fascia and island showcases full of frocks and gowns from a past era.

Trumper in Curzon Street (p107) with its plush red velvet interiors and private booths is a traditional barber shop catering for West End toffs, while in the City, Flittners at 86 Moorgate, and the nearby basement salon at No 1 Telegraph Street, both retain working period interiors, with traditional barbers' chairs, payment booths and mahogany display cabinets. Further afield, the New Century Barbers Shop in Muswell Hill has been trading for over 100 years, its walls decorated with mirrors and advertisements for Vaseline and Brylcreem. The famous Art Deco barber shop tucked away in the basement of the old Austin Reed store in Regent Street (now Superdry), with its sinuous, serpentine ceiling light snaking around the centre of the salon, chrome fittings, frosted mirrors and traditional barbers' chairs, has just been carefully restored as part of its reincarnation as Tommy Gunn's.

Walthamstow Stadium: Every dog has its day. Once a great landmark of north-east London, the future of the former greyhound track and its iconic listed signboard remains uncertain.

St James's remains an emporium of traditional retail delights for the cognoscenti – James Fox, cigar and tobacco merchants (p89), Lock's the hatters and milliners, Lobb's the bootmaker, Berry Brothers with its famous weighing scales (see *Panoramas of Lost London*, p68-9) and D R Harris the chemist's, which, although modernised, still boasts its original apothecaries' drawers – as does W C King at 35 Amwell Street, Finsbury, a chemist's founded in 1839, in an area renowned for its carefully conserved shopfronts.

In Stroud Green, W Plumb the butcher (p329) may now be empty, but Allens in Mount Street, Mayfair, and M & R Meats in Goswell Road still function as traditional butchers' shops with meat racks, tiled walls and marble slabs, although in South London, Kennedy's butchers ceased trading from its cream-tiled branches in Deptford, Camberwell and Bromley in 2007. Thomas Fox's umbrella shop at London Wall, established in 1868, with its sleek black Vitrolite and chromed steel fascia and red neon fox, sadly may now have closed, but James Smith & Sons Umbrellas in New Oxford Street (p147) continues to flourish behind the finest High Victorian shopfront in London, with gleaming gilt and glass fascias, stylised Victorian lettering and mahogany shop fittings.

For those wishing to depart in style, the distinctive blue lanterns of Frederick Paine's funeral parlours can still be found at various branches in south-west London. Their Kingston branch in London Road retains a rare panelled interior and a small museum. J Nodes in Ladbroke Grove has a good interior adapted from an early 20th century haberdasher's shop, with mahogany fittings and retractable shelves where the material was once measured and cut, while A France in Lamb's Conduit Street has a delightful office with stained-glass and hardwood fittings within a panelled, early 18th century London town house. Unfortunately, Francis & C Walters parlour in Limehouse with its distinctive iron-crested, gilt and glass fascia has now departed.

Elsewhere small specialist traders and craft workshops can still be found. When L Cornelissen & Son, the "artists' colourmen" founded in 1855, moved to Great Russell Street in 1987, the firm brought with it all the original black wooden drawers, antique cabinets, fixtures and fittings from its shop in Great Queen Street, Covent Garden. In Soho, W Sitch & Co (p122), a family-run business set up in 1776 and specialising in the restoration and reproduction of metal light fittings, is still trading from the 18th century town house it has occupied since 1903.

Discreetly located in the sedate environs of Berkeley Square, at No 50, is a house which was the scene of a notorious 19th century haunting. Maggs Bros Ltd (p102), one of the world's largest antiquarian booksellers, is full of hidden chambers lined with dusty leather-bound books slowly "maturing" on the shelves, whilst Daunt's in Marylebone High Street is one of London's most elegant bookshops with a top-lit gallery and stained glass window.

Throughout the 19th century, gentlemen eating away from home tended to frequent their clubs or make use of the numerous chop houses, pie shops coffee houses or taverns which provided plain

Tommy Gunn's Barber Shop, Regent Street: Hidden away in the basement of the old Austin Reed store (now Superdry) is the best-preserved barber shop in London, recently painstakingly restored to its original appearance.

wholesome fare, like Ye Olde Cheshire Cheese off Fleet Street (p284). London's oldest restaurant, Rules in Maiden Lane, established in 1798 and so beloved of Dickens, Thackeray, Conan Doyle, King Edward VII, and a whole flounce of actors from Henry Irving to Charlie Chaplin, was exceptional. The arrival of the purpose-built restaurant was a comparatively late phenomenon.

One of the earliest was the sumptuous Café Royal in Regent Street (1865), now being restored, but others followed, including the huge Criterion restaurant on the upper floors of the eponymous building at Piccadilly Circus with its famous Long Bar (now the restaurant) on the ground floor (p110). As eating out became more fashionable, increasingly Edwardian diners dressed for dinner in white tie or elegant gowns. Older small, select restaurants gave way to larger eating houses with orchestras, palm courts and sumptuous internal decorations on a scale that rivalled the great hotels, which also began to welcome customers who were not residents.

Romano's took over the Café Vaudeville in the Strand, and Simpson's in the Strand was rebuilt in 1904. Around Piccadilly Circus the Trocadero, Monico and Scott's opened, and further afield new venues like Pagani's in Great Portland Street, with its magnificent tiled Art Nouveau façade by Beresford Pite, and Frascati's in Holborn, had become famous London institutions. New catering chains like Slater's, the ABC (Aerated Bread Company) and, above all, Lyons & Co with their famous "Nippies" provided inexpensive meals for working people. By 1910 Lyons had opened 98 teashops and three of their grander Corner Houses, which were open all night in Coventry Street, the Strand and Oxford Street. Each offered good food at affordable prices

Daunt's Bookshop, Marylebone High Street: Flooded with light from its top-lit gallery and stained glass windows, Daunt's is one of London's most civilised bookshops.

in lavish interiors, all of which have now gone, although the gilt mosaic interior, caged lift and plush basement bar of its old Throgmorton Street branch still survives in the throes of refurbishment.

Conservation involves the adaptation of old buildings to new uses, so the Wolseley in Piccadilly (p98) is here as an imaginative recasting of a fine period interior. What started life as a swanky car showroom and later became a bank is now a sophisticated new restaurant. Les Trois Garçons in Bethnal Green (p320) triggered a trend for camp eclecticism which has been much copied and parodied since, a humorous stylistic thread of the last 20 years which offers a richly inventive counterpart to the clinical sterility of the interiors of so many minimalist restaurants.

At the other end of the spectrum, Manze's in Walthamstow (p338) is one of a number of superbly preserved examples of eel and pie shops that have served inexpensive and wholesome food in the poorer parts of London for the past 100 years. Its rival chain, Cooke's, still has two splendid outlets with cream tiles and sunburst stained glass in Broadway Market and Hoxton. What was once the flagship in Dalston is now a Chinese restaurant (the interior still remains).

The Quality Chop House in Farringdon Road (p225) is a rare survival of a working class restaurant, with bench seating and marble tables, now under new management and catering for a more upmarket clientele, while Pellicci's in Bethnal Green (p343) is the best of a dwindling number of popular cafés and coffee bars which were once commonplace in London's high streets from the 1930s to the 60s, but which are now rare. Others worth seeking out are the River Café opposite Putney Bridge tube station, located in the tiled interior of a former Express Dairy, and Lodi's in Blackhorse Road, a classic London "greasy spoon" with a similar Edwardian tiled interior.

Sadly, London's finest traditional fish and chip shop, W Burrows in East Acton Lane (p421), is no more, its unique listed interior destined for an outdoor museum, but the Golden Hind in Marylebone Lane, complete with its green and primrose Vitrolite panels and stainless-steel fish fryer, continues to flourish.

London's 3,400 or so remaining public houses have been celebrated exhaustively in all their different incarnations and styles in countless books and publications. Only a handful have been selected here, primarily on the grounds that each incorporates an extra hidden dimension.

Ye Olde Cheshire Cheese (p284) is one of London's oldest traditional taverns, with a multi-layered history and a wealth of literary associations and memorabilia of which even many regulars are unaware. The Viaduct Tavern (p279) with its coquettish mirrors is alleged to incorporate cells from Newgate Prison in the basement, although the story does not bear close scrutiny; but the cellars of The Morpeth Arms on Millbank do incorporate tunnels used until 1867 to move prisoners destined for transportation direct to the river from the old Millbank Prison, which was demolished in 1893. When The Old Queen's Head in Essex Road was rebuilt in 1829, the ceiling, panelling and Jacobean chimneypiece from the original building (frequented by Sir Walter Raleigh and Christopher Marlowe) were salvaged and reused in the new building, where they remain to this day. The Sherlock Holmes in Northumberland Street (p176) has an entire replica of 221B Baker Street on its upper floors, put together by Whitbread for the Festival of Britain in 1951. The Warrington Hotel in Maida Vale (p416) with its sensuous Art Nouveau murals was once a brothel, whilst the Arts and Crafts interior of The Black Friar (p292) is a playful evocation of Merrie England by some of the leading craftsmen of their day. Nearby in Holborn, The Cittie of Yorke, rebuilt in 1923, retains few fragments of its 1430 fabric, but its cavernous interior does boast a fireplace of 1815 ventilated by an under-floor chimney, and lines of private snugs for lawyers and clients. Gordon's Wine Bar (p178), one of London's most atmospheric and eccentric historic interiors, is allegedly the oldest purpose-built wine bar in London. A unique institution, it is hidden away in much earlier 17th century cellars at the bottom of Villiers Street. El Vino's in Fleet Street has a fine period interior, reputedly converted from an earlier hall of mirrors. Inter-war suburban pubs and roadhouses have fared less well, many, like The Railway Hotel, Edgware, a neo-Tudor extravaganza, having closed or else been adapted as family restaurants; but The Eastbrook in Dagenham (1937-8) continues to flourish with its armorial stained glass, Oak Bar, Walnut Bar and Music Room: a romantic celebration of English history in one of London's newest 1930s suburbs.

Many of London's finest institutions are closed to the public, which is why so many have been included here. In the City, five of the best historic livery company halls are illustrated – the Apothecaries (p276) the Drapers (p234), the Goldsmiths (p246), the Chartered Accountants (p238) and the Cutlers (p272) – as a representative sample of the 100 or so that exist in various guises.

Outside the precincts of the Tower of London, relatively little of London's secular mediaeval fabric survives. The private precincts of Charterhouse (p208) comprise one of the finest groups of mediaeval and Tudor buildings in London, but because access has been restricted in recent years, they remain comparatively little known. St John's Gateway (p212) nearby is more accessible, but few are conscious that the crypt of the adjacent St John's Priory (p214) has one of the finest 12th century interiors in the capital. Located a stone's throw from the runways at Heathrow is the "cathedral of Middlesex", Harmondsworth Barn (p396), built in 1426-7 and the largest surviving mediaeval timber-framed barn in England, now taken into care by English Heritage as London's most important Grade I listed building at risk.

In central London the College of Arms (p264), the home of heraldry for over 350 years; the Honourable Artillery Company (p226), the headquarters of the oldest regiment in the British Army; and the Library of St Paul's Cathedral (p268) are ancient institutions of which the public is only vaguely aware, with fascinating collections and superb interiors.

Cooke's, Kingsland High Street: Opened in 1910 with a palatial interior of Baroque domes and cream and green tiling, this was once the flagship of Cooke's empire of eel, pie and mash shops.

The private domains of the Inns of Court contain some of the capital's most glorious historic interiors, largely unknown other than to lawyers and their clients. Middle Temple Hall (p286), badly damaged in the Second World War, is the finest surviving secular mediaeval interior in institutional use in London, while to the north, the Library, Chapel and Hall at Lincoln's Inn (p154, 158) were hardly touched during the war. The Law Society in Chancery Lane (p198) has an annexe designed in restrained classical style by Charles Holden, with splendid Della Robbia plaques adorning the walls and war memorial sculpture by Gilbert Bayes.

All three of London's great law courts – the Royal Courts of Justice (p192), the Central Criminal Court (p274) and the new Supreme Court (p48) – are included since, other than for a few habitual recidivists who are hardly there to appreciate their architecture, their interiors are as unknown as their exteriors are familiar landmarks. The most accessible, the Supreme Court, has been carefully but controversially crafted out of the old Middlesex County Court in Parliament Square with considerable aplomb by the architects Feilden & Mawson.

For those unfortunates who face a custodial sentence, the architectural delights of London's prisons probably offer scant compensation. Looking north from Brixton Prison, an inmate might catch a glimpse of the old Brixton Windmill through the bars of their cell in one of London's more surreal juxtapositions. Those held in Wormwood Scrubs might find solace, if not redemption, in the largest prison chapel in England, a huge Romanesque cavern (p376) designed as part of Edward Du Cane's great penal complex between 1874 and 1891. Wandsworth (p376), once the Surrey House of Correction (1849), is typical of the 19th century prisons, built on a radiating plan derived from the original model at Pentonville, as were the haunting hidden underground vaults of the old Clerkenwell House of Correction (p218).

The arcane world of Freemasonry, resonant with mystical symbolism, is encapsulated not only in the awe-inspiring marble chambers of Freemasons' Hall, Great Queen Street (p164), but also in the secret delights of the obscure Masonic temple in the former Great Eastern, now ANDAZ, Hotel at Liverpool Street (p230) with its exquisite lotus-leaf capitals and zodiac ceiling.

Three of the great institutions that once regulated crucial aspects of London life are included – the palatial Port of London Authority building at Tower Hill (p260), where the first meeting of the United Nations was held, the old headquarters of the Metropolitan Water Board at New River Head in Finsbury (p222), which managed the supply of fresh drinking water to London for generations, and 55 Broadway (p54), Charles Holden's iconic stepped classical skyscraper designed for London Transport, which astonishingly is now threatened with displacement from its spiritual home to a rented office block, in a scandalous and short-sighted exercise of public asset stripping. What could be more sustainable than a large purpose-built office block directly above a central London tube station which was designed specifically for the needs of its occupier?

Freemasons' Hall, Great Queen Street: The vast echoing marble-lined chambers of Freemasons' Hall are imbued with mysterious spiritual symbolism and boast some of the most opulent Beaux Arts interiors in London.

Alongside the philanthropic – the Thomas Coram Foundation (p140) – the humanist – Conway Hall (p150) – and the overtly political – the Marx Memorial Library (p216) – a number of London's finest educational institutions boast interiors generally known only to their alumni: the Great Hall of the former City of London School, (p290), now part of J P Morgan bank; Westminster School (p50) with its ancient dining hall dating back to the 14th century; alongside the hidden splendours of Ashburnham House, one of London's finest 17th century interiors. At Dulwich College (p360) the James Caird, the boat in which Shackleton made his epic voyage across the South Atlantic in 1917, sits unobtrusively in the hallowed cloisters close to the Great Hall. At Harrow School (p434) the Fourth Form Room, carved with graffiti, is the best preserved 17th century schoolroom in England, but unknown to many is the relocated interior of Brooke House, Hackney, devastated in the Second World War but rescued and reassembled within Sir Herbert Baker's War Memorial Building, all of which remains unlisted.

University College, founded in 1826 as a secular alternative to Oxford and Cambridge Universities, retains the gruesome mummified remains of the philosopher Jeremy Bentham in an auto-icon exhibit in the public halls of the college (p137) near to the fine octagonal Flaxman Library. In the East End, the huge octagon which once formed part

of the People's Palace, much of which was gutted by fire in 1931, was later incorporated into Queen Mary College (p302). These, and a similar library in Gothic style at the former Public Record Office in Chancery Lane, reflect the huge influence on subsequent library design of the famous Round Reading Room at the British Museum (1854-7 by Sydney Smirke). Deep within King's College, Strand, is George Gilbert Scott's superb High Victorian Gothic chapel (p186), intended for the spiritual enlightenment of generations of students.

The philanthropic tradition runs strongly through London's history. Wealthy benefactors left substantial endowments for libraries, such as Dr William's Library in Gordon Square (p138), and institutions for the poor and sick. Of these, the most famous, the Thomas Coram Foundation (p140), was responsible for saving thousands of foundling children and orphans from a life or death on the streets. Today it still operates as a charity and museum from its home in Brunswick Square, the plain later neo-Georgian exterior encasing the original staircase, ceiling and principal rooms, which were dismantled and reinstalled in the new building when the hospital moved to Berkhamsted in 1926.

In the mid-19th century the superb mid-18th century house at the junction of Greek Street and Soho Square became the House of Charity, now the House of St Barnabas (p120), for the relief of the destitute and fallen women. At the rear, where it can be glimpsed from Manette Street, is an exquisite Gothic chapel modelled on the cathedral at Arles.

There has been a hospital at St Bartholomew's in Smithfield since 1123, so it is no surprise that it retains one of the finest hospital interiors in London, with a staircase decorated with murals by Hogarth and a magnificent Great Hall supported by some of the leading philanthropists of the day (p202). The Royal Hospital, Chelsea, and the former Royal Naval College at Greenwich, with its magnificent Baroque Painted Hall by Sir James Thornhill and Chapel by James Athenian Stuart, are world-famous and among London's greatest and most conspicuous glories. However, the more grisly aspects of early surgery can be gleaned from the Old Operating Theatre at the former St Thomas's Hospital in Southwark (p298). Built in 1821, it is the oldest in England, rediscovered in the bricked-up attic of the former chapter house of Southwark Cathedral in 1956.

Hospital chapels are one of the more obscure yet enchanting facets of London's hidden heritage. Thomas Guy lies buried beneath England's only surviving 18th century hospital chapel, an exquisite Georgian gem in the hospital that bears his name (p296). At the Hospital for Sick Children in Great Ormond Street, E M Barry's beautiful shimmering gold mosaic chapel of St Christopher (p142) was the centre of a major conservation project in 1992, when it was moved inch by inch in to its current position after its original site was redeveloped. By contrast, at the old Middlesex Hospital site in Goodge Street Pearson's wonderful High Victorian Gothic chapel (p130) currently stands marooned at the centre of a huge cleared site, its condition monitored regularly by English Heritage, its future uncertain, its fabric slowly deteriorating. St Thomas's was one of the first English hospitals to be designed with "Nightingale" wards, in the form of seven huge pavilions to promote natural ventilation and the dispersal of foul air and mephitic vapours. Deep within is a fine barrel-vaulted Italianate chapel designed by Henry Currey between 1868 and 1871. In St John's Wood is the radiant Italianate chapel at the Hospital of St John & St Elizabeth (p418), which once stood in Great Ormond Street before it was dismantled and rebuilt on its present site in 1898 for the Knights of St John of Jerusalem.

With the mass production of encaustic tiles in the 19th century, a cheap, easy-to-clean and highly functional cladding was found for many interiors, particularly hospitals, where a sterile environment was essential. Sometimes particular decorative themes were developed in ceramic tile, and a number of institutions like the Bolingbroke Hospital in Wandsworth have children's wards clad in enchanting nursery rhyme tiles depicting Little Bo Peep, Jack and the Beanstalk or Little Red Riding Hood.

The late 19th century was the heroic age of investment in London's infrastructure, in a concerted attempt to address its chronic public health and transport needs. It generated the construction of a whole series of buildings that have bequeathed a wonderful legacy of industrial archaeology.

Crossness Pumping Station (p348) and its northern equivalent at Abbey Mills are two of the greatest monuments of the period: huge cathedrals to sanitary reform, both of which played a pivotal role in Sir Joseph Bazalgette's visionary engineering solution for the disposal of London's waste. In the crepuscular world of subterranean London,

the Victorian sewers are hidden masterpieces of craftsmanship and engineering – miles of superbly crafted brick tunnels and chambers which still serve the city today.

As parallel measures were taken to improve London's water supply, capacious underground reservoirs were constructed to cater for the needs of rapidly expanding neighbourhoods. Filled with thousands of gallons of water, these monumental exercises in civil engineering can rarely be appreciated in their raw state, but at Claremont Square (p333) the quality of the Victorian brickwork was captured in its full glory in a rare moment when the reservoir was drained, its massive arched chambers buried beneath the centre of an early 19th century London square.

As private water companies were forced to clean up their act, they invested heavily in new infrastructure. Kew Bridge Pumping Station (p386) is perhaps the finest example of its type. Its elegant standpipe tower in the form of an Italianate campanile is a major local landmark. Inside lies the finest collection of steam pumping engines in the world.

At Wapping, the hydraulic pumping station (p309) was one of eight responsible for driving London's hydraulic main, which powered lifts and equipment across the capital. Decommissioned in the 1980s, it has been converted with real panache into a restaurant and performance space designed around the original industrial machinery. Tower Bridge may be a world-renowned icon of London, but deep beneath the river in Stygian gloom the colossal bascule chambers resemble something from a drawing by Piranesi – one of the capital's least-known and most awe-inspiring spaces.

However, perhaps London's greatest and most notorious industrial icon is Battersea Power Station (p372). While Bankside has been

Queen's Chapel, Greenwich: The Queen's Chapel and Painted Hall in Greenwich are among London's most famous architectural treasures. The chapel ceiling by James "Athenian" Stuart bears a remarkable similarity to his work in the Great Room at Spencer House.

St Thomas's Hospital: A typical Doulton nursery rhyme tile panel designed by Margaret Thompson and William Rowe in 1901-03 for the Lillian and Seymour wards, relocated following demolition in 1968.

converted into a fashionable powerhouse for Brit Art, Battersea, with its evocative interior like a set from Metropolis, continues to languish as the most challenging historic building at risk in the capital.

Few of London's factories or manufacturing buildings produced interiors of any great architectural consequence. The Clément-Talbot factory at Barlby Road, Ladbroke Grove (1905), however, was a notable exception, with a grand marble-lined administration block in front of its main factory and a production hall dominated by a huge cartouche of the Talbot crest. The Michelin building in Fulham Road, one of London's most colourful and imaginative compositions, was an early concrete Hennebique structure faced in Burmantoft's Marmo tiles. It was designed in 1909 by the Frenchman Francois Espinasse as a garage for fitting tyres, with advertising for Bibendum – the "Michelin Man" – embedded into every aspect. The glass cupolas resemble tyres, the tiled murals by Ernest Montaut depict early racing cars flying along the open road, and the interior has three humorous windows of Bibendum, now in the restaurant of the same name.

London's subterranean spaces are some of the most atmospheric, but inaccessible, places in the capital. At Chalk Farm beneath Camden Stables is a maze of tunnels and vaults once used by horses for the movement of goods between the canal, railway and road alongside the largest complex of Victorian industrial stabling in the country. Under the tracks on the west side lie the huge flooded chambers of the old Incline Railway Winding Engine House, where from 1837 to 1844 trains were wound up the incline from Euston to meet a waiting locomotive at the top, part of a wider complex of early railway buildings of world significance.

In 2004, a chronic failure to appreciate the potential of the subterranean Gothic vaults and Victorian carriageways at Bishopsgate Goods Yard triggered the unnecessary demolition of the entire northern range for the extended East London Line, but the original

Braithwaite Viaduct (one of the oldest railway structures in the world from 1839 to 1842) and the southern range still remain, providing a fantastic opportunity for the conservation-led regeneration of the whole area. Further down the line, Brunel's Thames Tunnel (1829-43), the world's first to be built under water, was relined as part of the upgrading works. Dubbed the eighth wonder of the world when it opened in 1843, over 1 million people – half the population of London at the time – walked through it in the first 10 weeks.

Elsewhere, a sprawling twilight world of hidden vaults lies under Waterloo. Three of the nearby railway arches were converted by Feliks Topolski in 1935 into an artist's studio which contains his vast 750ft linear mural *Memoir of the Century*, depicting all the key events and people of the 20th century.

Under Kingsway and Southampton Row the setted ramps, platforms and staircases of the old tram tunnel (p168) echo eerily with the distant sounds of traffic, which can be glimpsed intermittently in the darkness through the iron grilles above. Nearby, Aldwych epitomises the haunted world of the abandoned underground station (p181). Elsewhere, the disused Crystal Palace Low Level Station has a superb vaulted polychrome subway by E M Barry, while both Peckham Rye and Queenstown Road, Battersea, have abandoned station buildings with interiors frozen in time.

London's underground system is part of the capital's DNA, and rightly celebrated for its commitment to outstanding design, from Leslie Green's oxblood-coloured faience buildings to the progressive modernism of Charles Holden's iconic stations on the Piccadilly Line. From 1936 the management of the London Underground wanted to build a subsurface station reminiscent of the new system in Moscow, and in 1947 they succeeded with real verve at Gants Hill on the Central Line, with a 150ft-long concourse between the platform tunnels faced with moulded Stabler tiling decorated with chrome yellow banding.

Michelin Building, Fulham Road: Encaustic tiles were cheap and highly functional and lent themselves to imaginative decoration. At the Michelin Building exuberant designs celebrated the exciting new age of the motor car.

Of London's secret wartime tunnels, parts of the old Cabinet War Rooms have been opened up as a tourist attraction, but elsewhere many other shelters, bunkers and citadels have passed into private ownership or moulder away, inaccessible other than to nighthawks and urban explorers. Unbeknown to many, a huge public air raid shelter, now flooded, lies under the gardens of Soho Square. Under St Leonard's Court in Mortlake is a fine set of air-raid shelters with their original wartime fittings and notices, approached through a discreet entrance disguised as a conical brick garden building. The old Paddock bunker in Neasden (p424), only declassified in the past 10 years, remains closed other than for occasional group visits and for Open House London. Most atmospheric and profoundly moving of all is the Group 11 Operations Room at RAF Uxbridge (p440), which is preserved as it was on 15 September 1940 at the height of the Battle of Britain, the course of which was directed from Bentley Priory (p432) five miles to the north.

As the population of London more than doubled between 1831 and 1881, it ruthlessly exposed the inability of existing local authorities to address matters of public health and transport. By the mid-19th century London local government was a confused muddle of different authorities with independent boards of commissioners responsible for paving, lighting and cleansing, alongside a jumble of parish vestries. There were over 300 such bodies, empowered by over 250 local Acts of Parliament.

In 1855 the Metropolitan Management Act established the Metropolitan Board of Works as a strategic authority responsible for drainage, street improvements and building regulations, with a rearranged tier of local authorities. This in turn was replaced in 1889 by the London County Council. Ten years later, as a check on the powers of the LCC, Lord Salisbury abolished the district boards and parishes to create 28 metropolitan boroughs.

In the City of London, Mansion House, the traditional home of London's Lord Mayor, has famous interiors which rival those of the royal palaces, but between 1909 and 1922 County Hall, a vast new civic palace for London's government, was erected on the south bank of the Thames virtually opposite the Houses of Parliament as a new headquarters for the LCC. Designed by Ralph Knott in the grand classical manner, with a great monumental marble-lined entrance hall and council chamber and ranks of oak panelled corridors and offices, it remained the home of London government until the Greater London

Fleet Sewer: Hidden from sight in Stygian gloom far under ground, the London sewers are Victorian engineering marvels, as seen here at the Fleet river intersection.

Tower Bridge: Some of London's most awe-inspiring spaces lie out of the public gaze, like the astonishing bascule chambers sunk deep into the river to accommodate the opening leaves of Tower Bridge.

Council was abolished in March 1986, when the building was sold to a Japanese company and converted, in part, to a hotel, offices, aquarium and gallery space. Much remains vacant and unused, including the Council Chamber.

With the redefinition of London's civic geography in 1900, each of the new metropolitan boroughs celebrated their newly found municipal identity in an outpouring of local civic pride. New robes of office and insignia were made, to give tangible expression to this, alongside new town halls in a range of fashionable styles.

Some of these, like Battersea (1892-3) and Croydon (1892-4), which were highly eclectic in style, emerged in the last decade of the century, as did Finsbury (p220), a former vestry hall built in stages with its beautiful "Clerkenwell Angels" soaring up to embrace brachiated Art Nouveau light fittings. Many of those that followed reflected the revival of English classicism, and the lavish ornament of the Edwardian Baroque. Woolwich (p346), by Sir Alfred Brumwell Thomas, the architect of Belfast City Hall, was a bold statement of civic ambition in one of London's poorest neighbourhoods. Its triple-domed and galleried entrance hall is the finest of its type in London, but Deptford (1903-7, by Lanchester and Rickards), Lambeth (1906-8, by Septimus

Warwick and Herbert Austen Hall) and Marylebone (1914-20, by Sir Edwin Cooper) all followed in the same grand classical tradition.

Increasingly town halls were seen as one element of much larger civic complexes containing public halls, offices, libraries and community facilities. Hornsey (1933-5, by Reginald Uren) was revolutionary, the centrepiece of a wider composition embracing electricity and gas showrooms. It was the first of its kind in Britain, modelled on Willem Dudok's groundbreaking new Hilversum Town Hall completed five years earlier, with a marble interior, stylised bronze handrails, exotic woods and cool etched green glass. Greenwich (1938-9, by Clifford Culpin) followed the same precedent, but in a more overtly modern idiom. At Wandsworth (p367) a progressive Moderne-style block was added to the existing buildings in 1935-7 by Edward A Hunt, with an opulent entrance hall paved in onyx, and a staircase with a bronze scroll balustrade lit from above by a massive Art Deco chandelier.

At the national level, as early as 1725 Daniel Defoe complained that government "offices and palaces for business are scattered about". Thereafter for over 250 years a plethora of different schemes was advanced for the reconstruction of Whitehall to a single plan – from Sir John Soane to the megalomaniac modernist masterplan of Leslie Martin in 1965, which envisaged the comprehensive redevelopment of the whole area: the high-water mark of post-war philistinism.

By the late 19th century a series of new buildings had been erected incrementally over the previous 50 years to house the great offices of state alongside some of the more impressive individual buildings of previous generations such as the Banqueting House, 10 Downing Street (p70), the Admiralty (p43), Dover House and Gwydyr House.

Of this new generation of buildings, the Foreign Office (embracing the India and Colonial Offices) (p66) was bedecked with some of the most lavish interiors ever seen inside any government building in Britain. Designed by Sir George Gilbert Scott and Matthew Digby Wyatt and completed in 1875, this was architecture used overtly for political ends, intended to overawe visiting dignitaries with the majesty of Britain's burgeoning naval and imperial power.

The expansion of the government precinct in the late 19th century swept away some areas of shockingly dilapidated housing on the doorstep of Whitehall, but in 1936 the older aristocratic houses in Whitehall Gardens started to succumb to the tide of change and were levelled to make way for a colossal new building for the Air Ministry and Board of Trade, now the Ministry of Defence (1939-59, by Vincent Harris) (p74). Malmesbury House, Pembroke House, Cromwell House and Montagu House were all felled, but several rooms from Pembroke House and Cromwell House (see *Lost London*, p172-4) were salvaged and reassembled in the new building, along with Cardinal Wolsey's wine cellar (1514-16) (p75), an extensive vaulted fragment of the old Whitehall Palace that was lowered into place from its original position 19ft above in a massive engineering exercise undertaken in 1949.

Gants Hill Underground Station: London Transport has always embraced heroic design. Gants Hill is the only station on the entire network to be modelled on the great stations in Moscow.

Within the Palace of Westminster, the great chambers of the Lords and Commons, the historic Westminster Hall with the finest mediaeval roof structure in England, and the frescoes depicting stirring scenes from British history are well known to the visiting public, but outside of these areas are some of London's most stunning spaces where access is restricted.

Approached through a discreet staircase off Westminster Hall is the staggering St Stephen's Chapel (p40), completed in 1297 and retaining much of its mediaeval structure overlain with High Victorian Gothic polychrome ornament by E M Barry. At either end of the riverfront are two twin-towered pavilions; to the north is the Speaker's House (p38) and to the south the Lord Chancellor's residence (p38), the former completed after Pugin's death in 1858 with richly coloured Minton tiles and stained glass, and the latter with its splendid River Room faithfully redecorated in 1997-8 by Lord Irvine using Pugin fabrics and wallpaper, in the teeth of much misguided public criticism. At the centre of the Victoria Tower (p42) are the Parliamentary Archives with cast-iron spiral staircases arcing upwards between documents, rolls and Acts of Parliament passed since 1497. Although renowned the world over for its iconic external silhouette and the sonorous chimes of Big Ben (cast at the Whitechapel Bell Foundry, p312), the interior of St Stephen's Clock Tower (p36) surprisingly is better known more as the setting for the dénouement of John Buchan's novel *The Thirty Nine Steps* than for its intrinsic historic interest.

The reconstruction of the Palace of Westminster after the disastrous fire of 1834 ushered in the golden age of mural painting. In 1841 the Fine Arts Commission was set up under the enlightened chairmanship

County Hall: Once this was the inner sanctum of London's regional government, but since the abolition of the Greater London Council in 1986, the old Council Chamber has remained empty.

of Prince Albert to bring the history of the nation to life through the medium of murals, statuary, heraldry and painting. One result was the magnificent series of murals adorning the walls of the palace with works by G F Watts, Edward Matthew Ward, Frank Salisbury, John Byam Shaw and Frank Cadogan Cowper alongside mosaics by Sir Edward Poynter and Robert Anning Bell. This vogue for national romanticism was taken up for other government and civic buildings. At the Foreign Office (p66) Sigismund Goetze painted the stirring Britannia murals on the Grand Staircase between 1914 and 1919, Britannia Pacificatrix having to be amended by painting out Germany after the outbreak of the First World War, and India raised as a dignified standing allegorical figure. Other notable murals can be found at the Royal Exchange, by various artists including Lord Leighton between 1895 and 1922; the former P & O building in Cockspur Street from 1920 to 1921, executed by Frederick Beaumont; the Church of Notre Dame de France in

Leicester Place by Jean Cocteau completed in 1960; and the colossal 1951-4 abstract mural by Ivon Hitchens at Cecil Sharp House in Primrose Hill, the home of the English Folk Song Society.

Between 1910 and 1912 Sir Aston Webb's remodelling of the Mall and Buckingham Palace and the completion of the Queen Victoria Memorial transformed the ceremonial heart of London into a great new imperial capital. Alongside the Mall the historic buildings of previous generations were given a much improved setting as part of the backdrop to national events – Marlborough House (p84), for years the residence of Edward and Alexandra as Prince and Princess of Wales, St James's Palace with its exquisite Chapel Royal (p92), the Queen's Chapel (p93) by Inigo Jones and Clarence House, once the residence of Queen Elizabeth, the Queen Mother, now the London home of the Prince of Wales.

Webb's remodelling was carried out at a time of unprecedented national wealth and at the very moment when Edwardian architecture was at its most exuberant and self-confident. The great dominions of Empire were enshrined in bronze and stone in spectacular new edifices that reinforced London's place as a great global city. Australia House (p190) was completed in 1918 at a strategic location at the junction of the newly created Aldwych and Strand. India House (1930), with its subtle incorporation of Indian motifs and symbols, was raised nearby to the designs of Sir Herbert Baker, who worked with Lutyens on the creation of the majestic new imperial capital at New Delhi. It was Baker, the architect of so much underrated imperial architecture in South Africa, who designed South Africa House (1930-3) (p172) on the site of the old Morley's Hotel on the east side of Trafalgar Square. Opposite, Canada House was remodelled in 1924-5 within the shell of Sir Robert Smirke's old Union Club and Royal College of Physicians, symbolically located at the centre of the Empire for the oldest of the great dominions. Elsewhere, Africa House (1921-2) in Kingsway and British Columbia House (1915) in Lower Regent Street overtly expressed the Imperial ideal.

Nothing symbolised the transmutation of Empire into Commonwealth more strikingly than the extraordinary Commonwealth Institute (1962, by Robert Matthew, Johnson-Marshall & Partners) which arose on the edge of Holland Park. Its futuristic paraboloid roof and bold modern interior encapsulated the optimism of a new Elizabethan age and hopes for a new fraternity of nations sharing a common culture and heritage. Whilst the Commonwealth quietly flourishes and expands, after years of dereliction the building is planned to become a new home for the Design Museum, overseen by the minimalist architect John Pawson.

London's pre-eminence as a great world city was founded on commerce and trade, and some of the capital's finest interiors can be found in the temples of finance dedicated to the worship of Mammon. The architect Edward Maufe wrote: "A Bank should express aesthetically that security which we know it possesses as a fact. It should not only be strong, it should look strong."

The supreme example is the Bank of England (p242) – the "Old Lady of Threadneedle Street" – rebuilt by Sir Herbert Baker between

1921 and 1939 within Sir John Soane's massive perimeter walls; but many of the other great banks and insurance buildings of the period strove to outdo each other in the quality of their materials and opulence to convey an image of robust solidity and financial security. Gibson Hall (p232) is a remnant of the finest of the mid-Victorian banks in the City of London, whilst the former headquarters of the Midland Bank HQ in Poultry (1924-39, by Sir Edwin Lutyens) (p250) is a gigantic, vertiginous mass of stonework around a steel frame with a cavernous interior on a scale exceeded only by the adjacent Bank of England. Between 1927 and 1931 the commercial heart of the City of London around the Royal Exchange was rebuilt as the other great banks followed suit, each with glorious interiors: Lloyds in Lombard Street in1927, the National Provincial by Edwin Cooper on the corner of Poultry and Prince's Street in 1929, and the Westminster Bank in Throgmorton Street, completed in 1932 by Mewès and Davis, the architects of the Ritz.

In a number of cases, the headquarters of the great insurance companies rivalled even the banks for their ostentatious interiors. At Holborn Bars, Alfred Waterhouse's soaring red-brick cathedral was raised in stages for the Prudential Assurance Co (p206) over a period of

Foreign and Commonwealth Office: Architecture overtly deployed for political ends. Conceived at the zenith of Britain's economic and imperial power, the grandiloquent interior was designed to overawe foreign dignitaries.

almost 40 years with an entire sequence of interiors encrusted in various green and yellow hues of Doulton ceramic tile. Not to be outdone, at the western end of High Holborn the great rival Pearl Assurance Co built an equally impressive pile in full-blown Edwardian classical style in 1912-19, now the Chancery Court Hotel with a much-altered interior. In Southampton Row between 1921 and 1934 the Liverpool Victoria Friendly Society (p144) levelled an entire street block on the east side of Bloomsbury Square for a vast headquarters building with a magnificent Board Room and Directors' Offices and a full-blown Art Deco ballroom in the basement. In the City, Lloyd's Register of Shipping (p254) boasts a palatial interior and a marble staircase crowned by the superb sculpture of the Spirit of British Maritime Commerce by F Lynn Jenkins. Lloyd's of London (1978-86) by the Richard Rogers Partnership (p258) has been described as "the most consistently innovative insurance building the City has seen since

Commonwealth Institute: One of Britain's most innovative post-war buildings intended to convey a progressive image of modernity to the newly emerging Commonwealth; now empty and awaiting conversion as a new home for the Design Museum.

Soane's Bank of England". Lauded by some, excoriated by others, it is now London's most modern Grade I listed building, a bizarre juxtaposition of Rogers' gigantic atrium rising through the building with a boardroom by Robert Adam salvaged from Bowood House in 1955 for use in the earlier building on the site, and then reconstructed once again as a traditional inner sanctum within Rogers' building.

Alongside the great temples of finance and commerce is the fourth estate – the great newspaper offices, of which the riotous interior of the former Daily Express building in Fleet Street (p280) borders on the promiscuous. Lesser known and tucked away in nearby Carmelite House, the staircase of the former Daily Mail building still retains its caged lift and walls embellished with allegorical Art Nouveau decoration.

London's ecclesiastical heritage is so extensive and varied that it is impossible to even scratch the surface – from its ancient legacy of mediaeval parish churches in old urban villages to the Gothic splendours of inner-city Victorian churches. Seek and ye shall find. I have opted instead for a portrayal of London's spiritual diversity.

London has always flourished by being a tolerant, open city, assimilating wave after wave of newcomers, each of whom has left their mark on the city. This is most palpable in the spiritual sphere – German Lutherans within the plain confines of their chapel in Alie Street (p310); Jews in Bevis Marks (p252) and a host of synagogues

across the capital, from the hidden backland time capsule at 19 Princelet Street, Spitalfields, to the splendours of the New West End synagogue in Paddington; Greek Orthodox at the sublime St Sophia's in Moscow Road (p410); and Russian Orthodox off Knightsbridge. Behind the old Imperial Russian Legation in Welbeck Street (the plasterwork of its first floor rooms enriched with the arms of the Russian cities) lies an older Russian Orthodox church visited by Czar Alexander II in 1874.

In the unlikely environs of Neasden, the serrated outline of the Shri Swaminarayan temple (p422) can be seen rising over the unprepossessing inter-war houses lining the North Circular Road as a spiritual rejoinder to IKEA opposite. Equally surreal, the serene silhouette of a traditional Thai temple with its splendid contemporary murals can be glimpsed towering above the detached suburban houses in Calonne Road, Wimbledon (p384). It is a little-known fact that the purchase of the site of the future London Central Mosque and Islamic Cultural Centre in Regent's Park (p325) was authorised by Winston Churchill at the height of the Battle of Britain as a tribute to Indian Muslim soldiers who had died defending the British Empire.

Amongst the welter of smaller spiritual bodies is the unique expressionist Rudolf Steiner House in Regent's Park (p324), the little-known Welsh Baptist Chapel in Eastcastle Street, Marylebone (p124) and the Paget Memorial Mission Hall (p322) hidden away in the hinterlands of King's Cross. The Round Chapel in Clapton (p334) shows that even Non-conformists could build with style and bravura. Street's St James the Less, Pimlico (p52), is a lesser-known High Victorian Gothic gem in need of restoration, while Lutyens's St Jude, Hampstead Garden Suburb (p426), with its extraordinary murals by Walter Starmer, has one of the finest 20th century church interiors in the capital. Those with a particular interest in murals should visit the newly completed murals and carved fittings at the former Church of St Barnabas, Kentish Town, now the Greek Orthodox Church of St Andrew. The Georgian Orthodox Cathedral in Clapton (p334) was once the home of the Agapemonites ornamented with apocalyptic symbols and stunning stained glass by Walter Crane. Here in 1902 the vicar announced to an astonished congregation that he was Christ risen, causing not a little consternation amongst the good people of Clapton. At St Mary Magdalene, Paddington (p414), Ninian Comper's sublime crypt and Chapel of St Sepulchre is a twilight world with a beautiful star-spangled vault and stunning carved and gilded altar.

Of the funerary monuments, the surviving hydraulic catafalque beneath the Anglican Chapel at Kensal Green (p419), the astonishing Chandos Mausoleum and St Lawrence Chapel at Stanmore (p428) and the melancholy interior of the tomb of Sir Richard Burton at Mortlake (p381) offer their own very different perspectives on mortality and the afterlife, but the mummified remains of "Jimmy Garlick" in the tower of St James, Garlickhythe, in the City of London offer a very direct insight. The embalmed cadaver was found in the vaults in 1855 and, after residing at various points in the church, is now happily ensconced in a display case in the tower.

Moments from the commercial mayhem of Oxford Street is Tyburn Convent, a haven of soothing spiritual serenity and silence, home to a small community of Benedictine nuns in a plain white chapel reconstructed after war damage. The numinous air is palpable, but hidden in the crypt beneath is the Chapel of the English Reformation Martyrs, commemorating the 105 Catholics martyred for their faith in Tudor England. The altar is a rather gruesome interpretation of Tyburn tree, and the chapel walls are covered with human relics and body parts removed from the dead – vertebrae, bones, blood-soaked rags and even fingernails.

By its very definition street furniture is in the public domain, but nonetheless some items remain tantalisingly obscure. There are 13 surviving cabmen's shelters in London of the 61 erected between 1874 and 1914, all listed (p401). The Cabmen's Shelter Fund, founded by Lord Shaftesbury and friends, was intended to provide facilities at recognised cab ranks for cabbies in need of refreshment. Painted dark green with crowning ventilators, they resemble Victorian park kiosks, but each contains a small kitchen for the preparation of hot food, tables and chairs and space for a dozen people. For lovers of ephemera, sitting discreetly inside the western colonnade of the Royal Academy in Piccadilly what appears to be a conventional cast-iron K2 telephone box is in fact the 1924 competition-winning wooden prototype of Giles Gilbert Scott's famous kiosk.

Finally, the houses selected are united only by their diversity. The aim has been to illustrate and celebrate a broad range of periods and styles, with a strong emphasis on the decorative tradition.

Relatively few houses survive from before 1666, and of those that do, most are well known and managed by trusts or public bodies of various sorts. Canonbury Tower, Islington (c1520), the former home

of Thomas Cromwell, Francis Bacon and Oliver Goldsmith, has a set of panelled rooms completed between 1570 and 1610. Sutton House, which retains some rare linenfold panelling, was built in 1535 and is now managed by the National Trust. The interiors of Eastbury Manor House, Barking, built for the wealthy City merchant Clement Sysley sometime between c1556 and 1573, were extensively altered post-1841, although fragments of wall paintings remain. Charlton House, Greenwich, erected between 1607 and 1612 for Adam Newton, the tutor to Prince Henry, the son of James I, is the best surviving Jacobean house in London, with some good original plasterwork and chimneypieces. The eponymous Prince Henry's Room (p283) in Fleet Street (1610) was actually built as a tavern rather than for the prince, but it is a precious remnant of a timber-framed, pre-Great Fire house in central London. In Highgate, Cromwell House (1637-8), currently in private ownership, has a chunky oak staircase with huge handrails, pierced panels rather than balusters, and carved military statuettes on

New West End Synagogue: London has always been an ethnic melting pot, embracing waves of newcomers. The rich interior of this synagogue is in the Oriental tradition with exotic decoration over the Ark.

the newel posts replicated after the originals were stolen. Lauderdale House opposite has a timber-framed 16th century core overlaid by subsequent alterations.

Lambeth Palace (p44), the residence of the Archbishop of Canterbury, has some of the best surviving mediaeval fabric of any domestic building in London, including a 13th century undercroft and a 17th century prison in the upper part of the 15th century Lollards' Tower. Fulham Palace, once the summer residence of the Bishops of London, has a complete 16th century Tudor quadrangle with a roof structure over the Great Hall that has been dated to 1470.

Spencer House (p90) is the only great 18th century palatial aristocratic town house in London to survive intact, with its astonishing Palm Room of 1757 forming the architectural climax of the ground floor. Danson House, Bexley (p352), the epitome of an 18th century English country villa, was until recently one of London's most intractable buildings at risk, saved from certain ruin after direct intervention by English Heritage. John Murray's at 50 Albemarle Street (p96) retains all the ambience of an early 18th century town house in continuous daily use as a publishing house since 1768, while 11 Bedford Row (p152) shows that even the plain repetitive exterior of

Chapel of St Sepulchre, St Mary Magdalene Church, Paddington: The mediaeval style painted organ in the vaulted crypt chapel is one of the capital's most atmospheric sacred spaces.

the London terrace house can hide stunning set pieces. A comparable staircase compartment at 8 Clifford Street, Mayfair, has Grecian murals in the style of Sir James Thornhill. Similar obscure delights can be found at the Royal College of Nursing in Cavendish Square, which was remodelled in 1922-6 as the Cowdray Club but which retains an entire staircase compartment with landscape murals and grisailles of sculpture by John Devoto from an earlier 1720 house on the site. .

After years of decay, the fragile Gothick interiors at Strawberry Hill (p388), the Twickenham home transformed by Horace Walpole from 1749 to 1766, have been restored to their original splendour in a £9m project funded by the Heritage Lottery Fund and English Heritage.

Lancaster House (p94) is the grandest of all the great 19th century houses, conceived in 1825 as a home for the Duke of York, but only completed in the 1840s by Benjamin Wyatt for the 2nd Duke of Sutherland, and later sold to the soap magnate Viscount Leverhulme, who presented it to the nation in 1913.

In Kensington, Tower House, the wonderfully romantic Gothic sanctuary built by William Burges for his own use, has been sensitively maintained and restored by its current owner (see *Panoramas of Lost London*, p136-42). Linley Sambourne House in Kensington is a completely preserved Victorian time capsule and popular museum with all its furnishings and fittings, while Little Holland House in Carshalton (p382) shows how the succeeding generation reacted against the cluttered Victorian interior in favour of the plain craftsmanship of the Arts and Crafts movement. More exotic expressions of late 19th century taste can be found at Leighton House, the studio home of Lord Leighton (p398), nearby Debenham House (p402) with its fantastic Byzantine interiors and tiles (reputedly taken from the Czar of Russia's yacht *Livadia*) and the extraordinary Moorish garden room at Grove House, Hampton (p394), which conjures visions of the Alhambra.

For those who believe that the decorative tradition has died, overwhelmed by the clinical minimalism of the modern movement, three post-war interiors will come as a great surprise.

Externally 575 Wandsworth Road (p375) is simply one of a terrace of run-down late 19th century houses in a dog-eared part of Wandsworth, but the inside is a remarkable tribute to individual creative genius. Each of the rooms is dressed in delicately cut fretwork by the Kenyan poet and author Khadambi Asalache, who systematically covered the whole interior in elaborate Moorish-inspired fretwork over a 20 year period from 1981 until shortly before his death in 2006.

Charles Jencks's Thematic House in Holland Park (p404) is one of the great landmarks in the development of post-modernism and the rediscovery of symbolism and metaphor in architecture. Within the shell of an 1840s town house Jencks has created an entire interior based on cosmic symbolism, with 22 different levels of meaning expressed in a fantastic series of inter-related spaces, rooms and details which celebrate the sun, the moon and the seasons.

Most recently of all, at Crosby Hall (p368) in Cheyne Walk work is still in progress on a full-blown, authentic recreation of a Tudor

mansion for Christopher Moran to create a stunning new private house around the original mediaeval hall, which was relocated from Bishopsgate to Chelsea in 1910.

The impulse given by the conservation movement to the revival of craft skills has encouraged some to recreate authentic historic interiors from scratch by sheer artifice. Many who visit The Jerusalem Tavern in Britton Street, Clerkenwell, are incredulous that the "historic" interior with its old bar, fragments of tiles and atmosphere of past times is a fanciful recreation less than 20 years old behind a finely grained shopfront of c1800. Nearby at the Rookery in Cowcross Street a whole sequence of historic interiors has been crafted carefully to create a new "historic" hotel interior behind the reconstructed façades of a group of unlisted 19th century houses.

However, by far the most extraordinary is the fantasy house which can be found at 18 Folgate Street, Spitalfields (p316), an authentic recreation of an entire 18th century home within an original terrace house of the 1720s, conceived, controlled and orchestrated by the late Dennis Severs and now managed by the Spitalfields Historic Buildings Trust. Each room is furnished and lived in as it would have been at different points in time by a mythical family, the Jervises, where the visitor is tolerated only as a silent observer.

In counterpoint to this are a number of overtly modern buildings and interiors, including Stockwell Bus Garage (p374), the new Olympics Aquatic Centre by Zaha Hadid (p342) and Will Alsop's remarkable organic interior for the Blizard Institute of Cell and Molecular Biology at London Hospital (p304). Some of the most awe-inspiring spaces to

Strawberry Hill: Now restored to its former glory, Horace Walpole's house at Twickenham was hugely influential and launched a whole new eponymous style – Strawberry Hill Gothick. The exquisite Gallery forms its architectural climax.

have been built in the past 10 years are the great new roof structures now in daily public use, like Foster and Partners' huge roof over the Great Court at the British Museum, or John McAslan's stunning new semi-circular concourse at King's Cross Station.

This book is a plea for an appreciation of all traditions and styles, and a moving on from the style wars which have perpetually bedevilled rational discussion about architecture and new design in historic places. One of the great fallacies of the 20th century was the myth that architecture should be "of its time" and somehow express the "spirit of the age", or Zeitgeist, ignoring the very obvious fact that anything built in any age ipso facto must be representative in some way of its time. The corollary of this has been the very damaging belief that it is somehow "dishonest" to design new buildings that draw their inspiration and vocabulary from the past. To an historian this intellectual straitjacket is daft. As Professor David Watkin commented in his myth-busting book *Morality and Architecture*, "hostility towards inspiration from the past makes it impossible to understand the Renaissance with its tradition of imitating and copying antique works … Otherwise someone might say, 'I've got a fake. It's by Michelangelo.'"

The reason for the perpetuation of this myth is not hard to find. Many of the early pioneers of modernism promoted their ideas with a messianic fervour bordering on religious belief. All past styles

575 Wandsworth Road: Detail of the remarkable interior of Khadambi Asalache's house showing the intricate Moorish-inspired fretwork detail.

were rejected in favour of a new form of architectural expression – modernism. Modernism was equated with modernity, and nothing else, it was argued, should be tolerated.

Today, none of this would matter if it wasn't for the fact that this antiquated idea still holds a powerful sway over many in the architectural establishment and, by a process of osmosis, the planning profession and many local planning committees. It has had a deeply damaging impact on the form and design of our towns and cities and even on professional attitudes to the extension and adaptation of historic buildings. Even at an international level, the Vienna Memorandum on World Heritage and Contemporary Architecture, published by UNESCO in 2005, insists that "urban planning, contemporary architecture and preservation of historic urban landscape should avoid all forms of pseudo-historic design, as they constitute a denial of both the historical and the contemporary alike". It is a deep-seated prejudice, which should have been buried a long time ago, but it explains why those who produce buildings in the continuing vernacular or classical traditions are condescendingly dismissed as designing in "pastiche", even though ironically they may be the true radicals for daring to challenge outdated prejudices which have long since been discredited.

It is hardly surprising that the public as a whole seems bemused by all this intolerant rhetoric, which runs completely counter to burgeoning interest in the authentic restoration and adaptation of people's own homes and their interiors. Most people simply want to see the right

buildings in the right places and, unlike many design professionals, have no ingrained prejudice against any particular architectural style. This was poetically put by Spike Milligan in 1971:

> Beautiful Buildings
> No longer stand
> In Bloomsbury's
> Pleasant Land.
> The Land (it's said)
> Is sold. Who by? …
> A place that teaches
> Architectural Knowledge
> London University College!
> So when one stands
> And sadly stares
> At horrid new buildings
> In Bloomsbury's Squares
> We know the responsibility's
> Theirs.
> Envoi
> A lot of learning can be a little thing.

In an age of architectural pluralism, surely the time has come to consign old fundamentalist attitudes to the dustbin of history, and to celebrate artistic and stylistic diversity in all its forms and traditions. Modernism is just another style, and all styles are equally valid – vernacular, classical, Gothic, Islamic, post-modern and modern. None has a monopoly on truth. None is more honest than any other. In any situation there are myriad different options and styles to explore, and a proper understanding of context can and should provide a clear guide on how to proceed.

By celebrating London's rich heritage of interiors, I hope that a more sophisticated understanding might emerge of how to manage change better in a way that rejects prejudice in favour of tolerance and an appreciation of the extraordinary creativity of professionals from all backgrounds who produce works of art and architecture that are triumphs of individual expression. This book pays homage to the skills, imagination, craftsmanship and energy of past generations who have left their mark on London and who have not been afraid to deploy fantasy, humour, symbolism and allegory in the works they have created.

> In our city … street and square and crescent,
> We can feel our living past in our shadowed present,
> Ghosts beside our starlit Thames who lived and loved and died
> Keep throughout the ages
> London Pride.
> Grey city! Stubbornly implanted,
> Taken so for granted for a thousand years,
> Stay city! Smokily enchanted,
> Cradle of our memories and hopes and fears.
>
> (Noel Coward, "London Pride", 1941)

Author's note

With almost 1,700 photographs, *London: Hidden Interiors* is probably the most highly illustrated book about London ever published. The intention is to give the reader a true sense of having visited these places. In a real visit, the eye focuses on particular highlights for which an explanation is required, yet skims over other features as part of the background. In the same way, this book identifies many details but also allows the reader to take in a wealth of other visual information. Likewise the text singles out important features in the photographs yet often refers to other interesting details that could not be shown because of constraints on space.

The remarkable interiors in the pages that follow are organised as a geographical journey. Beginning in Central London, it spirals outwards from its starting point in Westminster through the West End and Mayfair. The reader then follows a route east through Soho, Covent Garden, Fitzrovia and Clerkenwell to the City and its fringes. Heading further east, the route then winds clockwise around the capital's southern suburbs, moving west and terminating in the north. It has not been possible in every case to keep fully to the geographic rationale but we trust the reader will be entertained and informed by the serendipity unveiled here.

Most of the places listed in this book are not open to the general public though may have special open days or participate in Open House, London. Each entry includes the street address, postcode and its listed status at the time of going to press, Grade I, Grade II* or Grade II. SAM indicates a Scheduled Ancient Monument. (For further explanation of the National Heritage List for England, visit the English Heritage website.) Readers who want to see the exteriors or perhaps to visit during an open day should find the organisation of the book helpful in planning a productive day out thanks to the grouping of nearby properties.

The related website www.londonhiddeninteriors.co.uk indicates any public access and gives links to information, where available, for each entry in the book. We remind readers that where the places listed in this book are occupied by individuals or companies, their privacy should be respected at all times.

St Stephen's Clock Tower
Palace of Westminster

SW1A 0AA
LISTED: GRADE I

Completed in 1858, the 316ft St Stephen's Clock Tower is a global icon renowned the world over for its instantly-recognisable silhouette and sonorous chimes. It stands close to the site of an earlier clock tower built in 1365 by Henry Yevele, the architect of the roof of Westminster Hall, and demolished under the direction of Sir Christopher Wren in 1698. Its bell, known as Great Tom of Westminster, was relocated by Wren to the north-west tower of St Paul's Cathedral.

The palace architect, Charles Barry, wrestled with the problem of how to give the clock sufficient prominence, and turned to Augustus Pugin for its design. It is widely believed that his innovative solution was derived from Pugin's earlier design for a clock tower at Scarisbrick Hall in Lancashire. The work at the palace finally drove the obsessive Pugin to insanity and a premature grave. "I have never worked so hard in my life for Mr Barry," he wrote of his designs for the clock tower.

Inside, the lower parts of the tower were used for the confinement of persons committed to the custody of the Serjeant at Arms, the last being Charles Bradlaugh, the rumbustious atheist Liberal MP, in 1880. A plain spiral stair of 334 steps winds up to the belfry and Big Ben, the nickname for the hour bell, supposedly named after Sir Benjamin Hall, the first Commissioner of Works, but more likely attributable to Benjamin Caunt, the well-known 17-stone prize-fighter, who fought his last fight in 1857 at the age of 42.

The original 16½-ton bell was cast at the Warner's foundry in Stockton-on-Tees and brought to London by sea from West Hartlepool in October 1856. However, a year later a 4ft crack was discovered, and a new contract was issued for its recasting to Mears of Whitechapel (p312). The new 13½-ton bell was hung in October 1858 and became operational in July 1859. When a short 4.3 inch crack appeared in this,

the bell was given a quarter-turn and the weight of the hammer reduced. It remains cracked. In 1957 the bells and the hammer were refurbished by the Whitechapel Foundry. The world-famous chimes, based on a phrase from Handel's "I know that my Redeemer liveth," were copied from Great St Mary's in Cambridge installed in 1793-4, and later, in a slightly altered sequence, at the Royal Exchange in 1845.

The installation of the clock was both complicated and controversial. In 1852 the contract was given to E J Dent, maker of astronomical clocks, and it was designed by the Astronomer Royal, Professor George Airy, and Edmund Beckett Denison QC (afterwards Lord Grimthorpe). The clock was completed by Dent's stepson and went into service on 31 May 1859. Each dial contains 312 panes of opalescent glass with 2ft-high numerals designed by Pugin. The minute hands are of hollow copper and the hour hands gunmetal. The clock weights almost 2½ tons, raised from nearly ground level by an electric motor. The clock is corrected for changes in barometric pressure by adjusting the weights in the tray at the top of the pendulum. The addition of one old penny causes the clock to gain two-fifths of a second over a 24-hour period.

On 5 August 1976 metal fatigue in the chiming gear increased the speed of the barrel, which smashed through the mechanism, fracturing the main frame. As a result about half of the original mechanism was replaced.

From 1885 the Ayrton light at the top of the tower has indicated whether either House is sitting at night. Since 1910 Big Ben has tolled for the funerals of Edward VII, George V and George VI. The chimes remained silent on the day of Churchill's funeral on 30 January 1965.

In 2012 the tower, which leans 9 inches from the vertical, was re-named the Elizabeth Tower to mark the Diamond Jubilee of H M The Queen.

The Speaker's House and Lord Chancellor's Residence
Palace of Westminster

SW IA OAA

LISTED: GRADE I

At the north end of the Palace of Westminster, between the Clock Tower and the river, is a projecting twin-towered pavilion overlooking Speaker's Green. It was designed around an inner courtyard to accommodate the official residences of the Speaker and Serjeant at Arms.

By the 19th century the Speaker was vested with much greater political authority than previously. The first Speaker's House was designed in a simple castellated Gothic style by James Wyatt in 1815 for George IV's Speaker, Henry Addington, but this was destroyed in the fire of 1834. Barry's new building ennobled the dignity of the office and enhanced its status by providing him with a palace within a palace, corresponding in grandeur with the Queen's Robing Room and Royal Gallery at the south end of the building, with interiors masterminded by Pugin.

Approached via a separate entrance in Speaker's Court, flanked by panels carved with the Mace and national emblems in stained glass, a splendid ceremonial staircase leads to a magnificent suite of reception rooms "emblazoned with ornament after the manner of the House of Peers". Barry had stipulated that "the style of its furnishings, fittings and decorations will be in accordance with the best examples of the Tudor period", and he succeeded. Lavish gilded coffered ceilings, panelling by Holland and Son, stained glass by John Hardman, floor tiles by Minton, elaborate Gothic chimneypieces by Pugin and the widespread use of heraldry displaying the arms and armorial bearings of past Speakers combine to create a romantic evocation of the glories of the Speaker's office.

The centrepiece of the entire enfilade of rooms is the State Bedroom. Until 1529 the Palace of Westminster was the principal royal residence, and the buildings played an important role in state ceremonial. It was customary for mediaeval monarchs to spend the night before their coronation in the palace. Although, with the exception of George IV, this practice had long since fallen into desuetude, a gorgeous state bed was provided, based on Pugin's designs, as a reference to past royal practice. Carved into the footboard are the royal arms, and its valance is embroidered with the emblems of the three kingdoms – the Thistle, the Tudor Rose and the Shamrock.

During the war and afterwards such ostentation became deeply unfashionable. Unbelievably the State Bedroom was dismantled and the bed sold off. It was rediscovered in a Welsh barn in 1985, purchased by the National Heritage Memorial Fund and restored by the Victoria & Albert Museum. The bed and bedroom were reconstructed in the former drawing room of the Serjeant at Arms' residence, adjoining the Speaker's Dining Room, which has a fine collection of the Speaker's state silver including two superb candelabra by Paul Storr.

In the matching south pavilion is the Lord Chancellor's residence with its superb River Room, controversially restored by Lord Irvine in 1997-8, with dark green monogrammed Pugin wallpaper and a fine collection of loaned paintings and neo-classical sculpture.

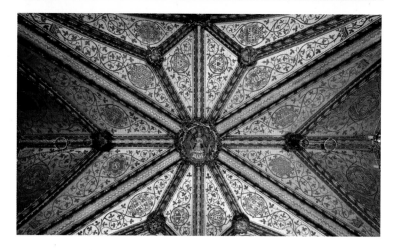

Chapel of St Mary Undercroft
Palace of Westminster

SW1A 0AA

LISTED: GRADE I

With its stupendous hammerbeam roof erected between 1394 and 1401 for Richard II, Westminster Hall is rightly celebrated as the finest timber-framed mediaeval structure in the world, but far less well known is the exquisite Chapel of St Mary Undercroft, which lies below.

St Stephen's Chapel was built as a double-storey royal chapel for Edward I in 1292-7 as a rival to La Sainte-Chapelle in Paris. Today only the former crypt, now known as the Chapel of St Mary Undercroft, survives, but it is of great architectural significance as its original master masons, Michael of Canterbury and his son, Thomas, were devotees of the complex geometrical forms in which lay the origins of the later Decorated Gothic style. Its lierne vaults, forming stellar and other patterns, are believed to be the oldest in England. The large central bosses (below left), restored by Barry after the fire of 1834, depict the martyrdoms of St Stephen, St John, St Catherine and St Laurence, and St Margaret and the Dragon. St Stephen is depicted being stoned to death by Jews dressed in the costume of the 14th century.

For a long period the chapel was used as the debating chamber of the House of Commons, but it also endured many indignities. Oliver Cromwell had the crypt whitewashed and used it as a stable for his horses, and it was also used as a coal cellar.

The internal restoration was carried out by Charles Barry's son, E M Barry, quietly over a 10-year period between 1860 and 1870 because of "rigid economic and ecclesiastical prejudice in the House of Commons", but the end result was a gorgeous, polychrome masterpiece encrusted with gold mosaics with stained glass by John Hardman Powell, an alabaster dado, and a floor of marble and Minton tiles. At the east end (middle left) the windows were replaced with full-length figures of martyred saints executed by J G Crace & Son. The altar rails and gates with their kneeling angels (opposite above), designed by Barry, were modelled on the grille made in 1294 for the tomb of Eleanor of Castile in Westminster Abbey. At the west end, in a beautiful octagonal baptistery, is a huge font with an alabaster bowl, shafts of Ipplepen marble and a base of Hopton Wood stone and Purbeck marble.

Just to the east of Westminster Hall, and north of the chapel, is another of the palace's obscure treasures hidden from the public gaze: the fan-vaulted St Stephen's Cloister, rebuilt in 1526-9 at the expense of John Chamber, Henry VIII's physician, with an early Tudor Gothic courtyard at its centre, later altered by Barry, and restored again after extensive bomb damage in the Second World War.

Today the principal entrance to the undercroft is via a staircase in the south-east corner of Westminster Hall. A bomb placed here by the Fenians in 1885 was discovered by a policeman and carried into Westminster Hall, where it exploded, blew out the great window and created a large hole in the floor. At the base of the staircase leading into Old Palace Yard a plaque marks the cupboard where the suffragette Emily Wilding-Davison concealed herself for 48 hours during the 1911 census in order to record her address as the House of Commons in protest at the exclusion of women from the vote. Two years later she planted a bomb at Lloyd George's house in Surrey, causing severe damage. Shortly afterwards she was killed after stepping in front of the King's horse at the Epsom Derby.

Victoria Tower
Palace of Westminster

SW1A 0AA
LISTED: GRADE I

Soaring 323ft above the streets of domestic buildings which once surrounded it, on its completion in 1860 the Victoria Tower was the largest and tallest square tower in the world, and a marvel of Victorian engineering. Designed by Charles Barry as a grand royal entrance and fireproof repository for the records of Parliament, the exterior and underside of its great entrance arch were richly carved with Gothic detail and symbolic commemorative sculpture. In the middle of the palace complex, the wildly romantic spires of the Central Tower disguised its more prosaic role as a gigantic ventilator, and later the Victoria Tower was adapted to improve the flow of air through the building. Barry was preoccupied with ensuring that the proportions of the two towers and the Clock Tower, and their relationship to the whole, were kept in harmonious balance. He succeeded perfectly.

Until 1497 the Clerks of the Parliaments, who were also Chancery clerks, took their records back into Chancery at the end of a session. These precious historical documents are now in the National Archives. In the late 16th century, the Lords archives were reorganised and kept in the Jewel Tower in the south-west corner of the palace, which still survives. This was very fortunate because when much of the palace was destroyed in a catastrophic fire on the night of 16 October 1834, the ancient Lords archives in the Jewel Tower survived. Many Lords papers which had not been transferred were saved by Henry Stone Smith, a Lords clerk, who hurled bundles of papers from the burning building into Old Palace Yard. Amongst these treasures were letters abandoned by Charles I during the Battle of Naseby, and the Declaration of Breda.

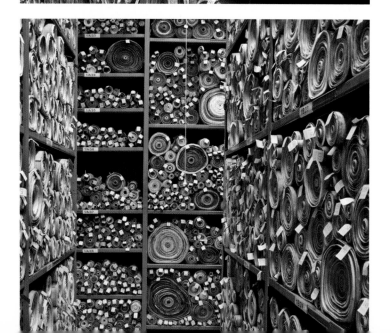

Barry's colossal tower was designed with eight fireproof strong-rooms served by a cast-iron spiral staircase of 553 steps winding twelve storeys through the building. The Archives hold copies of approximately 60,000 Acts of Parliament since 1497, and minutes, petitions and official records of both Houses, together with modern political papers and the historic archives of the Lord Great Chamberlain. Between 1948 and 1963 the old record rooms were reconstructed and air-conditioned. Further improvements and environmental controls were completed in 2004.

Amongst the three million records stored on 5½ miles of shelving are the Attainder of Catherine Howard, records of the trial of Mary, Queen of Scots, the Death Warrant of Charles I (1649), Habeas Corpus (1679), the Bill of Rights (1689), the Acts abolishing the Slave Trade (1807) and Slavery (1833) and the Great Reform Act (1832), alongside documents signed by generations of British luminaries from Elizabeth I and Oliver Cromwell to Samuel Pepys and Lord Nelson. Records held by the Parliamentary Archives may be consulted in the public Search Room at the Palace of Westminster, by appointment.

Old Admiralty Board Room
Old Admiralty Building

WHITEHALL, SW1 2PA
LISTED: GRADE I

The Old Admiralty in Whitehall is probably the oldest purpose-built office building in Britain. It was completed in 1725 to the design of Thomas Ripley in a U-shaped plan with a poorly proportioned pedimented Ionic portico deeply recessed behind a courtyard enclosed by two long wings. In 1760-1 Robert Adam linked the wings with an elegant arcaded entrance screen enriched with naval trophies by M H Spang, which now forms the principal road frontage.

Inside is the Admiralty Board Room, the nerve centre of the Royal Navy for almost 300 years, and the epicentre of some of the momentous events in British naval history from Trafalgar to Jutland.

The ceiling with its diminishing octagonal coffering was designed by S P Cockerell in 1788, but rebuilt in replica in 1947 after war damage in 1941. However the focal point of the entire room is the wind compass over the fireplace designed by Robert Norden which, together with the oak panelling, came from the earlier Admiralty Building and dates from 1708. It is driven by a metal vane on the roof and enabled the Admiralty Board to monitor wind direction. A semaphore system linked to a line of high points and church towers across southern England facilitated communication with the dockyard at Portsmouth in 12 minutes. On the dial is a plan of the seas around Britain and north-west Europe with ships, whales and allegorical figures in the waters. Prior to 1847, it stood on the north wall of the room.

Surrounding the fireplace are spectacular limewood carvings by Grinling Gibbons, which were installed in 1725, and relocated to their present position as part of the 1847 works. The carvings of nautical instruments from the 16th and 17th centuries include compasses, a ring dial, an astrolabe, a backstaff and a vovelle for computing tides. Some of the instruments are the only facsimile models of the originals now in existence. Surmounted by a crown and laurel leaves are the Sword of Victory and the Trumpet of Fame over the Eye in Glory signifying the Stuarts' belief in the divine right of kings. To the left of the fireplace, which contains Churchill's Box which he used as First Lord of the Admiralty in 1914-15, is a white mark called the Nelson Spot. At 5ft 4in, Nelson's height, it was used at interviews for candidates for the Royal Marines, which until 1847 stipulated minimum height requirements.

The clock by Langley Bradley (c1697) has stood in the room since 1725 and tells the date and time. The table and chairs were made in 1784, on which is a casket containing the flag of the Lord High Admiral, a post currently occupied by the Duke of Edinburgh.

Over the doors are seascapes by Vandevelde the Younger and William Nicol. The portrait of Nelson, by Leonardo Guzzardi, depicts the scar over his right eye following the Battle of the Nile. In a small frame on a side table is the original vellum appointing Samuel Pepys as Clerk of the Acts to the Navy Board in 1662. On the left side table is an original manuscript of the poem "The Fleet" by Lord Tennyson and a handwritten note by Theodore Roosevelt, which states: "Let us not owe our shameful safety to the British Fleet, let us do our own fighting."

The building is now occupied by the Cabinet Office.

Lambeth Palace

LAMBETH PALACE ROAD, SE1 7JU
LISTED: GRADE I

Lambeth Palace, a fascinating complex of picturesque mediaeval and later buildings, is the London residence of the Archbishop of Canterbury. Faced in diapered red brick and stone dressings, Morton's Tower, the castellated main gatehouse, has remained virtually unaltered since its completion in 1486. On the ground floor is a small prison with heavy iron rings embedded in the walls. The room over the gateway, lined with linen fold panelling, was Morton's audience chamber where the cardinal was served by his page, the young Thomas More. In the west tower is another fine panelled chamber bearing the 17th century coat of arms of Archbishop Tillotson (left).

The original mediaeval Great Hall (opposite) was dismantled by the regicides during the Commonwealth, but rebuilt after the Restoration by the aged Archbishop Juxon in 1660-3 with a magnificent hammerbeam roof 100 years after the fashion had passed – what Pepys called "Juxon's new old-fashioned hall". However its tall hexagonal lantern, cornice with garlands and modillions and internal classical nuances – coffering and pendants carved with foliage – prefigure the emerging classical style. Blackamoors' heads in the roof and over the fireplace were taken from Juxon's coat of arms. The hall, converted into the Palace Library by Edward Blore in 1829, contains a superb collection of early books including a Gutenburg Bible, a manuscript copy of Caxton's *Chronicles of England* and Charles I's embroidered leather gloves, handed to Juxon as the King mounted the scaffold.

The 13th century crypt, or undercroft (p46 bottom), is the oldest part of the palace: four double bays with a central row of Purbeck marble columns carrying chamfered arches and ribs reminiscent of Salisbury Cathedral. An 11th century fresco of Our Lord from northern Italy, a papal gift, sits in a niche beside the altar, adding to the air of timeless serenity. The Chapel, built in 1230, was gutted in the war and reconstructed, rather clinically, by Seely and Paget in 1955 with a vaulted plaster ceiling and modern murals by Leonard Rosoman (p47 top right). It was here that John Wycliffe was questioned in 1378 for his "heretical and depraved propositions". On the floor are rare surviving early 14th century floor tiles where Wycliffe may once have stood. The ornate carved oak screen with elaborate scrollwork and oval-shaped openings is part of Archbishop Laud's modifications of 1633, probably by Adam Brown. During the Commonwealth the Chapel was used as a drinking room by soldiers, who smashed Archbishop Parker's tomb and dismembered his body – "the corpse … stripped" and "conveyed to the outhouses for poultry and dung, and buried amongst the offal".

West of the Chapel, the Lollard's Tower (p46 top right) was built by Archbishop Chichele in 1434-5, and later added to by Laud to have rooms enjoying views of the river. A steep winding staircase leads to a small prison with a 3 inch thick, iron-studded oak door. Inside prayers and poignant pleas for help are carved into the panelling alongside formidable iron rings. Richard Lovelace, the poet who wrote "Stone walls do not a prison make, nor iron bars a cage", was imprisoned here in 1648-9.

East of the Chapel is the Guard Room, a four-bay hall with an impressive 14th century arched, braced roof structure carried on corbels with tracery to the spandrels (opposite bottom left). Until the 18th century this was the armoury, after which it became a dining room. Blore's reconstruction in 1829 preserved the roof intact, and it was restored again following bomb damage in the Second World War. Here Thomas More is believed to have faced examination following his refusal to take the Oath of Supremacy in 1534.

The main palace range is by Blore, who was appointed by Archbishop Howley in 1828 to assess the buildings, which he concluded were "miserably deficient". His wholesale reconstruction in the then fashionable Tudor Gothic style destroyed much mediaeval fabric including the cloisters, now the Picture Gallery. In a cabinet in the Gallery is the shell of Archbishop Laud's tortoise, which survived to the age of 120, before being inadvertently crushed by a gardener's wheelbarrow in 1753.

A handsome staircase and tracery balustrade lead to a screen beyond which is the Great Corridor and principal rooms (opposite middle and top left), mostly treated in a simple, understated Tudor Gothic style. The Dining Room and State Drawing Room were destroyed by wartime bombing.

The Supreme Court

PARLIAMENT SQUARE, SW1P 3BD

LISTED: GRADE II*

Established under the Constitutional Reform Act 2005, the Supreme Court took over the judicial functions of the Law Lords and the Judicial Committee of the Privy Council in October 2009. It is housed within the former Middlesex Guildhall on the west side of Parliament Square; a beautiful neo-Gothic building of 1911-13 designed by J G S Gibson and Peyton Skipwith, in deference to its historic neighbours, but with pronounced and innovative Art Nouveau nuances.

Faced in Portland stone with a large central tower and statuary in niches, an impressive relief frieze by the sculptor H C Fehr runs across the entrance portal, depicting scenes from English history including King John handing the Magna Carta to the barons at Runnymede, and the Duke of Northumberland handing the crown to Lady Jane Grey. Internally the building boasted the finest set of courtooms in the country and a remarkably intact Edwardian interior, which prompted SAVE Britain's Heritage to seek judicial review of the decision by Westminster City Council to grant listed building consent to make the necessary alterations.

Between 2007 and 2009 the building was adapted and converted sensitively for its new function as the Supreme Court. The entrance foyer was reconfigured with a new glazed screen and doors by Bettina Furnee, beyond which a new opening leads to the Justice's Library, crafted out of one of the former courtrooms with a gallery on four sides linked to the basement below by a new staircase. As the proceedings of the Supreme Court are very different from a conventional county court, significant changes were required to Gibson's splendid courtrooms, including the removal of some of the original fixed furniture and the creation of level floors, but the architectural character of the historic spaces remains, with richly modelled ceilings, panelling and stained glass. On the main staircase and the lobby to the former Council Chamber, tiled dados and historic light fittings have all been carefully conserved.

Beneath the fine hammerbeam roof in the former Middlesex Council Chamber (Court No.1), the original delicately carved bench ends by Fehr have been incorporated with great skill to terminate sets of new oak benches, and the original "throne" has been relocated to one of the galleries. The remaining original furniture from the other courtrooms has been removed and stored for reuse at Snaresbrook Crown Court. A fine bust of King Edward VII by P Bryant Baker has been relocated to the basement café, while paintings and objects from the Middlesex Art Collection have been cleaned, restored and relocated around the communal areas of the building.

Designed by Feilden & Mawson, and overseen by Gilmore Hankey Kirke for the Ministry of Justice, the project demonstrates that with specialist expertise, skill and flair even the most challenging historic buildings can be adapted to new uses without sacrificing their fundamental significance and integrity. Visitors are welcome to admire the work and observe the legal proceedings when the court is open on weekdays.

At the rear of the building is one of London's little-known historical curiosities. Grimly inscribed "For such as will beg and live idle", the rusticated entrance gateway (1655) from the Old Bridewell Prison, which once stood in nearby Greencoat Row, was relocated here in 1884.

Westminster School

LITTLE DEAN'S YARD, SW1P 3PF
LISTED: GRADE I

Inextricably woven into the mediaeval precincts of Westminster Abbey, Westminster School (the Royal College of St Peter in Westminster) is one of the country's most illustrious public schools. It owes its origins to a school for boys attached to the Benedictine Abbey of Westminster from at least 1179. After the dissolution of the monasteries, it was refounded in 1540 by Henry VIII, and again 20 years later, by Elizabeth I. In 1868 the school became self-governing under the Public Schools Act.

Now part of the wider World Heritage Site, the school is the steward of some of London's most important historic buildings, which are concentrated in and around Little Dean's Yard, an irregular courtyard enlarged from what was once a cobbled lane between ancient garden walls.

The oldest is "School", built in 1090-1100 and embracing part of the old monastic dormitory. An 11th century doorway survives in the west wall opposite some fragments of Norman windows, but the lofty hammerbeam roof of 1450 and the famous, original 17th century shell niche were destroyed when the building was gutted during the Second World War, following which it was reconstructed by Carden & Godfrey in 1957-9. From 1602 to 1884 the entire school was taught in this room, divided by a single curtain which separated the lower and upper schools hanging from the 16th century "Greaze" bar (the largest piece of pig iron in the world), over which on each Shrove Tuesday a horsehair-reinforced pancake is tossed, prompting a scrum of boys for the largest part. The panelled walls are painted with the arms of eminent former pupils.

A more complete mediaeval survival is "College Hall", built in 1369-76 as part of the Abbot's state dining hall, and now the school refectory, with a fine 14th century roof, and a later musicians' gallery from 1600 (left below).

"College", an early work of Lord Burlington, modelled on Palladio's Teatro Olimpico at Vicenza, was gutted in 1941 and reconstructed in 1947-50. Burlington was also responsible for the School Gateway (1734) which has been carved, as so many other surfaces in the school, with historic graffiti, often by moonlighting stonemasons commissioned by the boys.

Dr Busby's Library, approached via an inner vestibule with a huge Mannerist 17th century doorcase and *trompe-l'oeil* work (left middle), was built for the famous headmaster in 1657-9, also bomb-damaged in 1940 and also reconstructed after the war.

Ashburnham House, originally built as a residence for the Earls of Ashburnham in 1662, houses the school Library. It incorporates remnants of 14th century fabric from the mediaeval Prior's House, which accounts for some of its eccentricities. Most probably designed by John Webb, Inigo Jones's deputy, its attribution has been contested fiercely by generations of architectural historians as it is renowned for its unique, ingenious domed staircase and richly moulded plasterwork which continues into the Reading Room.

The school's notable alumni read like a roll-call of the good and great across the centuries from Ben Jonson, Robert Hooke and Christopher Wren to Jeremy Bentham, Edward Gibbon and A A Milne, plus seven former prime ministers.

Church of St James the Less

THORNDIKE STREET SW1V 2PS
LISTED: GRADE 1

The Church of St James the Less is one of London's finest, but lesser-known, Victorian churches, and the first work in the capital by George Edmund Street, later the architect of the Royal Courts of Justice.

Built in 1859-61, it was described by Charles Eastlake as "eminently un-English". Street was well versed in Continental architecture. Each year he undertook regular architectural study tours to Europe to immerse himself in the finer points of French and Italian gothic architecture. "The best mode of improving our style is the careful study of Continental styles ... we have to go to all those lands to discover in what that development varied from our own, in what it was superior, and in what inferior".

St James the Less is heralded by its distinctive, short pyramidal spire with four corner spirelets above a high tower in the manner of an Italianate campanile. The church, which forms part of a wider complex with a school and public hall, is enclosed by elegant railings (1866) by James Leaver of Maidenhead, modelled on the screen in Barcelona Cathedral. Inside it is pure muscular Gothic, with walls of banded red and black brick structural polychromy, a floor of red and yellow glazed Maw's tiles, and short, fat granite columns with stiff-leaf carved capitals by W Pearce carrying notched and moulded brick arches. Over the font is an exuberant gilded wrought-iron canopy made by Leaver and shown at the 1862 Exhibition. The carved stone pulpit is widely regarded as one of the finest works of Thomas Earp.

The architectural climax of the interior is a wonderful sexpartite brick vault over the crossing and chancel. Above is a vast mosaic of the Last Judgement (commonly called *The Doom*) by George Frederic Watts, which replaced an earlier painted fresco of his which had deteriorated. The entire nave roof is decorated with a now sadly faded painting of the Tree of Jesse by Clayton and Bell, who also executed most of the stained-glass windows which depict the Apostles and biblical scenes.

A wall plaque commemorates Canon Arthur Thorndike, the father of the actress Dame Sybil Thorndike, who was vicar of St James's until his death during a service in 1917.

The church is surrounded by the innovative, low-rise, high-density Lillington Gardens estate, built by Westminster City Council to the designs of Darbourne and Darke from 1964 to 1970.

55 Broadway

SW1H 0BD
LISTED: GRADE I

There is a handful of buildings which are so inextricably identified with their original function that to change their use should be unthinkable. No 55 Broadway, the iconic home of London Transport since its inception in 1933, is just such a case. It is part of London's DNA; a potent symbol of an organisation that put innovative design and corporate branding at its very heart through the inspirational work of its managing director and later vice-chairman, Frank Pick. The branding features on everything, from stylised posters of the period to the embossed tiles by Harold Stabler at many tube stations, so it is deeply disturbing that moves are afoot to sell it.

It was erected between 1927 and 1929 to the designs of Charles Holden (1875-1960), as the headquarters of the Underground Electric Railways of London Ltd over St James's Park underground station. Holden was extremely gifted and able to work in a whole range of styles. When it opened, 55 Broadway was the tallest building in London, built to an American scale and massed around a clever cruciform plan to maximise daylight to the offices.

Pick restrained Holden from adding ornamental classical detail, which accounts for the rather austere exterior, relieved only by the massing and 10 sculptures commissioned from the leading sculptors of the day – Jacob Epstein, Eric Gill, Allan Wyon, Henry Moore, Samuel Rabinovich, Eric Aumonier and Alfred Gerrard. Epstein's depiction of graphic nudity caused such a sensation that it prompted a public campaign to remove his two sculptures *Night* and *Day*. After Pick threatened to resign over the issue, the protests culminated in only minor modifications to the penis on *Day*. The other sculptors created eight nude reliefs representing the Winds on each of the principal faces of the building.

At ground level three arcades of shops originally met at the central hall, providing a direct route through the building, but this was modified in 1988-9. In the central hall are bronze-framed information boards with operational dials depicting train intervals, a map display case and clock.

Above, the interior is lined with travertine and bronze; the principal staircase with distinctive bronze balusters in the form of an Egyptian-style stalk with leaves. In the stair hall is a memorial bronze medallion of Lord Ashfield, 1874-1942: "Creator of London Transport". The lifts retain their original bronze surrounds and floor indicator panels, although the cars are modern replacements to a period design. On each floor adjacent to the lifts is a Cutler mailing chute for internal mail. The wings have large open-plan offices with copperlite glazing and bronze fittings.

At seventh floor level on the east wing are the boardrooms, which are disposed around a walnut panelled spine corridor culminating in the large boardroom. This has a jazzy geometric pink and grey ceiling, walnut dado panelling, decorated metal grilles to the clerestory lighting and French windows leading to a stone balcony.

Between 1932 and 1939 Holden designed a similar, taller building, for the Senate House of the University of London, with a vast stripped classical crush hall at its centre.

Institution of Civil Engineers

1 Great George Street, sw1p 3aa
Listed: Grade II

The Institution of Civil Engineers was the world's first professional engineering body. Although groups of civil engineers met under the aegis of Joseph Smeaton's Society of Civil Engineers, founded in 1771, and in a military context in the Corps of the Royal Engineers, it was not until 1818 that the present institution was established, at the Kendal Coffee House in Fleet Street. Ten years later, its first president, Thomas Telford, obtained a royal charter. In 1839 the organisation moved to 24-26 Great George Street, Westminster, where it remained until the entire street block was redeveloped for government offices in 1910. Following an architectural competition, a handsome new headquarters was erected opposite between 1910 and 1913 in a lavish Edwardian Beaux Arts style to the designs of James Miller (1860-1947).

Faced in Portland stone, the design conveys all the robust confidence of a profession which had been responsible for building Britain's infrastructure throughout the 19th century; and this supreme self-assurance permeates the interior.

From the entrance hall, a grand Imperial staircase rises through tripartite screens to the first floor. A huge glass dome allows light to pour into the staircase and ground floor through a circular central well.

On the landing is a moving bronze war memorial flanked by mourning female figures. The staircase newels carry busts of eminent engineers by H C Fehr, sculpted in 1897 and taken from the previous building.

At ground floor level are suites of meeting rooms panelled in a late 17th century style, stained glass by Hugh Easton (1956), and more recent engraved glass panels by Majella Taylor (1996). The Telford Theatre has a rare 17th century twin-fusee Grand Sonnerie Bracket Clock made by Thomas Tompion. In the library, which runs along the east side, are reused panelling and pilasters from Charles Barry Jr's earlier Institution building of 1895-6, and a chimneypiece with carved consoles in the form of gigantic bearded heads (far left). But the principal first floor space is the Great Hall, a vast chamber lined with giant pilasters in the style of Louis XVI.

At the centre of the ornate ceiling is a fascinating war memorial mural painted by Charles Sims in 1920, depicting an allegorical female figure swathed in the Union Jack with a background depicting a biplane and representatives of all the armed forces and services from the First World War. Sims had been an official war artist for the last year of the war, but the appalling scenes he witnessed, and the earlier death of his son in 1914, induced insomnia, hallucinations and increasing paranoia, culminating in his suicide by drowning in the River Tweed in 1928.

National Liberal Club

Whitehall Court, sw1a 2he
Listed: Grade II*

Renowned for its sublime romantic roofline of gables, spires and turrets, shortly after its completion in 1887 the National Liberal Club was hailed as "the most imposing clubhouse in the British metropolis"; and it was too. Not only was it the largest clubhouse ever built, until the ritzy Royal Automobile Club arrived (see pp 80-3) in 1910, it was also the first building in the capital to incorporate a lift and to be lit entirely by electricity.

The capacious club was founded by the Liberal grandee and Prime Minister W E Gladstone in 1882 to provide non-exclusive facilities for ordinary party members following the Third Reform Act, as "a home for democracy, void of the class distinctions associated with the Devonshire and Reform Clubs". G W E Russell wrote subsequently, "we never foresaw the palatial pile of terracotta and glazed tiles which now bears that name". H G Wells snorted, "The National Liberal Club is Liberalism made visible in the flesh – and Doultonware."

The architect was Alfred Waterhouse, who built a magnificent array of clubrooms behind an elevated outdoor riverside terrace, with over 140 bedrooms on the upper floors – a very early example of the use of a steel frame. The clubrooms are distinguished by the lavish use of patterned faience by Wilcock & Co in rich hues of green, yellow and brown, which impart a lustrous glow throughout the interior. This was not always appreciated. F E Smith, later the 1st Earl of Birkenhead, referred to it derisively as a useful public lavatory halfway between the Temple and Westminster. It was requisitioned for use by Canadian Army officers in the First World War. As part of the post–war refurbishments a rather swish electric escalator was installed to convey wine from the cellars to the dining room.

On 11 May 1941 the club received a direct hit from a German bomb, which destroyed the original main staircase. It was reconstructed in 1950-1 by Clyde Young and Bernard Engle as a splendid marble cantilevered oval staircase spiralling three storeys up through the building. Fortunately the bronze of John Prince (opposite below left) and the stained-glass portraits in the entrance hall of Harcourt, Rosebery, Gladstone and Morley survived, as did Onslow Ford's statue of Gladstone, which is now in the dining room. A painting of Churchill by Ernest Townsend was badly damaged, but restored and unveiled, much to his undisguised glee, in July 1943 by the Prime Minister.

In 1986 the adjacent Royal Horseguards Hotel took over the bedrooms, two vast opulent ballrooms and the old Gladstone Library, the books having been sold to the University of Bristol.

The club's wine cellar was adapted from a trench dug in 1865 for the world's first underground pneumatic tube railway from Great Scotland Yard to Waterloo. The putative Whitehall–Waterloo railway was abandoned three years later and the trench modified by the club for its present use.

Foreign and Commonwealth Office

King Charles Street, sw1a 2ah
Listed Grade: I

The Foreign and Commonwealth office is the grandest of all the great offices of government and a hymn to Pax Britannia.

Incomprehensible though it seems today, in the 1960s and 70s serious proposals were advanced for its demolition, but following a huge public outcry the buildings were listed, Grade I, following which an ambitious phased programme of restoration was undertaken from 1988 to 1992 to restore the interiors to their original glory.

Founded in 1782, originally the Foreign Office occupied a pair of houses in Cleveland Row, but in 1795 it relocated to the south side of Downing Street. Various proposals for a new building – initially by Decimus Burton in 1836-59, and then James Pennethorne in 1854-5 – were stillborn, but in 1856-7 an international architectural competition was held. The result was that the design of the new building became a political football in the notorious Battle of the Styles. After various of his Gothic designs were rejected, eventually Sir George Gilbert Scott was appointed to oversee the phased construction of a vast new complex of buildings in an Italianate style for the Home Office, Foreign Office, Colonial Office and India Office, all disposed around a spacious central quadrangle with four inner courtyards to each of the principal offices of state. Matthew Digby Wyatt, the surveyor to the old East India Company, was given responsibility for much of the India Office and its interiors, which included numerous artefacts from the old East India Company offices in Leadenhall Street, and the famous Durbar Court.

Gilbert Scott envisaged the Foreign Office as a "kind of national palace, or drawing room for the nation", designed to impress upon visiting foreign dignitaries the power and majesty of the British nation. Architecture was deployed for overtly political ends, which accounts for the lavish internal decoration and sheer bravura of the main rooms.

The Grand Staircase rises three storeys, culminating in a gilded dome decorated with allegorical female figures representing the 20 countries which had diplomatic relations with Great Britain at the time. The great coloured marble imperial stair divides into two as it soars majestically through the building, around it arcaded galleries with decoration by Clayton & Bell, mosaic pavements by Minton and Hollins and two splendid bronze gasoliers by Messrs Skidmore. Lining the galleries is the famous sequence of murals depicting allegories of Britannia by Sigismund Goetze, painted from 1912 onwards but only installed in 1921 after much controversy. Deeply unfashionable, they are wonderfully romantic evocations of British history and Britain's civilising mission.

Off to the north-west beneath a Sibyl adjuring silence is the entrance to the secretary of state's suite, which is decorated with stencilled gold stars on a green background. The ceiling is divided into three bays by iron beams covered in majolica, each bay covered with shallow octagonal painted plasterwork (p66 middle above). From this room Sir Edward Grey commented portentously in 1914, "the lamps are going out all over Europe. We shall not see them lit again in our lifetime."

The Locarno Suite comprises three large rooms sumptuously decorated in High Victorian style, originally by Clayton & Bell, and later restored in 1988-92 after the stencilling had been painted the colour of parchment (on the advice of the Royal Fine Art Commission) following the signing of the Locarno treaties in 1925. After occupation by the cypher branch of the department in the war, in 1945 the rooms were subdivided into office cubicles and the finishes hidden under false ceilings, until the groundbreaking restoration was completed in 1992.

The Grand Reception Room is a huge, vaulted, double-height space painted with the signs of the zodiac, stencilling and gilding. This leads to the Dining Room (above) with green walls and gilt stencilled stars, and beyond to the Conference Room (left middle) with an elaborate coffered ceiling with huge crossbeams and spandrels enriched with majolica plaques depicting the emblems of 20 nations.

The history of the Foreign Office is a textbook example of a failure to appreciate outstanding architecture during a period when it was unfashionable. What was so nearly lost is now a triumphant affirmation of the skill and expertise of the conservation teams involved, and also a fascinating insight into Victorian perceptions of Britain's place in the world at the height of its greatest power.

10 Downing Street

SW1A 2AA

LISTED: GRADE I

Between 1682 and 1684 the American-born Sir George Downing, political opportunist, profiteer and spy, employed Sir Christopher Wren to design a cul-de-sac of two-storey town houses between Whitehall and St James's Park. Forty years later it was described by Strype as "a pretty, open place especially at the upper end where there are four or five very large and well-built houses fit for persons of honour and quality". Downing's terrace was built directly behind a rather stately mansion occupied by the Countess of Lichfield, the daughter of Charles II. In 1732 King George II presented both houses to Sir Robert Walpole, who would only accept them if they could be used as an official residence for future First Lords of the Treasury, the title which remains engraved on the brass letterbox of the famous front door.

Walpole commissioned William Kent to unite and extend the buildings. The main entrance was created from Downing Street through to the "House at the Back", and a splendid three-sided staircase was added, which remains the most distinctive feature of the building. Over the next 250 years, its fortunes waxed and waned, with demolition contemplated on various occasions. Alterations were made by Lord North, and later Viscount Goderich, who employed Sir John Soane to design the State Dining Room and Small Dining Room, but by the late 19th century the building was in poor shape. Disraeli even paid for improvements to the bedrooms from his own pocket.

Churchill referred to the buildings as "shaky and lightly built by the profiteering contractor whose name they bear", while Margaret Thatcher extolled "the feeling of Britain's historic greatness which pervades every nook and cranny of this complicated meandering old building". A major reconstruction was carried out between 1960 and 1964 by Raymond Erith, and another in 1988-9 by Quinlan Terry.

The famous black entrance door was replaced in replica in blast-proof steel following an IRA mortar attack in 1991, a splinter from which remains embedded in the plasterwork upstairs. The entrance

hall with its chequerwork floor has a hooded watchman's chair with a drawer beneath for hot coals, to provide warmth for the occupant when it was deployed outside. Scratches to the right arm were caused by the watchman's pistols scraping the leather. To the left of the door is Wellington's campaign chest.

Once a quarter of mankind was ruled from the world-famous Cabinet Room, where a screen of Corinthian columns provides a small vestibule to the main room, part of a sequence of alterations by Sir Robert Taylor. On a side table is a ceremonial sword in a gold scabbard, a gift from the Emir of Kuwait, as thanks for assistance during the First Gulf War. Kent's superb staircase, its chrome yellow walls lined with black and white portraits of each prime minister, leads to three inter-linked rooms. The Pillared Hall, with a portrait of Elizabeth I over the fireplace, created by Taylor in 1796 (opposite below left), is used to receive guests; the Terracotta Room (below left), once Walpole's dining room, has plasterwork incorporating a straw-carrying "thatcher", a tribute to the then Prime Minister added during Quinlan Terry's 1989 renovation; while the White Drawing Room has a fine series of paintings by Turner and a bronze of Florence Nightingale.

The State Dining Room (opposite above), completed by Soane in 1826, has his characteristic shallow, starfish vault and ceiling, but double-height, creating a spacious, dark panelled room for formal entertainment overseen by a massive portrait of George II. Soane's Small Dining Room is used for more intimate gatherings. Deep in the basement, the two-storey vaulted Great Kitchen of 1732-5 remains.

No 10 is also the official residence of the cat of the Prime Minister of the United Kingdom, a post currently occupied by Larry. As a civil servant, the tenure of the Chief Mouser of the Cabinet Office runs with the office of Prime Minister, not the incumbent, which provides a reassuring sense of continuity at the heart of government. A predecessor, Wilberforce, saw off four prime ministers.

Ministry of Defence

HORSE GUARDS AVENUE, SW1A 2HB
LISTED: GRADE I

Originally designed by Vincent Harris for the Board of Trade and Air Ministry, this great stone leviathan marching along behind Whitehall houses the Ministry of Defence.

It was built in phases over a 20-year period, 1939-59, on a large quadrilateral site, its chillingly austere elevations linked by shallow-curved, copper-roofed cross wings terminated by angle pavilions with pedimented ends. Its construction involved the clearance of a whole series of historic houses in Whitehall Gardens, from which some of the best interiors were salvaged and reconstructed inside the new building.

The entrances are flanked by pylons, that to the north with huge sculptures of *Earth* and *Water* by Sir Charles Wheeler, *Fire* and *Air* having been vetoed for the south entrance on cost grounds. Inside at ground level is a double-height pillared hall in stripped classical style articulated by paired, octagonal columns faced in sombre polished black marble. At the mid-point is the Victoria and George Cross memorial in the form of a bronze sculpture by Marcus Cornish of a serviceman reaching out his hand to help others before a stained-glass window by Rachel Foster inscribed "They fled only from dishonour, but met danger face to face".

Beneath the building is one of London's hidden treasures – the undercroft from Cardinal Wolsey's Great Chamber in Whitehall Palace, now known as Cardinal Wolsey's Wine Cellar (opposite below). It was built in 1514-16 as part of the first phase of the Cardinal's work in Whitehall and is similar in form to one added later by Henry VIII at Hampton Court. Later the cellar was encased in stone-dressed brick and incorporated into a fine house built for Viscount Torrington in 1722, but it stood in the way of the new building and approach road. Following the direct intervention of Queen Mary in 1938 and specific undertakings in Parliament, in 1949 it was moved 9ft to the west and lowered 19ft in one of the most audacious exercises in conservation engineering ever undertaken at that time.

Approaching through a four-centred Tudor arched doorway carved with Wolsey's defaced arms, one enters a brick-vaulted chamber in two rows of five bays divided by four octagonal stone columns. At one end are restored platforms supporting large oak barrels. Other remnants of Whitehall Palace survive elsewhere, in particular in the Old Treasury and Cabinet Office, including parts of Henry VIII's covered tennis courts.

In the courtyard space at third and fourth floor levels of Harris's building are four elegant early 18th century interiors relocated from Pembroke House, one of London's first Palladian houses, three with delicate plasterwork ceilings designed by William Chambers and executed by the plasterer William Perritt, plus a room of 1722 from Torrington House.

Reform Club

104 Pall Mall, sw1y 5ew
Listed: Grade I

Four years after the great Reform Act of 1832, the Reform Club was founded by the Whig MP Edward Ellice to "promote the social intercourse of the Reformers of the United Kingdom". Ellice, known as The Bear, was a wealthy director of the Hudson's Bay Company and a prime mover behind the Reform Act, better known today for having the Ellice Islands named after him (now part of Tuvalu). He was determined to create a centre for radical liberalism where new members of both Houses of Parliament, who had been denied access to Brooks's, the inner sanctum of the old Whig aristocracy, could gather and promote progressive social thinking.

Following a limited architectural competition, in 1838 Sir Charles Barry was appointed to design a palatial new clubhouse in Pall Mall. Inspired by the Palazzo Farnese in Rome, but more closely influenced by his earlier work at the adjacent Travellers' Club, it opened in 1841. The result was a triumph and, arguably, Barry's classical masterpiece: nine huge bays of Portland stone marching serenely down Pall Mall.

Inside, Barry originally envisaged the large entrance hall, or Saloon, as a courtyard, or cortile, open to the sky, but given the inclement London weather, wiser counsel prevailed. The hall was covered with a huge coved cast-iron roof by Apsley Pellatt, a technological marvel comprising 770 lozenges of faceted lead crystal in 11 different sizes. Architecturally, it is the finest clubroom in London and was designed to accommodate the entire assembly of the Liberal Party; a breathtaking double-height space surrounded by colonnades of warm yellow scagliola offset by deep Pompeiian red walls and coloured marbles designed by Barry's son, Edward Middleton Barry – Ionic below and Corinthian above. Portraits of club founders and Liberal dignitaries gaze down from the walls.

The staircase is tucked away between solid walls with 90° turns at domed intermediate landings. Along the south garden front the Coffee Room is enriched with engaged Ionic columns and coffered ceilings. The Library above, converted by Barry from a drawing room in 1853, accommodates 75,000 books in Corinthian splendour beneath a coved plaster ceiling which echoes the form and detail of the glazed roof over the Saloon. The Morning Room boasts a stunning half-size copy of the Panathanaic frieze from the Parthenon (p79 top).

The club enthusiastically embraced the latest technology. Its famous chef Alexis Soyer was consulted by Barry on the design of the vast kitchens. A small steam engine under the front pavement pumped and heated water, and drove Faraday's Perfect Ventilation Apparatus, a fan ventilator which circulated heated air throughout the building via the cornices. Alas, this was less than perfect and something of a misnomer, one diner complaining that it produced "an atmosphere in which no animal ungifted with copper-lungs can long exist".

The Anti-Corn Law statesmen Richard Cobden and John Bright were early members, alongside Brunel, Palmerston and, later, Gladstone, who established the separate National Liberal Club (see pp 62–65) for Liberal grandees in 1882.

It was from the Reform Club that Phileas Fogg set off on his circumnavigation of the world in response to a wager with his fellow members in Jules Verne's *Around the World in 80 Days*. "Phileas Fogg was English to the backbone … he was simply a member of the Reform Club."

Inside is a vision of Edwardian opulence with a massive top-lit oval vestibule in Louis XV style lined in French stuc and surrounded by a gallery at first floor level.

Immediately beyond, overlooking the garden on the south front, is the former lounge (now a restaurant) decorated by Boulanger with a sky-painted ceiling, and a stage and musicians' gallery at opposing ends. The members' dining room is in the style of Sir William Chambers, and the billiard room based on an Adam ceiling from the old War Office. To the west the great smoking room (above) by Lenygon and Morant runs from front to back with a careful reproduction of the coffered ceiling and entablature of gryphons from Brettingham's Cumberland House. The corresponding room on the east side by M Remon of Paris is designed around a series of cut-up landscape paintings attributed to Jurriaan Andriessen, taken from an old chateau in the Midi.

In the basement, lit by torchères, is the famous Byzantine swimming pool overlooked from a niche on the stair by a fine bronze sculpture of a sea goddess by Gilbert Bayes, 1927. The 90,000-gallon concrete tank, lined with Sicilian marble, is surrounded by a peristyle with pairs of massive Doric columns covered in shimmering blue and gold mosaics.

The statue of Queen Victoria was unveiled by the Kaiser during a visit with his brother Prince Henry of Prussia. To commemorate the "first aerial looping the loop by Gustav Hamel and A V Hucks" an eccentric dinner was held at which everything was eaten in reverse, starting with liqueurs and coffee and ending with hors d'oeuvres. During the war Prince Olav of Norway, General Sikorski and General de Gaulle were all regulars, and it was at the RAC that the treacherous Burgess and Maclean had their last lunch together, in May 1951, before defecting to Moscow, the choice of club made, ironically, because the Reform was full.

Royal Automobile Club

89-91 PALL MALL, SW1Y 5HS
LISTED: GRADE II*

With its own rifle range, Turkish baths and spectacular indoor swimming pool resembling some exotic set from a Cecil B DeMille epic, the Royal Automobile Club was the last and grandest expression of the great age of club building. Its flamboyant French façade in the style of Louis XIV is unlike any of the other gentlemen's clubs, which took their architectural inspiration from Grecian antiquity, or the elegant palazzi of Rome and Venice. This is hardly surprising as the architects were Mewès and Davis, who designed the Ritz, and Francophilia was at its height in the wake of the Entente Cordiale.

The Automobile Club of Great Britain and Ireland was founded in 1897 by Frederick Richard Simms as "a Society of Encouragement for the motoring movement and the motor and allied industries in the British Empire". After temporary sojourns at Whitehall Court and 119 Piccadilly, in 1907 it became the Royal Automobile Club under the patronage of Edward VII. A year later it acquired the site of the old War Office at Cumberland House, Pall Mall, designed by Matthew Brettingham, in a deal with the Commissioners of Woods and Forests, which stipulated that the new buildings should cost not less than £100,000. What arose cost £250,000, and an army of French craftsmen, sculptors and blacksmiths crossed the Channel to impart an authentic Parisian quality to the entire building in *la grande manière*.

Carved into the pediment over the front entrance is an allegorical sculpture of *Science as the Inspiration of the Allied Trades* by Ferdinand Faivre, complete with a primitive motor car. The wrought-iron gates and lamps are by Maison Vian of Paris.

Marlborough House

PALL MALL, SW1Y 5HX
LISTED: GRADE I

Currently the headquarters of the Commonwealth Secretariat, Marlborough House remains a royal palace, its last royal resident being Queen Mary, who is commemorated by a simple stone plaque on the garden wall facing The Mall.

The house was built by the redoubtable Sarah Churchill, Duchess of Marlborough, on the site of the old pheasantry in the garden of St James's Palace. Designed by Sir Christopher Wren and his son, it was described at the time as "in every way answerable to the grandeur of its master". Approached by a broad flight of steps, and faced in red Dutch bricks with rusticated stone quoins, originally it comprised two tall storeys with a crowning stone cornice and balustrade over a basement with projecting wings, between the windows of which are shallow niches. The duchess originally intended the main access to be from Pall Mall, but this was foiled by her implacable enemy the Prime Minister, Robert Walpole, who bought the site between the newly completed house and Pall Mall, thereby blocking the access, but Wren's fine entrance screen still survives hard up against the rear of the buildings in Pall Mall.

The imperious duchess survived her husband for over 20 years and terrorised Court circles, referring to the King as "neighbour George" and manipulating a series of advantageous marriages for her daughters. "What a glorious sight it is to see such a number of branches flourishing from the same root", she trilled at a family gathering. "Alas," whispered Jack Spencer to his cousin, "the branches would flourish far better if the root were underground."

After the death of the 4th Duke in 1817, the Crown reacquired the property, and from 1853 to 1861 it was used as the National Art Training School, the forerunner of the Royal College of Art. In 1860 it was remodelled and enlarged by Sir James Pennethorne with two additional attic floors as a residence for the Prince of Wales and Princess Alexandra, throwing the whole composition into imbalance. For over 40 years it was the scene of wild parties and numerous indiscretions by the heir to the throne. The future King George V was born here in 1865. In the gardens is Queen Alexandra's poignant pet cemetery, and Queen Mary's thatched revolving summer house.

However, the great glory of Marlborough House is its lavish interior, which reflects the changing fashions of each period of its use. The main entrance through Pennethorne's hall leads to a double-height cube – the Saloon around which runs a balcony, over which are paintings of the Battle of Blenheim by Laguerre. On the ceiling above is a cupola surrounded by paintings by Orazio Gentileschi (1635-8) intended for the Queen's House, Greenwich, but adapted and moved here in 1711. They depict Peace, surrounded by the Liberal Arts and Virtues. Below are framed tapestries. To the west and east of the Saloon are two grand staircases with huge murals – that to the west illustrating the Battle of Ramillies, and that to the east Malplaquet. The remaining interiors were remodelled by Sir William Chambers in 1771-4, and later by Pennethorne in 1860-2. The State Dining Room by Chambers has a pair of chimneypieces embellished respectively with male and female herms. The State Drawing Room along the garden front was formed by uniting three rooms with Corinthian columns. At first floor level the Prince of Wales' Smoking Room, lined with false books, survives.

The primary interest of the interior is the mural paintings which, although rather leaden in execution, celebrate one of Britain's greatest military commanders in his original, if altered, London house, together with the historical associations with King Edward VII and his circle when Prince of Wales.

Outside on the boundary wall to Marlborough Road is Sir Alfred Gilbert's profoundly moving bronze masterpiece the Queen Alexandra Memorial, completed in flowing Art Nouveau style as late as 1932.

Oxford
& Cambridge Club

71-77 Pall Mall, sw1y 5hd
Listed: Grade II*

The Oxford & Cambridge Club was founded for members of both universities in 1829, after the waiting list for the older United University Club (1821) became too long. The inaugural meeting at the British Coffee House in Cockspur Street was presided over by no less a person than Lord Palmerston. Initially located at 18 St James's Square, in 1835 the club took the decision to build a new clubhouse. Sir Robert Smirke was appointed as architect, assisted by his younger brother, Sydney.

The result was a bold and imposing Graeco-Roman frontage with Italianate nuances, considered to have an "air of monumental grandeur … which, from its connexion with the Universities awakens attention to those proud features of our Constitution". Appropriately, above the upper windows are panels of terracotta bas-reliefs by William Grinsell Nicholl depicting "the exalted labours of the mind" based on the designs of Robert Smirke RA, the architect's father. Homer, Bacon and Shakespeare, and Milton, Newton and Virgil, lie either side of a central panel depicting Apollo, Athene and the nine Muses.

The interior is capacious and well-proportioned in the Greek style. The principal floors are linked by a giant marble staircase with a massive balustrade. On the landing is a fine bronze copy of Donatello's *David*. In 1907 the staircase was enhanced by Sir Reginald Bloomfield, who lined the walls in light brown marble and added the large Doric Venetian window to the landing, flooding the space with light.

Beneath the withering gaze of a portrait of the Duke of Wellington, the morning room has a ceiling rose which functions as a ventilator and chandelier boss decorated with acanthus buds and anthemion ornament.

The coffee room extends for the full depth of the building, lit by three huge chandeliers installed in 1867. Above lie the north and south libraries with birchwood bookcases containing a fine collection of over 24,000 books, one of the best in clubland. The large smoking room adjacent is the most handsome of the club's rooms, with a richly decorated coffered ceiling and dado-high bookcases specifically designed for the space.

In 1950-1 the club acquired the adjacent building (opposite left), which had been remodelled by Thomas Henry Wyatt for the 2nd Marquess of Ailesbury. In 1902 it became the home of Queen Victoria's daughter Princess Christian, and later her two daughters Princess Helene Victoria and Princess Marie Louise. The long, narrow ballroom and supper room beyond created by Wyatt now provide elegant additional clubrooms.

During the war a bomb fell on the kitchen, but fortunately, given the 44,000 bottles of wine kept in the cellars, it failed to explode. Illustrious past members include Edward VII, Canning and Palmerston, Clement Attlee, Harold Macmillan and Benazir Bhutto. Gladstone's name appears in the earliest surviving list of members in 1833. He demanded repeatedly that the staff should be allowed to attend church on Sundays, until a pew was reserved for their use at St Philip's Church, Regent Street.

In its early days two officers from the Guards Club, which was then next door, sought the club's hospitality during the summer cleaning period. Seated opposite an elderly gent immersed in his newspaper, one merrily exclaimed, "These middle-class fellows know how to do themselves well." Slowly the paper lowered. Opposite sat the Duke of Wellington, the Iron Duke, Chancellor of Oxford University.

James J Fox / Robert Lewis

19 St James's Street, swia ies
Unlisted

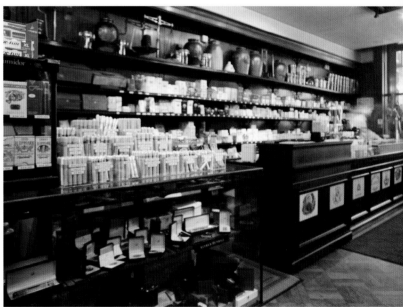

"Robert Lewis is the most beautiful cigar shop, barring none – in London or elsewhere … The odour of Havanas is overpowering to the heathen but myrrh and mirth to the initiated. If I had to live in a shop I would dwell in Robert Lewis forever"

(G Cabrera Infante, *Holy Smoke*)

James J Fox is claimed to be the longest-established cigar merchant in Britain. Located behind an elegant, angled oak shopfront in the heart of St James's, it is the place of pilgrimage for aficionados of the cigaresque.

The firm was founded as a stockist of snuff, pipes, pouches, vestas and other smoking sundries by Christopher Lewis at 14 Long Acre in 1787. "Tobacco wrapped in a leaf" was brought back to England by troops returning from the Peninsular Wars and, as its popularity increased, the firm moved to Great Newport Street to capitalise on the interest. In 1855-6 Robert Joseph Lewis took over the firm and relocated to St James's Street, where he, and later his son Henry, rapidly built up a clientele drawn from a wide cross-section of British society, acquiring the first of eight royal warrants from the second son of Queen Victoria, HRH the Duke of Edinburgh, in the 1880s.

Amongst its more colourful regulars was Major Walter Clopton Wingfield, founder of Le Cordon Rouge, the inventor of musical formation bicycling and, perhaps more notably, the game of lawn tennis, which originally he called Sphairistike. Wingfield devised his own smoking mixture and gave Lewis's exclusive rights in exchange for 1lb of the mixture each month for life. Oscar Wilde was an habitué, ordering special cigarettes, on each of which he had painted the name Oscar in red letters. The original ledgers show he left a sizeable debt of £37. 17s. 3d.

For over 60 years Winston Churchill was a customer, having been introduced by his mother, who had a particular penchant for the firm's handmade, gold-tipped Alexandra Balkan cigarettes, which she smoked through an amber holder.

The shop retains all the accoutrements of a traditional tobacconist, complete with a carved wooden figure of a Red Indian and a smoking room for clients. In the basement is a fascinating museum of memorabilia including the oldest box of cigars in the world, made for the Great Exhibition of 1851, Churchill's chair, a hand-blown Bristol glass pipe of 1787, hookahs, commemorative cigar bands, Edward VIII's humidor and correspondence from well-known satisfied customers.

Now trading as James J Fox, the firm continues to offer 18 marques of Havana in over 350 different shapes and sizes. It is a measure of London's extraordinary global reach that it is the cigar capital of the world.

Spencer House

29 St James's Place, swia inr
Listed: Grade I

Today it seems inconceivable that London's finest 18th century mansion should have been allowed to become one of its most conspicuous buildings at risk, but following war damage and years of sad decline, the house descended into a parlous state. In 1985 it was acquired by R.I.T. Capital Partners plc and under the chairmanship of Lord Rothschild a team of specialist advisers was assembled to undertake an ambitious programme of restoration executed by Rolfe Judd between 1987-90.

The house was built between 1756 and 1766 as the London residence of the 1st Earl Spencer and his wife, Georgiana. The exterior and ground floor interiors, designed by John Vardy with advice from Colonel George Gray, Secretary to the Society of Dilettanti, are rooted in the Palladian tradition, but are one of the earliest examples of the development of neo-classicism in England. In 1758 Vardy was replaced by James "Athenian" Stuart, a master of detail of Greek and Roman classical antiquity, and it was he who was responsible for the superb first floor interiors. The leading craftsmen of the day were employed for the furnishings – chimneypieces by Scheemakers, plasterwork by Joseph Rose, and joinery by Thomas Vardy, the architect's brother. On its completion, the writer Arthur Young remarked that there was not "a house in Europe better worth the view of the curious in architecture, and the fitting up and furnishing of great houses, than Lord Spencer's".

In addition to the Spencer's magnificent collection of European art, the second Earl added a library of early printed books, regarded as the greatest private collection in the world. In 1788 he appointed Henry Holland to remodel the interiors.

For over 100 years the house was the setting for lavish balls, sumptuous suppers and refined receptions for leading members of fashionable society from the arts, politics, aristocracy and royalty. In 1857 a ball was held for Queen Victoria – "a magnificent fete … marked by … princely liberality and good taste" with the house "illuminated with singular brilliancy".

The Spencers remained in occupation until 1895, when the house was let, before finally departing in 1927, after which began a period of long, slow decline.

The cool classical entrance hall is embellished with a Doric frieze of swags and bucrania from the Temple of Jupiter the Thunderer. The Ante-Room has a great niche coffered in the manner of the Temple of Venus and Rome and adapted later by Holland to form an entrance (left middle). Beyond the Library, the Dining Room boasts a ceiling by Vardy based on Inigo Jones's work in the Banqueting Hall in Whitehall with a frieze modelled on the Temple of Fortuna Virilis in Rome. The stunning Palm Room (opposite above) is one of London's most magical spaces derived from John Webb's drawing for the King's Bedchamber at Greenwich, the palms symbolising marital fidelity and the frieze taken from the Roman Temple of Antoninus and Faustina. Corinthian half-columns swathed in palm fronds frame an arch, which leads to a domed central space surrounded by three coffered apses.

The open-well, stone staircase is a marriage of Vardy and Stuart with a Venetian window at half-landing level and a cut metal balustrade painted in trompe l'oeil – all lit by a magnificent Venetian lantern from the Doge's barge acquired by Lord Rothschild in 1999. At first floor level Lady Spencer's Room has one of Stuart's most beautiful ceilings based on the baths of Augustus in Rome and a frieze from the Erechtheoin in Athens. The enfilade of rooms leads on to the Great Room (right), which is lined with red damask rising to a coved coffered ceiling, comparable to Stuart's work at the Queen's Chapel in Greenwich (see p23), with four bronze medallions portraying Bacchus with panthers, Apollo with griffins and Venus and the Three Graces framed by putti. The Painted Room beyond (1759) is an exquisite neo-classical space and the earliest example of its style in Europe (opposite below), its green walls decorated with painted scenes depicting the Triumph of Love, some painted by Stuart himself. A screen of Corinthian columns frames a perfectly symmetrical apsidal space divided by fluted engaged columns with ribbons of painted floral scrolls to the pilasters inspired by Raphael.

The repair and restoration of Spencer House as offices and reception space was a conservation triumph since when it has provided the setting for conferences, concerts, charitable events, political meetings and royal receptions. The house is open to the public every Sunday except in January and August.

The Chapel Royal
St James's Palace

SWIA IDH

LISTED: GRADE I

St James's Palace is the official residence of the sovereign, which is why high commissioners and ambassadors are still formally accredited to the Court of St James. Built in 1531-6 by Henry VIII on the site of a leper hospital, it was the home of the Kings and Queens of England until the ascension of Queen Victoria in 1837, who chose to live at Buckingham Palace. Substantial parts of the original Tudor fabric survive, including the great red-brick gatehouse facing St James's Street, emblazoned with Henry VIII's royal cipher, and parts of the courtyards and state apartments, including the Chapel Royal.

The term Chapel Royal referred to the peripatetic body of priests and singers who served the needs of the travelling sovereign, but later it came to be applied to various buildings used by monarchs for worship. The two principal Chapels Royal are at St James's Palace – the Chapel Royal itself and the later Queen's Chapel.

The Chapel Royal is one of London's hidden gems. It was decorated by Hans Holbein in honour of the King's marriage to Anne of Cleves. The ceiling, completed in 1540 and panelled in interlocking hexagons of cast-lead mouldings, depicts the arms of Anne of Cleves and the mottoes of Katharine of Aragon and Anne Boleyn. It demonstrates how the painted decorative traditions of the Italian Renaissance adumbrated by Serlio were absorbed and reinterpreted at the English Tudor court by local heraldic artists – possibly Antonio Toto del Nunziata, or Andrew Wright. The west end was reconstructed by Robert Smirke in 1836-7 with a new entrance, royal closet, side galleries and ante-chapel bearing the ciphers of William IV and Queen Adelaide in matching Tudor style. The pews were installed later in 1876.

The chapel has been the scene of some of the most momentous events in English history. The heart and bowels of Mary I are buried beneath the choir stalls. Elizabeth I prayed for divine intervention here in 1588 against the threat of invasion during the Spanish Armada, receiving messages via beacons across the country from Cornwall. Charles I received Holy Communion in the Chapel Royal before his execution in Whitehall in 1649. Prior to the funeral of Diana, Princess of Wales at Westminster Abbey in 1997, her coffin lay in the chapel for her family and friends to pay their respects.

On a happier note, Queen Victoria married Prince Albert in the chapel on 10 February 1840. She wrote ecstatically of her wedding: "I NEVER, NEVER, spent such an evening!!! He clasped me in his arms and we kissed each other again and again … bliss beyond belief! Oh! This was the happiest moment of my life.!" A copy of her signed marriage certificate hangs in the vestry.

The Chapel Royal was also the birthplace of English church music. Thomas Tallis, William Byrd, Henry Purcell and George Frederick Handel are among the chapel's most illustrious composers and organists. The organ was designed by Aston Webb in 1924-5.

The chapel was restored in 2001-2 when new stained glass by John Napper depicting the tree of the Commonwealth was installed to mark the Golden Jubilee.

Queen's Chapel

Marlborough Road, SW1A 1DH

Listed: Grade I

The Queen's Chapel was once an integral part of the St James's Palace complex, until 1809 when the connecting buildings burned down. In 1856-7 Marlborough Road was created, severing the chapel from the palace.

The Queen's Chapel is one of the glories of English Renaissance architecture: the first church in England to be built in a wholly classical style, and one of the best surviving works of Inigo Jones. It was built by James I for his son Charles as a Catholic chapel in 1623 and completed two years later for use by his French queen, Henrietta Maria.

Externally it is a plain, pedimented brick box faced in render with Portland stone quoins and dressings. At the east end the broad Venetian window with square Corinthian columns is believed to be the earliest to survive in the country.

The interior is exceptionally fine, with an elliptical painted and gilded coffered vault in timber rather than plaster, modelled on Palladio's Temple of Venus and Rome. The furnishings are principally later, following modifications carried out for Catherine of Braganza in 1662, 1679-80 and later by Wren in 1682-4. However, the Royal Pew in the West Gallery (top right), with its large hybrid chimneypiece with segmental half-pediments and festoons, is part of Jones's original decorative scheme. The reredos with its quadrant wings of 1682-4 is by Grinling Gibbons, although the pedimented centrepiece containing a 17th century altarpiece of the Holy Family by Annibale, or possibly Agostino Carracci, is from the Royal Collection. Overhead the Stuart and Portuguese royal arms are framed by gilded angels and festoons. The balustraded altar rails were given by Queen Anne in 1702.

Lancaster House

STABLE YARD, ST JAMES'S, SW1A 1BB

LISTED: GRADE I

A palace is not merely a large house, but a building specifically designed for formal ceremony with a sequential progression of spaces and features intended to impress upon the visitor the wealth and status of its owner. Lancaster House has been described as "the only true private palace ever built in London". Originally known as York House (1825-7), subsequently as Stafford House (1827-1914), and now as Lancaster House, it has had a chequered history.

Construction began in 1825 for the Duke of York and Albany – "the Grand Old Duke of York" – initially to designs by Sir Robert Smirke, but the headstrong duke soon sacked his architect and appointed Benjamin Dean Wyatt in his place. When the spendthrift duke died in a sea of debt in 1827, the unfinished shell of the house was sold to one of the wealthiest men in England, the Marquess of Stafford (later 1st Duke of Sutherland), whose eldest son brought it to fruition, adding a rather cumbersome attic storey in 1833-6 to Smirke's design.

Situated in a large private garden adjacent to the Green Park and facing St James's Park, externally its Bath stone elevations are understated, but the opulent interiors are staggering, prompting Queen Victoria to remark to her friend Harriet, the 2nd Duchess, "I have come from my house to your palace." Lavishly designed in the style of Louis XIV, the interiors are a melding of the work of Benjamin Dean Wyatt, Sir Robert Smirke and Sir Charles Barry.

The colossal entrance hall and staircase lit by an oblong lantern is lined in yellow and black scagliola with inset paintings of 1841-8 by G G Lorenzi in the manner of Paolo Veronese. The intricate cast-iron staircase balustrade is by J Bramah & Sons.

At first floor level the Music Room has a circle-coffered ceiling with borders derived from Palmyra (left). Beyond, the vast Picture Gallery (left above), also with Palmyrene decoration, once held the Sutherlands' magnificent art collection in "the most magnificent room in London" with works by the great European masters including Van Dyck, Rembrandt, Rubens, Titian and Murillo. In the lantern is Guercino's painting of *St Chrisogonus Borne by Angels* (1622) taken from Rome (opposite below left). Between two recesses with carved lunettes is a grandiloquent green marble chimneypiece by Crozatier of Paris, lavishly ornamented with gold caryatids beneath a gilded overmantel and sumptuous French clock (opposite below middle). Over the north-east Ante Room is a fine 16th century painting of the *Three Graces* attributed to Battista Zelotti (left below). Another superb chimneypiece (c1837) by Richard Westmacott Jr, with children representing winter and autumn, can be found in the Green Room, which was once the boudoir of the 2nd Duchess. Unusually there are more fine state rooms at ground floor level, including the splendid State Dining Room (1828-9) (opposite below right).

As liberals and patrons of the arts, the Sutherlands received a galaxy of 19th century celebrities at the house, including the social reformer Lord Shaftesbury, the anti-slavery campaigner Harriet Beecher Stowe and the Italian revolutionary Giuseppe Garibaldi, whose stay in April 1864 is commemorated by a roundel by Luigi Fabbrucci unveiled 20 years later.

In 1912 the house was purchased by Sir William Lever (later 1st Lord Leverhulme), the Lancastrian soap magnate, who promptly presented it to the nation. Between the wars it was the home of the London Museum, but in 1950 it was taken over by the Foreign Office for receptions and international conferences.

The Queen's coronation banquet was held here in 1952. Subsequently it was the venue for several conferences to settle the future of various colonies of the British Empire including Malaya in 1956, Nigeria in 1957-8, Kenya in 1960, 1962 and 1963 and, most famously, the independence of Southern Rhodesia as Zimbabwe, through the Lancaster House Agreement of 1979.

50 Albemarle Street

W1S 4BD

LISTED: GRADE II*

50 Albemarle Street was built by Benjamin Jackson, Master Mason of the Crown, between 1717 and 1719 on the site of Albemarle House. In 1720 the levelled area was described as "looking like the ruins of Troy", but over the next 30 years it was developed into a select aristocratic quarter close to the Court of St James.

No 50 is a well-preserved early Georgian town house, half of a pair, retaining a beautiful original cantilevered oak staircase with three twisted balusters per stair and fluted Corinthian columns to the newel posts. But what makes the house so special is that for decades it was the most prestigious and influential literary salon in London, a meeting place for writers, scientists, politicians and explorers.

In 1812 the house was acquired by the publisher John Murray II, a highly gregarious man who was the friend and confidant of many of the leading writers of the day. He was the publisher of, amongst others, Jane Austen, Sir Walter Scott, Washington Irving and Lord Byron. Murray's home cum office was renowned for his "Four o'clock friends" – where he held afternoon tea with his writers gathered around the fireplace in the first floor room beneath the dazzling plaster ceiling in the style of Inigo Jones (below left). It was here on 17 May 1824, shortly after Byron's death at Missolonghi, that together with five of Byron's closest friends and executors Murray burned Byron's memoirs, in the belief that they were so outrageous they would destroy his reputation. Only Tom Moore demurred.

Notwithstanding the literary outrage it caused, the firm flourished under John Murray III, who published Charles Eastlake, Herman Melville, David Livingstone and, in 1859, two bestsellers on the same day – Charles Darwin's *The Origin of Species* and Samuel Smith's *Self-Help*. Its list of authors is a roll-call of generations of eminent Britons – the great explorers Franklin, Livingstone, Barrow, Schliemann and Isabella Bird; the scientist Charles Babbage; the political economist Thomas Malthus; and the geologist Sir Charles Lyell. More recently John Betjeman, Osbert Lancaster, Mary Renault, Freya Stark, Patrick Leigh Fermor, Kenneth Clark and, not least, yours truly all published under the John Murray imprint, before the family business was sold in 2002. Its historic archive was acquired by the National Library of Scotland for £31 million.

The rooms are hung with portraits of eminent Murray authors interspersed with an extraordinary collection of literary memorabilia. It was here that Byron met Sir Walter Scott for the first time after their famous feud. Scott's cane and travelling writing desk form part of the collection, together with scarabs from Egypt, militaria from the battlefield of Waterloo, tiger claws from India, the inner linings from Byron's boots and other personal possessions and a lock of hair from the stunning Lady Caroline Lamb, who still haunts the staircase.

There is nothing quite like it anywhere in London – a truly historic interior imbued with the shades of generations of literary geniuses from over a quarter of a millennium.

The Wolseley

160 PICCADILLY, W1J 9EB
LISTED: GRADE II*

The Wolseley is now in its third incarnation, having been built in 1921 as a prestigious West End showroom for Wolseley cars. Set within the ground floor of a monumental classical building designed by William Curtis Green, the lavish vaulted Florentine interior and exquisite Chinese lacquer work provided a sumptuous upmarket setting for the swanky marque. The cars were displayed on the black and white marble floor with its centrepiece of radiating black and white stars. However, as early as October 1926 the venture had failed, and the company went into receivership with debts of £2m.

The building was sold to Barclays Bank, who promptly recalled Curtis Green to convert the building into a sumptuous new banking hall, which opened in April 1927, and which reflected the commercial might of one of the "big five" British banks.

Barclays had never adopted a coherent house style. The commissioning of new banks was left to local managers, who were given considerable latitude, and, doubtless in the interests of economy, at Piccadilly the interior was adapted to reinforce the exotic Chinese theme which had been executed by Walter Brierley. The panelled counters were crafted in black and red lacquer with Chinese motifs, and bespoke furniture designed by Curtis Green included black cane and lacquer work chairs, a Chinese chest, a post box and stamp machine.

The 1920s were the heyday of British commercial influence in the treaty ports of China – Shanghai, Hong Kong and Canton. Chinese design filtered back and was seen, albeit briefly, as a modish expression of Britain's global wealth and power. The nearby contemporaneous shopfronts of Jackson's of Piccadilly, tea merchants, which still survive albeit in new uses, have pagoda-style tops adorned with Chinese figures.

In 1999 Barclays closed, and the interior was converted with great sensitivity into the Wolseley restaurant by David Collins, architects, reopening in November 2003.

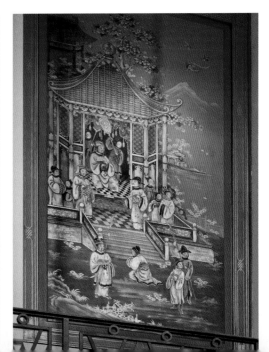

Park Lane Hotel

PICCADILLY, W1J 7BX
LISTED: GRADE II

Overlooking Green Park and faced in white Burmantoft 'Marmo' faience, externally the Park Lane Hotel is a rather incoherent composition, with a deeply recessed centre and black columns to the entrances, but the interior is a complete revelation.

Beyond the main entrance the restaurant in the west wing has reset panelling and boiseries in Louis XV style, designed in 1904 by Carlhian and Beaumetz of Paris for the American financier Pierpoint Morgan's house in Princes Gate, Kensington. To the east, the Oak Room is a copy of the Globe Room of 1637 from the Reindeer Hotel in Banbury, but these are a mere prelude to the amazing 1920s Silver Gallery, staircase and ballroom, which form the largest and most sumptuous unbroken sequence of Art Deco spaces in London.

Designed by Kenneth Anns and Henry Tanner in 1927, the rooms are approached through a separate entrance from Piccadilly. The large entrance hall, or Silver Gallery, in pink mauve and silver hues is breathtaking. Clustered vertical tubes of light frame the entrances beside arched mirrors in silver gilt frames. The staircases beyond are marked by triple-tiered, annular lights which form exotic capitals to the silver gilt columns beneath. Glowing cylindrical stairlights match the geometrical brass handrails.

On the staircase walls are paintings by a Miss Gilbert. One depicts stylised classical female figures, daringly topless, but striking the carefree poses of giddy young flappers of the 1920s – all in silver leaf lacquered to the walls in gold. Another symbolically depicts nymphs with wild beasts. The staircases lead down to a gallery overlooking a huge basement ballroom finished by Higgs and Hill with wall panelling enriched with winged horses and youths, pink-tinted shaped mirrors, fountain wall-lights, frosted-glass chandeliers and palmette-decorated plasterwork. Surrounding rooms, lavatories and their details in full period style are all part of the total aesthetic experience. It is sensational.

Here in the Jazz Age London's *jeunesse dorée* would trip the light fantastic to the Charleston, shimmy and Black Bottom. With characteristic bobbed hair, "the badge of flapperhood", frivolous flappers would "trot like foxes, limp like lame ducks, one-step like cripples, and all to the bizarre yawp of strange instruments". Freed from the constraints of stays and corsets, and dressed like boys with flattened chests, etiolated young women flaunted their sexuality, scandalising their elders and ushering in the age of the new, "modern" woman.

Maggs Bros Ltd

50 Berkeley Square, w1j 5ba
Listed: Grade II

Discreetly located in a fine town house of c1750 on the west side of Berkeley Square, No 50 was once the home of George Canning, Britain's shortest-serving prime minister, who died in the house in 1827. Maggs Bros, which holds the royal warrant, is one of the oldest antiquarian booksellers in the world. Founded by the delightfully named Uriah Maggs in Paddington in 1853, after various peregrinations via The Strand and Conduit Street it arrived in Berkeley Square in 1937.

Behind the reticent façade is a bewitching interior full of hidden rooms and odd chambers lined with leather-bound volumes and manuscripts which are allowed to "mature" slowly on the shelves. In this paradise for bibliophiles can be found countless priceless volumes from a first edition of Captain Cook's journals and charts to Trevelyan's *The Indian Mutiny and Massacre* cheek by jowl with the selected contents of the library from Sherborne Castle, Oxfordshire. On the staircase landing racks of old glass panels display copies of ancient manuscripts from the firm's collection, the walls lined with portraits of the Maggs family, who still own the business.

The elegant mid-18th century rooms have fine late 18th century marble chimneypieces, possibly relocated from demolished houses on the east side of Berkeley Square in the 1930s, interspersed with sundry mahogany cabinets and bookcases relocated from earlier premises. At one of the tables a pile of letters in envelopes complete with Victorian stamps and beautiful copperplate handwriting has been sifted carefully as though it were the incoming post rather than part of the archive. Another table is that on which Dickens penned the opening chapters of *The Pickwick Papers*.

In the basement is a rare original service tunnel connecting the house to the mews at the rear – a crepuscular shaft of lime-washed brick swathed in cobwebs and crammed with old books, boxes, grates and dead storage. The mews is screened by an entirely separate secondary façade, seemingly erected simply to mask a later staircase insertion rather than as an architectural eyecatcher. In the mews dusty old storage rooms still retain mid-19th century wallpaper alongside a more contemporary gallery and exhibition space.

The air of other-worldliness which pervades the building belies a shrewd business acumen. In 1932 Maggs Bros pulled off one of the great bookselling coups of the 20th century when it not only purchased a rare Gutenberg Bible from the Soviet government, but also the famous *Codex Sinaiticus*, a priceless ancient handwritten copy of the Greek Bible, for £100,000, the highest price ever paid for a book at that time. In 1998 the firm once again set the record for the world's most expensive book when it bought a copy of the first book ever published in England – William Caxton's imprint of *The Canterbury Tales*, for £4.2m. Such forays are not unusual. In 1916 Maggs Bros purchased the desiccated penis of Napoleon Bonaparte from the descendants of Abbé Vignali, his priest, who, having administered the last rites to the exiled Emperor, without further ado then surreptitiously chopped off the imperial member, no doubt thinking that it might come in handy. Having handled (as it were) the appendage for over eight years, in 1924 the firm sold it on.

As if all of this were not enough, 50 Berkeley Square was once notorious as the most haunted house in London – the attic purportedly visited by the spirit of a young woman abused by her uncle who hurled herself from the top floor window into the street below. In the late 19th century at least two intrepid souls who spent a night in the room died in convulsions without ever revealing the cause. Even Canning claims to have heard strange noises in the house, but following an exorcism by a bishop, nothing paranormal has disturbed the quiet repose of Maggs Bros during their occupation.

Clermont Club

44 BERKELEY SQUARE, W1J 5AR
LISTED: GRADE I

In 1696 the 3rd Lord Berkeley of Stratton sold his house in Piccadilly to the Duke of Devonshire with an explicit undertaking not to allow buildings north of its gardens, a commitment which was honoured for almost 200 years. The result was a continuous sweep of open landscape from Berkeley House, through the gardens of Lansdowne House (built in the 1760s) and on through the central gardens of Berkeley Square to the edge of the Grosvenor Estate beyond.

In 1738-9 a group of large houses was erected on the eastern side of the square, followed immediately by an even more opulent group on the west side. Of these, No 44, now the Clermont Club, is widely regarded as the finest terrace house in London. It was designed by the elderly William Kent for Lady Isabella Finch, the 7th daughter of the 7th Earl of Winchelsea, known as Don Dismal for his swarthy appearance. Bel, as she was called, was a middle-aged spinster and maid of honour to Princesses Amelia and Caroline, daughters of George II.

The reticent brick exterior and large rusticated arched entrance give little clue to the splendours which lie inside. Beyond the plain, stone-flagged entrance hall and tiny former porter's lodge is the dramatic centrepiece of the whole house – a staircase which has no equal in Palladian architecture and which was widely admired by contemporaries. Horace Walpole described it: "as beautiful as a piece of scenery, and considering the space, of art as can be imagined!"

It was revolutionary. There had never been anything like it. At a time when staircases conventionally were either square or spiral, Kent produced a highly complex series of interpenetrating spaces: an exercise in pure theatre, creating the illusion of a palatial interior within the confines of a terrace house. The curved flights of stairs break back in on themselves to a bridge across the first floor landing and a screen of Ionic columns, behind which the stair rises to the second floor. Above is a coffered dome reminiscent of Santa Maria Maggiore in Rome. The scrolled ironwork resembling seahorses evokes Kent's earlier work at Holkham Hall.

The staircase is but a precursor to one of the finest rooms in London, the Saloon or Great Chamber, with a coved and coffered gilded geometrical ceiling inset with grisaille paintings on blue and red grounds, depicting the *Loves of the Gods*, probably painted by Kent himself before his death in 1748. At each end are matching fireplaces by Joseph Pickford surmounted by pier glasses and trophies, the walls lined with dark blue damask introduced as part of John Fowler's restoration for the Clermont Club in 1962.

Behind the Saloon is Lady Bel's bedroom and boudoir, remodelled by Henry Holland in 1790 after the house was sold to Lord Clermont following her death in 1771. Lady Clermont, a friend of Marie Antoinette, was an ardent Francophile, which accounts for the stylistic change. Sympathetic restoration and alterations were carried out by John Fowler and Philip Jebb between 1962 and 1964, including the octagonal Gothick garden pavilion.

From 1962 the Clermont Club was the haunt of a wealthy group of buccaneering British gamblers including five dukes, five marquesses, nearly 20 earls and two cabinet ministers, alongside such luminaries as Ian Fleming, Lucien Freud, James Goldsmith and Lord Lucan. In the basement is Annabel's, the private members' restaurant and nightclub.

Geo F Trumper

9 CURZON STREET, W1J 5HQ

UNLISTED

Geo F Trumper is that rare commodity – a surviving example of a traditional gentlemen's barbershop with a beautifully presented period interior, complete with individual mahogany cubicles and glass display cases from the early 20th century full of fragrant scents bearing the names of great British figures: Marlborough, Wellington and Curzon among others.

George F Trumper opened his first barbershop in Curzon Street in 1875, although the present handsome, stone-faced building was not erected until later, c1912. The plain polished oak shopfront with its black and gilt lettering on the windows and sill boards epitomises the understated urbane elegance of old Mayfair. Given the aristocratic and military clientele he attracted, Trumper made his shop feel like more a luxurious gentlemen's club than just a functional barber's shop, an ambience which continues to this day.

Inside, the individual private cubicles are divided by glazed mahogany screens with dark red velvet curtains; the walls lined with hunting scenes and shelves of the firm's world-famous colognes, grooming products and shaving accessories. Beneath the display cases is a dado lined with plush studded green leather.

Home House

20 Portman Square, w1h 6lw
Listed: Grade I

Elizabeth, Countess of Home, the daughter of William Gibbons, a wealthy Jamaican planter, was a formidable old battleaxe who swore like a trooper and was christened by William Beckford the "Queen of Hell". She married twice – first to James Lawes, the son of the island's governor, from whom she inherited a fortune in 1734, after which she moved to England, where eight years later she married the 8th Earl of Home. Phenomenally wealthy, but childless, in her late 60s she commissioned a magnificent private palace from Robert Adam. Completed in 1776, it is his finest surviving London town house.

The restrained five-bay-wide façade is chastely enriched with band courses and panels of garlands over the windows. Inside is the famous top-lit Imperial staircase, shown here before (opposite above left) and after (opposite middle) restoration, influenced by William Kent's revolutionary staircase completed 35 years earlier at 44 Berkeley Square (see Clermont Club p104). Set in a circular well, and serving only the first floor, it rises full height through the house. The warm burnt sienna marbled walls slowly lighten in colour towards the skylight, enriched with stucco trophies and painted panels from *The Aeneid*, although the large grisaille panels around the landing are almost certainly additions by Philip Tilden for Lord Islington in the 1920s.

The principal rooms are decorated in distinctive Adam style, with panels of delicate painted plasterwork, and the clever use of shallow curves and recesses to modulate the surface planes. At ground floor level the front parlour (opposite below left) has a large central oval motif with paintings by Angelica Kauffman. Behind the staircase in the Library, the painted panels over the doors and mantelpiece are signed by Kauffman's husband "Antonio Zucchi 1776" with portraits of British worthies including Drake, Newton, Bacon, Locke and, rather immodestly, Adam himself.

At first floor level the sumptuous Ballroom is approached discreetly through a jib door in the apse. The room is surrounded by a rich inlaid mahogany dado and crowned by one of Adam's most intricate ornamental plaster ceilings (below left). Across the front of the building the Music Room (opposite right above middle) is a confection of circles with paintings of musical subjects. The Etruscan Room with its shallow curved walls, semi-domes and striking decoration is both unusual and a rare survival of what Adam described as "a mode of Decoration which differs from anything hitherto practised in Europe" (opposite below right).

Some of the rooms in the upper floors retain early silk and paper wall-hangings, most notably the current Patricia Portman Room (opposite middle below) with superb 1820s Chinese Chi Lung silk in shades of indigo and coral and a palm-tree chimneypiece now covered in silver gilt.

After the death of the countess, the house was passed through various hands – most notably the French Ambassador, the Duke of Atholl, Earl Grey and the Dukes of Newcastle. From 1932 to 1989 the house was occupied by the Courtauld Institute of Art. From 1947 to 1974 its director was Anthony Blunt, Master of the Queen's Pictures and the notorious Soviet spy. In his rooms at the top of the house he consorted with politicians, academics and his fellow spies Philby, Burgess and Maclean. Allegedly MI5 installed a secret listening device in the wall of 21 Portman Square to eavesdrop on his conversations. After his exposure as a Soviet agent, Blunt confessed to his former wartime boss at MI5 "it gave me great pleasure to have been able to pass the names of every MI5 officer to the Russians". Quite how many died as a result of his treachery is difficult to discern. Had the Germans had a successful spy in Soviet intelligence, he could have lost Britain the war.

Between 1989 and 1996, the house lay vacant as one of London's most vulnerable buildings at risk, but in 1996 it was acquired by Berkeley Adam Ltd and meticulously restored.

Criterion Restaurant and Theatre

224 Pɪᴄᴄᴀᴅɪʟʟʏ, ᴡ1ᴊ 9ʜᴘ
Lɪsᴛᴇᴅ: Gʀᴀᴅᴇ II*

In 1871 the railway caterers Spiers & Pond held a competition for the design of a new entertainments complex comprising a restaurant, dining rooms, smoking room, grand hall and theatre for a site on the south side of Piccadilly Circus occupied by an old galleried coaching inn, The White Bear. Thomas Verity was selected as architect. The complex was the first of a new generation of monster restaurants catering for the newly affluent middle classes. Designed in French Second Empire style and influenced by Charles Garnier's work in Paris, it opened in 1874 and was an instant success. Eight years later it was extended by Verity's son, Frank.

Beneath the huge restaurant, which catered for over 2,000 diners, is "an underground temple of drama" – the Criterion Theatre, which Verity modelled on the Athenée in Paris. This was made possible by modern services such as lifts and mechanical ventilation, and fireproof separation from the restaurant above. The theatre entrance (below left) retains its original appearance with a painted ceiling, mirrors and tiles made by W B Simpson & Son and cartoon figures by A S Coke. Critics claimed that "the effect would be like a butcher's shop" but, having experimented with tiling at the Mansion House Station Restaurant, the clients were determined to adopt it. Verity concluded that it was "bright and clean, practically indestructible, and not too expensive, and what is more important, it will wash".

The theatre was given an illusion of space by the clever use of mirrors and decoration, although shortly after its opening a young actress, Violet Vanbrugh, described acting there as being "something like an isolated race of submerged beings from one of H G Wells' imaginative novels".

To the left of the main entrance is the former buffet area, known as the Long Bar, now the Criterion Restaurant. In 1899 this was extended to include a raised smoking room to the rear (p113 above). At the same time the interior was remodelled by Frank Verity to form a spectacular neo-Byzantine "Marble Restaurant" resembling an Aladdin's cave. Beneath a glittering gold mosaic, tunnel-vaulted ceiling by Burke & Co are walls sheathed in Tennessee and Vermont marbles, their first use in England. By 1980 the interior was believed to be no longer intact, but in 1983 it was rediscovered beneath the Formica-covered walls of the Quality Inn. I recall well the thrill of its rediscovery on removing some of the ceiling panels and finding the hidden splendours beneath, and the subsequent battle to prevent the demolition of the jewel-like smoking room at the rear. The entire interior was restored with great aplomb in 1984.

It was at the original Long Bar in the Criterion that Conan Doyle imagined the meeting between Sherlock Holmes and Dr Watson.

Regent Palace Hotel
Quadrant 3

GLASSHOUSE STREET, W1B 5DN
LISTED: GRADE II

Resembling the prow of a great Edwardian liner wedged into a tight berth behind Piccadilly Circus, the former Regent Palace Hotel (now Quadrant 3) was designed in 1911 for J Lyons & Co by Henry Tanner Jr and W J Ancell, and completed in 1915 after Ancell's death by his assistant, F J Wills. Faced in "Burmantoft's Marmo" faience over a steel frame, its huge bulk meant that the corner pavilions and details were always more important than the overall composition, which is hard to comprehend from the narrow streets of Soho. With over 1,000 rooms, on its completion it was the largest hotel in Europe. After years of post-war decline, what was once a rather dowdy hotel has been transmuted by the Crown Estate into a mixed-use building providing offices, flats, shops and restaurants transforming the blighted Piccadilly Circus hinterland into a destination in its own right. An integral part of the scheme has been the sensitive conservation and restoration of some of London's finest early 20th century interiors, including a superb set of Art Deco bars designed by the stylish Oliver Bernard in 1935.

Bernard (1881-1939) was a stage designer and leading proponent of the Art Deco style who began his career with J Lyons & Co, designing ceramics for the 1924 British Empire Exhibition. A year later he was the technical director of the British Pavilion at the Exposition Internationale des Arts Décoratifs et Industriels Modernes, from which the style takes its name. His work at the Regent Palace was described at the time in *Building* as "just a trifle dissipated and naughty, but not sufficiently as to be vulgar". His Chez Cup Bar, the critic purred, was "slick and smart and quite the last thing in interior decoration".

Under the expert guidance of Donald Insall & Partners, the former coffee and dining room, remodelled by Bernard and known most recently as The Titanic Bar (opposite and below left), was carefully dismantled and re-erected at lower ground floor level to sit alongside Bernard's other great space, latterly known as The Atlantic Bar (p116 top and middle), now the Sherwood Street restaurant. Guided by Bernard's original drawings and photographs, both interiors have been restored with meticulous attention to detail. Timber veneer, marble, brass, silver and gold leaf finishes, mirrors and swanky Art Deco lighting have all been restored or reinstated to create a dazzling ensemble of 1930s rooms alongside Ancell's surviving classical interior – the former grill room of 1915 (p117).

Although the recasting of the hotel as a new mixed-use building involved an exceptional degree of intervention into the fabric of the building, the benefits far outweigh the losses. The sensitive conservation and reinstatement of the jaw-dropping interiors, and retention and refurbishment of the key corner pavilions, coupled with the insertion of new flank elevations in blue, green and cream faience by Dixon Jones, has revitalised a seedy quarter of the West End in desperate need of regeneration.

Algerian Coffee Stores

52 Old Compton Street, W1D 4PB
Unlisted

A great city can be measured by the quality and extent of its historic shops and cafés, which coalesce to confer a very distinctive sense of place. At a time when so many high streets are under siege from clone stores and corporate chains, it is doubly important to ensure that those that remain are safeguarded and cherished. Unlike Paris, in London historic shops and uses are at the mercy of market forces and not accorded preferential business rates.

Established in 1887, the Algerian Coffee Stores is one of those delightful specialist shops that make London such a rich and diverse world city. Behind its distinctive pillar-box-red shopfront in the heart of Soho, many of the original late 19th century fittings survive including the mahogany counter, display cases and shelves.

The shop is permeated with the pungent aromas of over 80 different coffees from across the globe and more than 120 exotic teas with wildly romantic names – Silver Snail, Rose Congou and, best of all, Dragon's Whiskers.

London has still not produced an effective mechanism for protecting historic shops and uses for the benefit of future generations.

House of St Barnabas-in-Soho

1 Greek Street, wid 4nq
Listed: Grade I

No 1 Greek Street is one of the best surviving mid-18th century houses in London. Its plain, understated façade offers no hint of the Georgian exuberance which can be found within. Built in 1744-6, the house remained an unoccupied shell for eight years before it was sold to a Jamaican planter, Robert Beckford, the younger brother of Alderman (later Lord Mayor) William Beckford, who completed the interior.

Approached through a simple bracketed stone doorcase flanked by a pair of obelisks, the impressive double-height entrance hall is dominated by a magnificent stone staircase with a lyre pattern wrought-iron balustrade. The walls and ceilings are a riot of moulded stucco masks and cartouches in an elaborate Rococo style, a treatment which is continued with Palladian nuances into the three main rooms. The ceiling of the main saloon facing the square has an oval centrepiece with four rather overweight putti depicting the four elements. Although executed to the highest quality, tantalisingly the designer of the interior remains unknown, although comparisons have been made with the Mansion House.

In 1861 the building was sold to the House of Charity, which had been established 15 years earlier in nearby Manette Street for the relief of the destitute and homeless poor. Although ambitious plans were drawn up for a chapel, refectory, dormitory and cloisters, only the chapel was built, tucked away at the rear; a muscular early French Gothic gem designed by Joseph Clarke, the architect to the charity. Inside, bands of red and white stone are juxtaposed with coloured marbles to create a place for quiet contemplation beneath a dark blue ceiling punctuated by gold stars. The stained glass designed by John Hayward is post-war – installed in 1957-8 to replace the original windows, which were destroyed in the Second World War.

The charity continues to flourish as a life skills centre and events venue in an innovative partnership between the business and charitable sectors.

W Sitch & Co

48 Berwick Street, w1f 8jd
Listed: Grade II

The historic terrace houses of 18th and 19th century London are immensely adaptable and capable of accommodating a multitude of different uses from housing, offices and commercial space to public houses, clubs and workshops. As a result many light industries and craft workshops in central and inner London can still be found in what were once elegant Georgian and Regency houses.

W Sitch & Co, art metal and lighting specialists, is a wonderfully atmospheric example. Founded in 1776, the year of the Declaration of American Independence, it has been located in an early 19th century town house in Soho since 1903, and specialises in the restoration, renovation and replication of historic lighting and fittings from any period.

Every surface of the interior of the building is crammed with light fittings, lamps and specialist metalwork. A fine early 18th century staircase with turned balusters and ancient timber treads worn smooth by the passage of time leads to a veritable treasure trove. The upper floors are lined with a bewildering array of sconces, wall lights, chandeliers, lanterns, lamps and candelabra in a plethora of designs and styles. At the rear is a fully operational workshop and forge for the manufacture and polishing of individual artefacts. The basement resembles a burial crypt – piled high with metalwork, fixtures, fittings and accessories.

Amongst the company's august clientele are the National Trust, English Heritage and 10 Downing Street.

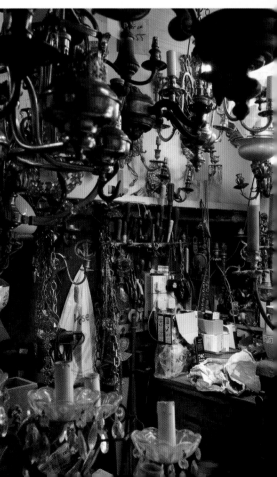

Welsh Baptist Chapel

EASTCASTLE STREET, W1W 8DJ
LISTED: GRADE II

Situated a stone's throw from Oxford Circus, the Welsh Baptist Chapel is one of London's more obscure but intimate treasures.

The Baptists first arrived in Castle Street East, as it was then called, in April 1865 as one of a number of groups that rented the Franklin Hall for the purposes of worship. Fifteen years later they acquired the site and adapted the building for their own purposes, but such was their success that they soon outgrew it. In 1888 they commissioned a new building as a spiritual home and social centre for Welsh exiles in London. "It was fitting that He, for whom the heavens are but his thrones, and the earth is but a footstool, should have a better house in which to dwell," expounded the Welsh Baptist paper *Seren Cymru*.

The architect of the new chapel was Owen Lewis (Owain Dyfed), the son of an eminent Welsh preacher and hymn-writer, Titus Lewis. He had worked his way up through the building trade to become an architect, and later a highly influential president of the Welsh Baptist Union and the first director of the Welsh Baptist Insurance Company, which he established.

Lewis produced a rather peculiar but fetching design with a tall, three-bay-wide stone Corinthian colonnade across the lower floors enclosing a double flight of balustraded stairs. Inscribed proudly in the frieze of the portico are the words "Capel Bedyddwyr Cymreig". The interior is truly delightful – a beautifully preserved preaching box with a gallery around three sides enclosed by decorative iron balustrades and stained glass. The organ enjoys pride of place over the pulpit. Beneath is a lecture hall cum schoolroom.

A major benefactor was D H Evans, the businessman who created the eponymous Oxford Street department store, a deacon of the Church and son-in-law of its first minister, Reverend William Harris. Lloyd George was an occasional visitor on Flower Sunday, accompanied in 1901 by Winston Churchill.

Lewis was lavished with praise for the meeting house that he created. "And what a building! It is an edifice worthy of a West End reputation. Exquisitely chaste in design, commodious, without apparently a fault in the important matter of sound, and every inch of room sensibly utilised. Lavatories, tea-making and other conveniences in abundance!" extolled the *Baptist* with uncharacteristic hyperbole.

Today the chapel provides a home and social centre for the United Welsh Church in central London.

Sanderson Hotel

50 BERNERS STREET, W1T 3NG
LISTED: GRADE II*

The former headquarters and showroom of Arthur Sanderson & Son, the wallpaper and paint manufacturer, were built in 1959-60 by R H Uren of Slater, Moberly & Uren to celebrate the firm's centenary. The building rapidly became a nationally recognised icon of go-ahead, modern Britain after featuring in the opening credits of the TV series *Danger Man* between 1960 and 1962.

The building was configured around a Japanese-style courtyard garden landscaped by Philip Hicks with a long curtain wall of glass and Portland stone to the principal elevation facing Berners Street. Internally the space was designed to be highly flexible with removable partitions between the rooms to facilitate multiple uses. Contemporary artwork was included in the principal communal spaces as an integral part of the overall design.

Behind the open staircase is a fine abstract stained-glass window by John Piper and Patrick Reyntiens. Elsewhere are glass and marble mosaics by Jupp Dernbach-Mayern.

After the firm vacated the building, it was converted to a stylish new hotel – a fantasy dreamworld with an eccentric, contemporary décor which acts as a perfect foil to the international modernist design. The architects were Denton Corker Marshall and the theatrical interior by Philippe Starck.

Cleverly executed with humour and irony, the fantasy décor is a blend of kitsch and contemporary design with a bold use of primary colours to offset the cool minimalist spaces. In the lobby and reception area Salvador Dalí's red lips sofa is juxtaposed with hand-carved African furniture and a Baroque silver-gilded chair with arms in the form of swans. Tinted cut-glass windows frame the lifts. The former retail counter is now a long bar with a line of bar stools, each decorated with a single seductive eye, while beneath the original staircase and Piper window the billiards room, adjacent to the Purple Bar, has a purple baize table surrounded by velvet chairs crafted from antlers and horn.

The Sanderson shows how with flair, style and wit a building can be enhanced rather than diminished through intelligent, informed conservation and the sensitive introduction of an appropriate new use.

Middlesex Hospital Chapel

Nassau Street, w1n 8hn
Listed: Grade II*

Marooned at the centre of the vast Middlesex Hospital site, lying isolated, exposed and vulnerable, is one of the finest chapels in Britain; its future frustratingly unresolved.

The spectacular chapel of the former Middlesex Hospital was designed by John Loughborough Pearson and begun in 1891, although it was not completed until 1930 by his son, Frank. Built as a memorial to Major Alexander Ross MP, a chairman of the Board of Governors, funding was provided by his family for a lavishly decorated interior in a rich eclectic mixture of Italianate, Byzantine and neo-Romanesque styles.

Pearson returned from a study tour of Italy in 1874 as a passionate enthusiast for the elaborate polychrome pavements of mediaeval Italian churches, which later he deployed to great effect in his own work.

At the Middlesex Hospital the chancel floor is a sumptuous juxtaposition of green, yellow and black marble Cosmati work complemented by green onyx slabs to the walls of the nave and sanctuary. Above is a band of chevron-patterned marble and rich mosaic work. Soaring overhead, the groin-vaulted ceilings shimmer with gold mosaics and blue stars in a stunning display of craftsmanship by Robert Davison, whose Decorative Arts Studio was in nearby Marylebone. To complement his unified vision for the interior, for the stained glass Pearson turned to his favourite artists, Clayton & Bell.

On his death in December 1899, Pearson's son Frank took over, completing the last two bays of the gold mosaic ceiling with icons of the Apostles either side of the sacred monogram IHC. With the reconstruction of the hospital in 1929, additional space was created to form a narrow baptistery which Frank Pearson embellished in full-blown Byzantine style with a lapis-lazuli dome and angels bearing scrolls.

In 1936 Rudyard Kipling lay in state here. Until its closure in 2005, the chapel provided daily solace and hope for many at their hour of greatest need.

Pollock's Toy Museum

1 Scala Street, W1T 2HL
Listed: Grade II

"If you love art, folly or the bright eyes of children, speed to Pollock's!" wrote Robert Louis Stevenson after a visit to the rival firm of W Webb in the 1880s. His advice is just as pertinent today. Pollock's Toy Museum is not just a house of wonders, but a hidden gateway into the magical world of childhood.

Benjamin Pollock (1856-1937) was a Hoxton furrier who, whilst still in his teens, married Eliza Redington, whose family were printers and bookbinders with a "Theatrical Print Warehouse". The Pollocks inherited the business, which contained a mass of copperplate engravings, lithographs and souvenir "pin-ups" of the stage stars of the time. Prints of theatre scenery and the cast of successful plays were supplied in miniature for home entertainment – for "a penny plain" or "two pence coloured". Pollock adopted the lithographic press, rather than copperplate, which he operated personally for over 60 years, continuing the family business he had inherited.

By the 1870s intense competition from German companies had reduced the traditional English toy theatre to just two firms – Webb's and Pollock's – both operating from Hoxton, both producing hand-coloured, folk-art designs. By the 1920s Pollock's was legendary. Leading lights of the London stage beat a path to its door – Ellen Terry, Gladys Cooper and Charlie Chaplin all visited. Diaghilev, who had been taken there by Sacheverell Sitwell, promoted his Russian ballet in 1927 with décor "after Benjamin Pollock".

In 1944 the family business and stock were sold to a flamboyant entrepreneur, Alan Keen, but by 1951 the firm was in receivership. Three years later, in search of some slides for her son's toy theatre, Marguerite Fawdry bought the entire stock, and together with three other friends who were collectors of toys and dolls, she established a small museum in Monmouth Street, Seven Dials. In 1969 it moved to an evocatively dilapidated early Georgian house in Scala Street, where it has flourished ever since as one of London's genuine curiosities.

Up the narrow winding staircase is the timeless enchanted world of childhood. Every surface of every room is lined with delightful displays of toys, dolls and childhood memorabilia – board games, mechanical and tin toys, wax and composite dolls, teddy bears, folk toys, tableaux, and even a young girl's nursery of 1900.

Petrie Museum of Egyptian Archaeology

MALET PLACE, WC1E 6BT
UNLISTED

Housed above a set of 19th century stables, the Petrie Museum of Egyptian Archaeology is one of London's most captivating hidden gems; a veritable treasure trove of over 80,000 objects which comprise one of the world's finest, and little-known, collections of Ancient Egyptian and Sudanese artefacts.

Much of the initial collection was donated by the writer Amelia Edwards, who in 1882 co-founded the Egypt Exploration Fund, dedicated to the research and preservation of Egyptian ancient monuments. On her death in 1892 she bequeathed her library and collection of antiquities to University College, London, and endowed the Edwards Chair of Egyptology, the first to be established in Britain. The first Edwards Professor was (Sir) William Flinders Petrie (1853-1942), one of the titans of early Egyptology, who excavated many of the most important Egyptian sites including Tanis, Abydos and Amarna, the city founded by the monotheistic Pharaoh Akhenaten.

Petrie's collection was arranged in galleries and intended primarily for reference by scholars, students and academics rather than the public. After his retirement in 1933, his successors added to it extensively. In the early 1950s it was recovered from wartime storage and moved into its current home in Malet Place, adjacent to the Science Library of University College.

Petrie was notorious for his extreme right-wing views and was an ardent believer in eugenics. On his death in Jerusalem in 1942 his body was buried in the Protestant Cemetery of Mt Zion, but rather conceitedly he bequeathed his head to the Royal College of Surgeons, so it could be studied for its intellectual capacity. Unfortunately it went AWOL, and was only discovered in London many years later.

The collection is full of some of the oldest Egyptian artefacts and many 'firsts', including the earliest example of worked metal, the first worked iron beads, the earliest example of glazing, the oldest wills on papyrus and one of the earliest fragments of linen along with a beadnet dress of a dancer from 2400BC, a suit of armour from the royal palace at Memphis and the world's largest collection of Roman mummy portraits from the first and second centuries AD.

Grant Museum of Zoology

21 University Street, wc1e 6de
Listed: Grade II

It is not often that one comes face to face with the reproductive organs of a duck-billed platypus, but that is one of the many delights that await the visitor to the Grant Museum of Zoology.

On entering the newly relocated museum, it is somewhat disconcerting to be greeted by a human skeleton and three simian companions seemingly engaged in casual conversation as they survey the room below from the balcony, but the Grant Museum is full of such wondrous things. There is the skeleton of a quagga – the rarest in the world – a dodo and a Tasmanian tiger, all of which were hunted to extinction; the skulls of an African and an Asian elephant; the bones of a gorilla, rhinoceros, wolf and lion; and countless jars full of extraordinary artefacts including a large container full of pickled moles. The collection of 67,000 specimens includes Sir Victor Negus's bisected animal heads in an arresting display of which Damien Hirst would be proud.

Robert Edmond Grant (1793-1874) was born and educated in Edinburgh. He later became the first professor of zoology and comparative anatomy in England, with radical evolutionary views which influenced a young Charles Darwin. On his arrival at University College, London, he found no teaching materials, so immediately began his own collection, which forms the basis of the current museum. The collection was augmented and catalogued by his successors, including Sir Edwin Ray Lankester and W F R Weldon.

After repeated threats of closure, the museum relocated to the former University College Medical School building, now known as the UCL Rockefeller Building, in March 2011.

The building was designed in 1907 by Paul Waterhouse (1861-1924), the son of Alfred Waterhouse (1830-1905), with whom he had collaborated on the adjacent University College Hospital a year earlier. Faced in Portland stone and red Bracknell bricks, its dignified classical elevations are articulated by large windows which light what were once chemical, bacteriological and histological laboratories. The building embraced three separate functions – the Medical School, Maternity Students' House and a Nurses' Home, which was connected by a tunnel to the hospital opposite and incorporated the latest technology: electric lights and central heating.

The former Medical School Library, later the Thomas Lewis Room and now the museum, has a fine balcony which was once decorated with a set of busts of eminent men associated with medicine and surgery at the hospital or college. The museum collection, which is still used for teaching purposes, is calculated to bring out the ghoulish inner nine-year-old in every visitor.

Jeremy Bentham
Auto-Icon

University College London, Gower Street, WC1E 6DE
Listed: Grade I

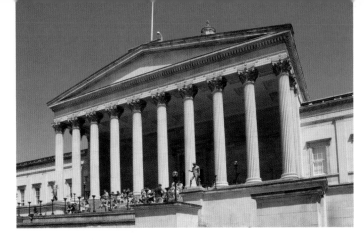

Known as "the godless college" because it was founded as a secular alternative to Oxford and Cambridge, University College was formed in 1826. Its foundation is commonly, but erroneously, accredited to the philosopher, jurist and reformer Jeremy Bentham (1748-1832). In fact he took no part in it. The myth is derived from a mural (1922) by Henry Tonks in the dome over the Flaxman Gallery, which lies behind the portico, showing him approving the plans of the university buildings.

Bentham believed that education should be more widely available and kept separate from religion. Theology, he argued, should have no bearing on morality or legislation. Inspired by his free thinking, the college was founded by James Mill (1773-1836), the father of the philosopher John Stuart Mill, and Henry Brougham (1778-1868).

As a scientific rationalist, Bentham did not believe in life after death so on his demise in 1832 he left instructions that his body should be used for dissection by medical students and afterwards made into an auto-icon or self-image.

His wishes were carried out by his friend Thomas Southwood Smith, who took responsibility for preserving Bentham's head and articulating his skeleton. The auto-icon was kept at Smith's home until 1850, when it was presented to the college and placed in a mahogany cabinet resembling some sort of gruesome telephone box at the end of the South Cloisters. Bentham specified that his head should be preserved by a process of desiccation favoured by Maoris, but it was not successful. The result proved too grisly to display, so Smith commissioned a modeller, Jacques Talrich, to make a wax head for the auto-icon, which is what can be seen today.

The auto-icon contains Bentham's skeleton dressed in his own clothes stuffed with straw "in the attitude in which I am sitting when engaged in thought". The only part of his body visible is his hair. His real head, now extremely fragile, is stored at UCL under controlled atmospheric conditions.

Bentham's passing was described by his friend and literary executor John Bowring on 6 June 1832: "It was an imperceptible dying. There was no struggle – no suffering – life faded to death – as the twilight blends the day with darkness".

The college has a superb collection of casts of the work of the sculptor John Flaxman in the Flaxman Gallery beneath the dome with a full-size piece of St Michael conquering Satan, commissioned by Lord Egremont in 1821 for Petworth House.

Close to the auto-icon in the South Cloisters is an unusual panel of coloured marbles (1865) depicting scenes from Homer by Baron Trinqueti, the designer of the Albert Memorial Chapel at Windsor.

Dr Williams's Library

14 Gordon Square, WC1H 0AG
Listed: Grade II

Situated on the west side of Gordon Square, Dr William's Library is the pre-eminent research library of English Protestant Non-conformity, with a wealth of manuscripts, books and polemical works embracing theology, ecclesiastical history, mysticism, philosophy, language and literature.

Dr David Williams was born in or near Wrexham in 1643; he became Chaplain to the Dowager Countess of Meath, and later a leading London Presbyterian minister. On his death in 1716, he was buried in Bunhill Fields, but most of his estate was bequeathed for charitable purposes, including the foundation of a public library. Initially the library remained at his home in Hoxton, but in 1729 it was moved to Cripplegate, where it flourished as a meeting place for Dissenting bodies. In 1864 the library was displaced by the Metropolitan Railway Company and, after temporary homes in Queen Square and Grafton Street, it moved into its present building in 1890.

The handsome, neo-Jacobean Gothic building in Gordon Square was designed by Thomas Leverton Donaldson in 1848-9 as University Hall, a hostel for students of the adjacent University College, London, at which he was the first professor of architecture.

For over 35 years from 1853 it was shared with Manchester New College, but when the college moved to Oxford in 1889, the building was acquired by Dr Williams's Trust, at which time the fine cast-iron gallery and spiral stairs were installed.

Amongst its 300,000 titles and 90 major manuscript collections are a Wycliffite New Testament, a psalter apparently made for Philippa of Hainault, the wife of Edward III, and the papers of eminent 17th century Non-conformists, including Roger Morrice's *Ent'ring Book*, a political diary covering the period 1677-91. There is an extensive collection of correspondence from Wordsworth, Lamb, Coleridge, Southey, Sir Walter Scott and Harriet Martineau, which provides a precious resource for scholars.

Laid out in the Reading Room are the original reference catalogues with copper-plate, handwritten entries in ancient leather-bound volumes.

Over the past 120 years little has changed. The muted interior, suffused with watery light filtered through stained-glass windows enriched with armorial bearings, remains an extraordinary time capsule, and one of London's little-known treasures. An atmosphere of quiet, scholarly repose permeates the entire building, broken only by the measured ticking of the 18th century longcase clock.

Thomas Coram Foundation for Children

40 Brunswick Square, WC1N 2QA
Listed: Grade II

The Foundling Hospital, like the Great Hall at St Bartholomew's Hospital, encapsulates 18th century attitudes to philanthropy, where the elevating nature of art and music played an important part in providing "hospitality" to the poor and less fortunate.

When Captain Thomas Coram returned from life at sea he was appalled at the sight of children abandoned on dungheaps in the streets of Georgian London, so in 1741 he established the Foundling Hospital for "the education and maintenance of exposed and deserted young children". A charter was granted for a new hospital, and between 1745 and 1753 a large new complex with a chapel, entrance screen and lodges was erected in Bloomsbury to the designs of Thomas Jacobsen. It rapidly became London's most popular charity, attracting the support of some of the most eminent men of the day. William Hogarth and George Frideric Handel were both governors, the latter frequently performing his *Messiah* in the chapel, while the former designed the children's uniforms and coat of arms. In addition to Hogarth, Thomas Gainsborough, Sir Joshua Reynolds and Francis Hayman all decorated the walls of the hospital with their paintings.

In the 1920s the hospital decided to relocate to a healthier rural location, and in 1935 it moved into a new complex at Berkhamsted. The historic hospital buildings could have made genteel accommodation for the University of London, but they were sold to a property developer and eventually demolished, after which Lord Rothermere launched a successful campaign to purchase the site as an open space for children.

However, three rooms and some of the most important contents from the original buildings were preserved in the foundation's offices – a new, understated neo-Georgian block of 1937 by J M Shepherd.

Behind the plain exterior is the original massive oak staircase from the former Boys' Wing, with heavy handrails and balustrades. This leads to the Court Room which has a lavish Rococo ceiling by William Wilton, and a fireplace with a delightful overmantel by Rysbrack of foundling children gainfully employed in husbandry and navigation. Around the walls is the foundation's art collection from the former hospital, with large biblical canvases and medallions showing other London hospitals. In the adjacent picture gallery is another original interior complete with a coloured marble chimneypiece. The sculpture collection includes a terracotta bust of Handel by Roubiliac (c1739), a reclining baby by E H Baily and a terracotta group of a girl and foundling by George Halse of 1874.

The recently refurbished Foundling Museum offers a fascinating insight into the work of the former hospital and foundation. Among the most heart-rending artefacts are the distinguishing tokens put on each child by their parent before their permanent separation – coins, trinkets or simply scraps of cotton or paper.

Over the period of 200 years up to the Second World War, the Foundling Hospital took in and educated over 27,000 children; the boys eventually going into the army, the girls into domestic service.

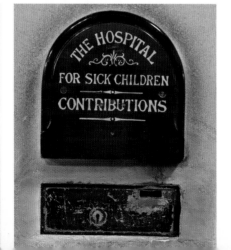

St Christopher's Chapel
Hospital for Sick Children

GREAT ORMOND STREET, WC1N 3JH
LISTED: GRADE II*

Dedicated to St Christopher, the patron saint of children, the chapel at the Hospital for Sick Children is not only profoundly moving, but also one of London's most unexpected and beautiful interiors.

The exquisite interior, resembling a mediaeval jewelled reliquary, was designed by Edward Middleton Barry in memory of his sister-in-law, Caroline, the wife of William Henry Barry, the eldest son of Sir Charles Barry, who with Pugin co-designed the Palace of Westminster. On her death her husband donated the staggering sum of £40,000 for the chapel, with a stipend for the chaplain to cater for the spiritual needs of impoverished children from the surrounding slums.

Unveiled in 1875, the tiny neo-Byzantine chapel was designed to inculcate Christian faith and religious awe in children who could not read through vibrant polychrome detail and the use of spiritual iconography. "We cannot regret the expenditure, as one thinks how the little ones will revel in the beauty," wrote a contemporary observer in *Christian World*.

The central dome is painted with an orchestra of 12 angels, each playing musical instruments, at the centre of which is the Christian symbol of a pelican plucking blood from her breast to feed her young – an allegory of Christ shedding his blood for humanity.

On the north wall is a heart-rending mural of children from all historical periods called to Christ above the quotation "Suffer the little children to come unto me". Opposite, on the south wall, Jesus instructs his disciples to "Feed my lambs. Feed my sheep." Below are poignant short rows of black ebonised pews designed for children.

The columns of rare pink Devonshire marble carrying the central dome are carved with gilded flowers, owls, squirrels and mythical beasts designed to captivate and stimulate children's imaginations. The sanctuary is divided from the nave by a rich marble screen with brass gates inlaid with glowing coloured glass ornament. Beyond, the ceiling of the apse shimmers with gold stars against a dark blue sky above eight intertwined angels depicting the Christian values – faith, truth, patience, purity, obedience, charity, honour and hope – over rich stained-glass windows by Clayton & Bell illustrating the boyhood of Christ. The elaborate Cosmati work floor is by Antonio Salviati and allegedly modelled on a pavement in St Mark's, Venice.

In 1992 the chapel was relocated from its original position on the first floor of the hospital in one of the most audacious exercises ever undertaken in conservation engineering. After underpinning on an enormous concrete raft, the chapel was moved inch by inch using greased slides and hydraulic rams into its current position, where it was reopened as part of a complex of new hospital buildings by the late Diana, Princess of Wales on St Valentine's Day, 1994.

Victoria House

SOUTHAMPTON ROW, WC1B 4DA
LISTED: GRADE II

The shocking mortality rates of Victorian Britain prompted the less fortunate to form burial clubs, so they could afford a decent funeral for their loved ones as an alternative to the pauper's grave.

Trade unions, churches and other associations formed benefit societies, whereby for a regular monthly payment, funeral expenses would be covered irrespective of how long a person had been a member. This led to widespread abuse. Often sickly children were enrolled in multiple clubs in anticipation of a handsome payout on death. In some of the poorest areas of the great conurbations wilful neglect and even murder occurred.

The early societies were unregulated. Many collapsed from mismanagement or fraud, but a number of reputable societies emerged, one of which was the Liverpool Victoria Friendly Society. It was formed as a burial society in 1843, and its business was based on "penny policies" collected by door-to-door insurance agents. A number of these friendly societies, like the Co-operative, Prudential, Pearl and Liverpool Victoria, grew into huge financial institutions accommodated in buildings which vied for sheer opulence with the great banks.

Victoria House, the headquarters of Liverpool Victoria, involved the clearance of an entire street block of Georgian houses on the east side of Bloomsbury Square, for a huge Grecian-style Beaux Arts palace.

Designed by Charles W Long and erected over 13 years between 1921 and 1934, it exuded the twin values of dignity and security which came to be expected for the headquarters of the great financial institutions.

Externally, it resembles a great stone and bronze leviathan moored at the head of a fleet of smaller, but nonetheless impressive, structures anchored to the south along Southampton Row and Kingsway, its great central pediments carved with sculptures by H W Palliser. Although the company only occupied the northern end of the building, no expense was spared. It is lavishly appointed throughout in marble, mahogany, travertine and bronze.

Beneath the heroic marble entrance hall (now marred by an inappropriate modern glass floor) is a large basement ballroom and foyer (opposite above and p146) fitted out totally differently in pure Art Deco style in chrome, silver leaf and mauve-coloured lighting in sharp contrast to the chaste Greek classicism of the upper floors.

At third floor level is a suite of superb mahogany-panelled Grecian-style boardrooms (opposite below), some of which have fine 18th century marble chimneypieces salvaged from the houses which once stood on the site, and all served by a splendidly preserved, marble-lined directors' washroom with inlaid basins and original brass taps.

Shortlisted in 1998 as a potential new City Hall for the Mayor of London, later it was refurbished around its two inner light wells by Will Alsop, while retaining the historic interiors.

James Smith & Sons

Hazelwood House, 53 New Oxford Street, WC1A 1BL
Listed: Grade II*

Jonas Hanway (1712-86), the traveller and philanthropist, was reputed to be the first Londoner to carry an umbrella, much to the derision of hackney coachmen, who regularly greeted him with the shout of "Frenchman, Frenchman! Why don't you call a coach?" Hanway Street, linking Oxford Street and Tottenham Court Road, is named after him. In one of those peculiar chronological resonances which reverberate through London's history, James Smith established the famous firm of umbrella makers, James Smith & Sons, a stone's throw away from Hanway Street, in Fouberts Place, off Regent Street, in 1830.

In 1857 his son, also called James, opened a shop in New Oxford Street, which had recently been laid out by Sir James Pennethorne. It was followed rapidly by six other businesses elsewhere in London, including a hatter and barbershop. From their branch in the tiny passageway at Savile Place they sold umbrellas to many of the leading figures of their day, including Lord Curzon, Gladstone and Bonar Law.

The company was one of the first to use the famous Fox steel frames, named after Samuel Fox, who created the first steel umbrella frame in 1848. In addition to umbrellas, Smith's has specialised in making canes and military swagger sticks, as well as more bespoke items such as ceremonial maces for tribal chiefs in South Africa, Nigeria and elsewhere.

Their superb shopfront and interior is a beautifully preserved example of a high-class Victorian West End shop, with cast-iron cresting to the faceted gilt and glass fascias, inscribed brass sills, elaborate black and gilt lettering to the upper panels of the windows and a splendid traditional box sign. Inside, the original mahogany counters and display cases are stocked with an array of canes, sticks and umbrellas, most of which are still manufactured in the basement.

James Smith & Sons is the largest and oldest umbrella shop in Europe, and its shopfront and interior one of the landmarks of central London.

Baptist Church House

2–6 SOUTHAMPTON ROW, WC1R 4AB

LISTED: GRADE II*

Depicted here vacant and derelict, Baptist Church House is a salutary illustration of how once-elegant interiors can deteriorate once they fall out of use, and the vital importance of keeping buildings weathertight pending adaptation and conversion.

Completed in 1903 for the Baptist Union by the architect Alfred Keen (a pupil of Norman Shaw), the building was one of the most accomplished fronting the newly widened Southampton Row, before the subsequent formation of the grand new boulevards of Aldwych and Kingsway to the south.

Standing sentinel outside is a statue of John Bunyan by Richard Garbe, set in a pedimented niche above which rises a fine Baroque composition with a lively skyline of Flemish gables and tall stacks crowned by a central clock tower. Inscribed beneath the statue are the opening lines from *The Pilgrim's Progress*:

> As I walk'd through the wilderness of this world,
> I lighted upon a certain place, where was a Denn;
> And I laid me down in that place to rest:
> And as I slept I dreamed a dream.

Inside, a conventional stone staircase leads to a sequence of fine Arts and Crafts rooms. Over the fireplace in the Visitors' Room is a splendid Doulton terracotta panel by George Tinworth portraying Freedom from Sin from *The Pilgrim's Progress*. The adjacent Shakespeare Room, named after a former Union secretary, boasts a fine barrel-vaulted ceiling with superb Arts and Crafts plasterwork by Lawrence Turner. Turner was a major figure of architectural decoration and craftsmanship. On his death in 1959, he was compared in the *Times* obituary to the great craftsmen of the days of Sir Christopher Wren and Robert Adam. Over the fireplace is another fine terracotta plaque by Tinworth celebrating the liberation of Jamaican slaves in 1834; both plaques form the gift of Scott Durant, a local Baptist, in 1903.

Tucked away at the rear of the whole complex is a large double-height octagonal chapel with enriched ornamental plasterwork by Garbe featuring biblical trees. Garbe taught sculpture at the neighbouring Central School of Art and Crafts from 1901 to 1929 before becoming Professor of Sculpture at the Royal College of Art. In 1939 the chapel was divided at gallery level to create a council chamber, the site of the foundation of the British Council of Churches in 1942. By 1961 it attracted only a handful of worshippers and closed shortly afterwards.

After lying vacant for several years, it is now being converted to hotel use.

Conway Hall

25 Red Lion Square, WC1 4RL
Listed: Grade II

Conway Hall occupies a unique position in the intellectual life of London. It was built in 1929 as the headquarters of the South Place Ethical Society and is the only remaining example of its kind in the country. It owes its origins to a group of Christian Dissenters who established themselves in Bishopsgate in 1793. The congregation became Unitarian and built a chapel at South Place, Finsbury, in 1823 where, under the ministries of William Johnson Fox and Moncure Daniel Conway, it became a centre for progressive religious thought.

Conway was an American abolitionist, Unitarian clergyman and follower of Thomas Paine. A friend of Charles Dickens, Charles Darwin, Thomas Carlyle and Robert Browning, he led the society from 1864 to 1885 and again from 1892 to 1897. In 1888 the society became aligned with a wider American-led movement for promoting non-theistic religion established by Felix Adler in New York.

From 1897 it started appointing lecturers rather than ministers to give the Sunday address, preceded and followed by music. Throughout the 20th century it became a centre for radical thought and social theory. The secularist Joseph McCabe, the socialist reformer Herbert Burrows and John Hobson, the social theorist and economist, were all connected with the society's early work, which took its name from its earlier home in Finsbury.

In 1927 plans were prepared to build a new headquarters "where men and women of advanced thought could meet and enjoy the amenities of social discourse with facilities for writing, rest and refreshment". As the centre of intellectual radicalism in the 1920s, Bloomsbury was an obvious choice for the new building.

The architect was Frederick Herbert Mansford (1871-1946), who had worked with Alfred Waterhouse. He produced a plainly detailed but highly distinctive building in an inventive union of Arts and Crafts and classical styles. Built on the site of the old Raglan Music Hall, and a later Edwardian successor, the irregular site subsumed part of an earlier Victorian terrace in Theobalds Road. The principal entrance from Red Lion Square has a large round-headed French window set in gauged red and grey brickwork with a curved balcony and urns to the parapet and to the side along Lambs Conduit Passage.

The interior is a time capsule from 1929. The capacious entrance hall is a plainly treated but impressive space. A line of Arts and Crafts seats with carved backs commemorate Frank Andrade Hawkins, the treasurer of the South Place concerts. The reconstituted stone staircase is cantilevered and divided from the foyer by a two-bay arcade and Tuscan column. The balustrade is solid with a seat at first floor landing level. The first floor Humanist Reference Library facing the square is the most important of its kind in Europe, with over 10,000 volumes on ethics, humanism, rationalism and philosophy. It retains its original fittings, including a clock and inscribed chimneypiece, panelling, bookcases and parquet flooring.

Over the proscenium arch in the main assembly hall are Polonius's words from Hamlet, "To Thine Own Self Be True"; flanked by pilasters with reliefs to the capitals showing, to the left, a man, a woman and a child holding a light, and to the right the same group, but holding a mirror; a reference to self-knowledge and the free-thinking humanist ideology of the society. The panelling behind the stage was the gift of Ann Mansford.

11 Bedford Row

WC1R 4BU
LISTED: GRADE II*

11 Bedford Row is a rare surviving example of an early Georgian town house with a painted staircase compartment at the front of the building.

Bedford Row was commenced in the 1690s by the builder-developer Nicholas Barbon, who laid out an unusually broad street with a terrace of houses on the west side which enjoyed an open aspect across the gardens of Gray's Inn opposite. In 1716 leases were granted by the owner Margaret Skipwith for the development of the east side, part of a speculation by a carpenter, Robert Burford, and a plumber, George Devall.

No 11 was the most impressive house in the street, four bays wide, and completed in 1718. Two years later the house was sold to Dame Rebecca Moyer, the wife of the eminent MP, judge and City alderman Sir Samuel Moyer. Two moulded lead cisterns adjoining the conference room bear her initials and the date 1720. Although she occupied the house for only three years prior to her death in 1723, it was almost certainly she who commissioned the portrait artist John Vanderbank (1694-1739) to decorate the stairs with a set of handsome murals in the fashion of the time.

Vanderbank studied under Sir Godfrey Kneller, after which he established his own academy in St Martin's Lane. When this failed he fled to France, but later returned to serve a sentence in "the Liberties of the Fleet", a group of town houses surrounding the Fleet Prison, not far from Bedford Row, where privileged prisoners could serve their time in comparative comfort. He died in 1739 and was buried at St Marylebone Church, his promise largely unfulfilled. His contemporary, the engraver and antiquary George Vertue, wrote: "only intemperance prevented Vanderbank from being the greatest portrait artist of his generation".

The staircase by Burford is a magnificent example of Georgian joinery, with Corinthian column newels, three twisted balusters per stair, swept handrails and a raised and fielded panelled dado. On the party wall is an equestrian figure of George I heralded by cherubs in a frame of painted Corinthian columns and pilasters. Adjacent is Britannia receiving tribute. Opposite on the landing are allegorical figures of the arts. Above, Mercury, History and Justice are portrayed in a huge oval medallion.

Other fine painted staircase compartments of the period can be found at 8 Clifford Street, Mayfair (c1719), probably by Sir James Thornhill; 76 Dean Street, Soho (1732) and 20 Cavendish Square (1730), both by the theatre-painter John Devoto; and at St Bartholomew's Hospital (1735-7) by William Hogarth (see pp 202-5).

As early as 1835 the house became the business premises of various firms of solicitors, and it has remained in office use ever since, narrowly escaping damage in the Second World War, when over 20 neighbouring buildings were gutted by incendiary bombs.

New Hall and Library
Lincoln's Inn

WC2R IEP
LISTED: GRADE II*

By the early 19th century membership of Lincoln's Inn had expanded so much that the Benchers resolved to build a whole new range of facilities. The result was a dramatic new complex of wonderfully romantic neo-Tudor buildings soaring above the boundary walls to Lincoln's Inn Fields – complementing and enhancing the adjacent 17th and 18th century collegiate courtyards of the older parts of the Inn.

The New Hall and Library were designed by Philip Hardwick in 1842 and completed by his son, Philip Charles, in 1845. John Loughborough Pearson oversaw much of the detail, which was executed in bright red diapered brick with stone dressings to echo the character and texture of the oldest part of the Inn. A huge central lantern breaks the roofline to reinforce its romantic external skyline of crenellations and towers. Seen in conjunction with the spires of Street's Royal Courts of Justice beyond, it is one of the most sublime views in London.

The interiors are breathtaking. The Hall is over 60ft high with a false hammerbeam roof, which is actually hung from metal rods with painted pendant beam ends. Commanding the entire hall is a huge fresco of *The Lawgivers* (1852-3) by George Frederick Watts, featuring the great lawmakers of history from Moses and Muhammad to Edward I and Charlemagne. The walls are panelled and carry the arms and portraits of past Benchers and grandees.

A lofty octagonal lantern links the Hall with the Library, which is rightly considered to be one of the most beautiful in the world – a phalanx of bookcases and iron galleries dividing the spaces into bays under another superb hammerbeam roof, all lit by great Perpendicular stained-glass windows in canted bays at each end of the L-shaped space; the original library having been extended by George Gilbert Scott in 1871-3, who reused Hardwick's original east window. At the centre of the space stands a statue of Lord Erskine (1830) by Westmacott. With over 80,000 books, it holds one of the world's oldest collections on law and jurisprudence.

Hardwick's work at Lincoln's Inn, and Scott's sensitive later extensions, are an eloquent demonstration of how an understanding of context and a mastery of style can create new buildings for new generations which enhance rather than diminish local character and a sense of place.

Old Hall and Chapel
Lincoln's Inn

WC2A 3TL
LISTED: GRADE I

The precise date of the establishment of Lincoln's Inn is unclear. It stands on the site of the mansion of Lincoln de Lacy, the 3rd Earl of Lincoln, which, on his death in 1310, he left as a residence for lawyers whom he had encouraged to come to London. Its oldest records date from 1422 and, following a decree of 1414, it became a recognised place of legal education. Thomas More was admitted as a student here in 1496. The east courtyard, gatehouse and Old Hall are the oldest parts, with large areas of fabric dating from the late 15th century.

Built in 1489-92, the Old Hall replaced a smaller chapel of the Bishop of Chichester, but its fabric bears witness to a whole series of alterations – principally in 1625, 1652, 1706 and 1819 – culminating in major structural interventions and a comprehensive restoration by Sir John Simpson between 1924 and 1929. Simpson saved the building from collapse. He removed a barrel-vaulted plaster ceiling to expose the elaborate arch-braced roof beneath, with collar beams, two sets of moulded purlins and cusped windbraces. Against the south end is an elaborate carved timber screen designed by Robert Lynton in 1624 with a large central clock. The former gallery openings are infilled with heraldic paintings, which were added in 1819 when the screen was relocated against the wall. On the corresponding north wall is Hogarth's painting of *St Paul before Felix* from 1750. Until the opening of the Royal Courts of Justice in 1882, the Lord Chancellor's Court of Chancery sat here from 1734. Charles Dickens used it as the setting for the opening scenes of *Bleak House*, and the never-ending case of Jarndyce v Jarndyce.

Adjacent to the Old Hall, but separated from it by a covered passage and a relocated 13th century arch from the earlier building on the site, is the Chapel. This dates from 1620-3 and is highly unusual as it is raised on an open Gothic undercroft with lierne vaults executed by the mason John Clark. It has been attributed to Inigo Jones, but there is scant evidence for this. It underwent major alterations in 1797, and again in 1883. Until 1852 Benchers and members of the Inn were permitted to be buried in the undercroft, which was used as a crypt as well as a meeting place. John Thurloe, Cromwell's Secretary of State, was buried here in 1668, as was Sir John Anstruther, the Chief Justice of Bengal, in 1811.

Inside is a large vaulted nave with beam ends carried on carved and painted stone corbels. Beneath lie ranks of pews with 17th century carved timber pew ends, a 17th century communion table and communion rails, and an 18th century pulpit. The south window has early 17th century stained glass of the Apostles by the Van Linge brothers. The main east window in Perpendicular style, remodelled by James Wyatt in 1795-6, has a fine display of armorial glass commemorating distinguished Benchers and members.

John Donne laid the foundation stone of the Chapel. Past members of Lincoln's Inn include 15 prime ministers from William Pitt to Tony Blair, including Spencer Perceval, the only prime minister to be assassinated, to whom there is a plaque on the entrance to the chapel.

Sir John Soane's Museum

13 Lincoln's Inn Fields, WC2A 3BP
Listed: Grade I

Sir John Soane's labyrinthine treasure house has been the haunt of students of art and architecture for nigh on 200 years; the repository of an extraordinary collection of architectural fragments and curiosities all displayed in a fantastic sequence of rooms and spaces for maximum theatrical effect to surprise, delight and mystify the visitor.

Born in 1753, the son of a country bricklayer, Soane was a peculiar cove. Exceptionally tall, and with a face once likened to a "picture on the back of a spoon", he was irascible, demanding and a voracious collector. He was also one of England's most brilliant and original architects, a febrile genius who developed a unique architectural style of his own. A pupil of both George Dance and Henry Holland, he studied architecture at the Royal Academy and then spent two years in Italy perfecting his art. Just eight years after returning to England, he was appointed architect to the Bank of England. After an advantageous marriage to Elizabeth Smith, a builder's heiress, in 1792 he acquired No 12 Lincoln's Inn Fields, which he rebuilt as his family home and office. In 1813 he moved next door to No 13, which he rebuilt as a museum for his burgeoning collection. Ten years later, he bought No 14, which he rented out, using the stable yard at the rear to extend his museum. On his death in 1837, the entire complex was bequeathed to the nation by an Act of Parliament passed four years earlier.

The visitor passes through a procession of carefully-contrived spaces intended to induce particular effects and moods. On entering via No 13, to the right of the narrow stone staircase with its distinctive Soanian iron balustrade, is the Dining Room and Library painted Pompeiian red and lit by coloured glass with artfully concealed mirrors conveying an illusion of space. The ceilings were painted by Henry Howard; over the fireplace, a portrait of Soane by Sir Thomas Lawrence. The Library has a flat ceiling with peculiar pendants and cleverly-conceived hanging arches.

The Study and Dining Room contain a collection of antique marbles acquired in Italy in the 1790s by Charles Heathcote Tatham for Henry Holland, and later secured by Soane. Both rooms overlook the Monument Court, a light well crammed with antiquarian fragments assembled as a "pasticcio", or monument to architecture with a bust of Soane at the centre. The Corridor, covered in plaster casts and original marbles, leads to the Picture Room, built in 1824 on the old stable yard at the rear of No 14. Here are over one hundred pictures ingeniously displayed on "movable planes" with works by Canaletto, Hogarth, Fuseli, Turner and Hodges, and some fine drawings by Piranesi.

The Monk's Parlour (p162 below right), contrived as a series of rooms for an imaginary monk – "Padre Giovanni" – is a pure flight of gothic fantasy, designed to induce melancholia; a tightly constricted space lit by stained-glass with mediaeval masonry and carvings taken from the Palace of Westminster salvaged during Soane's supervision of alterations there, and continued into the Yard. The Crypt continues in the same vein intended to evoke the atmosphere of Roman

catacombs and surrounded by plaster models of classical monuments, many by Flaxman. In the Sepulchral Chamber, pride of place is given to the Egyptian sarcophagus of Seti I, discovered by Giovanni Belzoni, and purchased by Soane, after the British Museum declined to buy it.

The Colonnade and Dome (p160 below) are encrusted with archaeological fragments and casts including a 5th century BC female torso from the Erechtheion on the Acropolis, and full size Roman statues of Apollo Belvedere, Aesculapius and Diana of Ephesus. An 1829 marble bust of Soane by Chantrey ("I have never produced better") sits under the Dome surrounded by myriad corbels, cornices, urns and busts. In the Breakfast Room (below), beautifully lit from above through a canopied dome of coloured glass and mirror fragments, are portraits of Napoleon and coloured engravings of a Roman villa discovered in the grounds of the Villa Negroni in Rome.

Upstairs, beyond the "Shakespeare" recess, the first floor Drawing Rooms are finished in the then fashionable "Turner's Patent Yellow". The loggia was created by Soane in 1834 when he glazed the open balcony in the Coade stone screen wall he had created earlier across the facade of the house.

Among the curiosities in the eclectic collection are pistols belonging to Napoleon and Peter the Great, a scold's bridle for nagging wives, slave shackles and a giant sea sponge from Sumatra. Soane's collection, and also Horace Walpole's at Strawberry Hill (p388), bear witness to the role of the gentleman antiquarian collector in fostering a greater appreciation and understanding of history in the late 18th and early 19th centuries.

Sir John Soane's Museum is one of London's greatest treasures and widely regarded as the "supreme example of the house museum in the world". A £7millon, three-year restoration project commenced in 2011.

G Smith & Sons

74 CHARING CROSS ROAD, WC2H 0BG
UNLISTED

G Smith & Sons was one of the first shops to be opened in the newly constructed Charing Cross Road, which had been driven through the slums of St Giles by the Metropolitan Board of Works to improve traffic-flow in central London, and lined with dour yellow-brick tenements.

The firm was established in 1869, and began trading from its current premises in 1874 as tobacconists and purveyors of snuff. Snuff was taken by all classes and age groups, and snuff and tobacconist shops were once commonplace, traditionally marked by the figure of a Highlander.

Externally the shop retains its original deep cobalt, gilt and glass fascia and lettering to the shopfront and stall riser. Inside are display cabinets full of pipes and smoking utensils, prints and gilt and glass mirrors extolling the pleasures of tobacco.

Since the demise of Fribourg & Treyer in Haymarket, G Smith is one of the few remaining traditional tobacconists in London with its original fixtures and fittings. Inexplicably it remains unlisted.

Freemasons' Hall

60 GREAT QUEEN STREET, WC2B 5AZ

LISTED: GRADE II*

Known as the Masonic Peace Memorial, Freemasons' Hall was built as a tribute to its 3,000 members killed in the First World War. At an Especial Grand Lodge held on 27 June 1919 at the Royal Albert Hall, the Duke of Connaught resolved "to create a perpetual Memorial of its gratitude to Almighty God to render fitting honour to the many Brethren who fell during the War".

In 1925 an international architectural competition was launched, assessed by Sir Edwin Lutyens and two leading Freemasons, Walter Cove and Alexander Burnett Brown. It was won by Henry Victor Ashley (1872-1945) and Francis Winton Newman (1879-1953), who had extensive experience designing banks, factories, housing and hospital extensions. On 8 August 1925 the largest ever catered meal in Europe raised £825,000 for the Masonic Million Memorial Fund from 7,250 Brethren dining at Olympia.

The Grand Lodge of England, founded in 1717, had been based in Great Queen Street since 1774. Two years later Thomas Sandby designed the first purpose-built Masonic hall in the country in the form of a Roman Doric temple embellished with Masonic symbols. The complex was added to in the 1820s by Soane, and later by F P Cockerell, who remodelled the frontage to Great Queen Street in stages between 1863 and 1869.

Originally Ashley and Newman intended to retain Sandby's hall, but after serious defects were found, it was demolished in March 1932. The gigantic new complex was faced in Portland stone and designed on an heroic scale in stripped classical style. No expense was spared on the sumptuous interior, which was finished in neo-Grecian style in marble, bronze, mosaic and stained glass imbued with Masonic symbolism.

Set on a diagonal axis, the ground floor is occupied by the grand entrance hall and museum. An elegant marble staircase lit by full-height stained-glass windows leads to a huge marble-lined vestibule. Facing west is the war memorial window and Roll of Honour housed in a beautifully crafted bronze casket by Walter Gilbert (1871-1946). Gilbert, the director of the Art Department of H H Martyn of Cheltenham, designed most of the metalwork throughout the building. The Roll of Honour is contained within a bronze casket resting on an ark amongst reeds, the boat symbolising a journey which has come to an end. In the centre of the front panel the soul of man rests in the hand of God. At the four corners stand four winged seraphim carrying golden trumpets. Across the front are gilded figures portraying Moses the Law Giver, Joshua the Warrior Priest, Solomon the Wise and St George.

The entrance to the awe-inspiring Grand Temple is through huge bronze doors, each cast in one piece and weighing 1¼ tons. On the outside are panels showing the building of King Solomon's Temple. On the inner face the handles are made by the hilts of swords whose blades are embedded in the doors as symbols of peace.

The colossal Grand Temple has a gallery, raked seating, dais and Willis organ; the walls are lined with Ashburton and Botticino marbles. Above lies a celestial canopy surrounded by a mosaic cornice 15ft deep, which depicts allegorical figures with different orders of classical architecture. In each corner are figures representing the four cardinal virtues – prudence, temperance, fortitude and justice. Elsewhere the Boardroom is panelled in hardwood and lit with stained glass. Lodge Room No 10 has huge arched bays carrying a domed roof.

The museum has a fine collection of Masonic objects including jewellery, regalia, clocks, furniture and porcelain.

Tram Subway

KINGSWAY, SOUTHAMPTON ROW, WC2
LISTED: GRADE II

Hidden just below the surface of Kingsway is one of London's most haunting underground spaces. Abandoned about 60 years ago, the old Kingsway Tram Subway is unique in Britain.

After decades of discussion, in 1905 the London County Council finally began the long-awaited Holborn-Strand improvement scheme to drive a new boulevard through the decaying slums of Holborn. It was the largest single clearance of buildings since the Great Fire 240 years earlier. An integral part of the strategy was to provide a new subterranean connection between its tramway systems north and south of the river in a cut and cover tunnel.

From the north in Southampton Row, the subway is approached through an open cutting with a 1:10 gradient, so steep that even experienced tram drivers regularly ran into difficulties, rolling back disconsolately into the tunnel to Holborn tramway station. With the Fleet sewer at the north end, and the District Line beneath the Embankment to the south, the site constraints were such that for over 20 years special non-flammable, single-deck trams were deployed, built by the United Electric Car Co. of Preston.

Services commenced on 24 February 1906 between the Angel, Islington and Aldwych, and were soon extended to Tower Bridge and Kensington Gate. After leaving the subway beneath the western wing of Waterloo Bridge, trams turned sharp right along the Embankment to Westminster Bridge, or left on a separate service from Bloomsbury to the Hop Exchange in Borough.

In 1929 the original tram tunnels were enlarged to take double-height trams, with a grand reopening by King George V on 14 January 1931. However, with the foundation of the London Passenger Transport Board two years later, the decision was taken to phase out trams in favour of "more modern vehicles" – trolleybuses. The last tram ran through the subway on 5 April 1952, three months before London's final service was withdrawn on 5 July.

In 1964 part of the south end of the subway was re-engineered to form an underpass, the remaining truncated section later becoming a restaurant and bar. After brief use as the London Flood Control Centre, today the entire central and northern sections remain eerily abandoned: disused platforms, echoing faintly with the noise of the traffic above. It is one of London's neglected assets – a strange troglodyte world used for the storage of street furniture and materials, and as an occasional film set.

Beefsteak Club

9 Irving Street, wc2 7ah
Unlisted

Since the 18th century there has been a long gastronomic tradition of private gentlemen's dining clubs in London, many with a reputation for quaint eccentricity. Within the august realms of clubland, the Beefsteak, and Pratt's in St James's, are two of the most exclusive. At one time, to be a member of the Beefsteak one needed to be "a relation of God – and a damned close relation at that".

There have been numerous Beefsteak Clubs, the first founded in 1705 by a group which seceded from the Kit-Kat Club. Another, the Sublime Society of Beef Steaks, followed in 1735, but was dissolved in 1867. The present club was established in 1876 as a successor to the Sublime Society. Its members hoped to rent the society's dining room at the Lyceum Theatre, but in the event took the lease on some rooms in King William IV Street above the Folly (later Toole's) Theatre. In 1882 it moved upstairs and had a vaulted ceiling constructed. When the lease expired in 1896, it moved to its current home in Irving Street and carefully copied its previous clubroom with a lofty open-timber oak roof designed by Frank Verity incorporating the club's gridiron motif.

The heart of the club is the dining room, with a long communal table for convivial dining and conversation. Previous members have included Harold Macmillan, John Betjeman, Edward Elgar, Rudyard Kipling and Edwin Lutyens.

At Pratt's, where traditionally all the staff are referred to as "George", great consternation was caused in the 1980s when a woman was recruited. The dilemma was resolved when it was decided to call her "Georgina". At the Beefsteak the steward and waiters are all called "Charles". Whilst Pratt's has a more eclectic collection of club "lumber"; including a duck-billed platypus, assorted stuffed birds and fish and the disconsolate front end of a rhinoceros, the more intellectual Beefsteak has the original gridiron rescued from the ashes of the Lyceum Theatre (the home of the Sublime Society) when it burned down, as well as a jaunty silver cockerel presented by the actor Sir Squire Bancroft.

South Africa House

Trafalgar Square, WC1N 5DP
Listed: Grade II*

The finest buildings of the British Empire and Commonwealth lie overseas, but in the 40 years between 1890 and 1930 London was refashioned into a great imperial city. When the decision was taken to erect a new South Africa House in Trafalgar Square, it was no surprise that the architect selected was Sir Herbert Baker (1862-1946). Baker was prolific in South Africa – where he designed the magnificent Union Buildings in Pretoria – as well as in 15 other countries, producing buildings which not only expressed imperial ideals but also responded inventively to the climate, topography, craftsmanship and culture of the host country.

At South Africa House Baker produced a finely conceived and executed classical building, which sits comfortably in the London townscape next to St Martin-in-the-Fields (the architectural model for so many colonial churches), but embellished with subtle symbols of the flora and fauna of South Africa – heads of elephants, lions, antelope and wildebeest to the sill brackets, and mimosa and protea on the keystones – all carved by Joseph Armitage to the designs of Sir Charles Wheeler RA. Over the southern corner is the famous gilded springbok by Wheeler; above, a life-size statue of Bartholomeo Diaz carved in situ by Coert Steynberg.

The interior is a little-known masterpiece of 1930s classicism. The double-height, twin-domed vestibule and entrance hall symbolise the old Dutch republic and the British colonies which came together to form the Union of South Africa. Beneath the motto "Unity is Strength" are marble floors and columns using stone from northern Transvaal, and red jasper, verdite, crocodilite and serpentine from Witwatersrand.

Overlooking Trafalgar Square, the High Commissioner's office (above left) is a showcase of Baker's enthusiasm for native craftsmanship with panelling and furniture in stinkwood, so called because of the smell when it is cut. The adjacent Chief Secretary's room is panelled in tambotie from the Transvaal, the wood from which the voortrekkers made their furniture. The Dutch Room (left) is a recreation of a Cape Dutch farmhouse with a beamed ceiling and Delft tiles. In the anteroom outside is a fine set of landscapes by Gwelo Goodman. The teak-panelled Reading Room (below left) evokes the atmosphere of a captain's cabin in a sailing ship with an alabaster relief by Charles Wheeler depicting the discovery of the Cape based on the epic Portuguese poem *The Lysiads*. The fireplace is flanked by two clocks in which a map of each hemisphere revolves around two poles with a fixed hand perpetually pointing to the sun at noon. In the basement, the cinema (opposite middle) reflects the maritime theme of the Reading Room with symbolic gilded heraldry and friezes by Lawrence Turner. The exhibition hall has pictures by Jan Juta and J H Pernieef.

The interior is a repository of superb South African art. At first floor level murals by J H Amshewitz depict the travels of Bartholomeo Diaz and Vasco da Gama; while above on the fourth floor the Zulu Room (opposite below left) depicts scenes from the life of the Amazulu, including the *Feast of the First Fruits* (1938) painted in egg tempera by Le Roux Smith Le Roux and Eleanor Edmonde-White.

At South Africa House Baker drew together architecture, sculpture, symbolism, iconography and art into a seamless, integrated whole. The spirit of South African sovereignty is encapsulated in the emblem of the flying springbok, which lies in the very centre of the entrance hall floor. It was devised by Baker and derived from the Persian golden-winged ibex at the Louvre. "Give the swift creature the wings of the imagination and might it not become the national symbol?" he subsequently wrote in his memoirs.

ARMY SPECTACLE DEPOT.

British Optical Association Museum

41-42 Craven Street, wc2n 5ng
Listed: (No 41 – Grade II)

Founded in 1901 by the optician J H Sutcliffe (1867-1941), the British Optical Association Museum is now hosted by the College of Optometrists, after a peripatetic existence over the past 100 years.

It was first opened to the public in 1914 at Clifford's Inn Hall, prompted by Sutcliffe's desire to establish "An Optical House Beautiful" in line with the fashionable concepts of the Aesthetic Movement. Later it moved to Brook Street and then to Earl's Court before arriving at its current location in 1997, a fine early Georgian house built c1730, with a replica extension erected in 1988. Sutcliffe's legacy is a quirky collection of over 18,000 items relating to ophthalmic optics, the human eye and visual aids, as well as archival material, paintings and prints.

The Print Room is covered with portraits, prints and paintings all on an ophthalmic theme, including the first illustration of a pair of swimming goggles in a print of 1590. Amongst the allegorical pictures and satires by Stradanus, Cruikshank and Gillray is a caricature depicting a revolving top hat with assorted pairs of glasses suspended from the brim. On the end wall is an oil painting of St Lucia, the patron saint of those suffering from eye diseases, traditionally depicted holding her eyes on a golden plate. At the rear is the college's collection of oil paintings, including a 16th century portrait of St Jerome in his study with spectacles, a rare 17th century Venetian canvas with the sitter wearing glasses, and a fine portrait of Benjamin Franklin, who lived nearby at 36 Craven Street.

The museum display is a fascinating juxtaposition of old and new objects, including the spectacles of famous personalities from Dr Johnson to Ronnie Corbett, and the sides of Dr Crippen's glasses, the lenses missing after he tried to use them to cut his own throat in prison in a failed suicide attempt. The cabinets house an extensive collection of porcelain eyebaths, binoculars, spyglasses and jealousy glasses with sideways mirrors to allow the owner to discreetly eye up potential suitors. Look for the dark adaptation goggles with red lenses used by Second World War pilots to adjust their night vision prior to take off, and the early revolving self-service cabinet of spectacles (1889) made by the Automatic Sight Testing and Optical Supply Co Ltd.

The real highlights are the trays of glass eyes, one of which (not for the faint-hearted) has 160 models of diseases and ocular malformations. Another is a selection used as ocular prostheses for troops during the First World War. Alongside artificial eyes from Ancient Egypt to allow the dead to see into the next life is the earliest British contact lens (1933), and an alien Long-Necked Jedi eye from *Star Wars – The Attack of the Clones* (2002).

The Sherlock Holmes

10-11 NORTHUMBERLAND STREET, WC2N 5DB
UNLISTED

Only three British characters from fiction have achieved universal renown – Sherlock Holmes, James Bond and Harry Potter. Such is the reputation of Sherlock Holmes and the evocative appeal of Victorian and Edwardian London that overseas many believe he actually existed. This is perhaps understandable, as a complete recreation of his lodgings was built by Marylebone Borough Library and the Abbey National Building Society for the Festival of Britain in 1951, and subsequently it went on a world tour. In 1957 the entire exhibit was acquired by Whitbread & Co, who installed it in The Northumberland Arms (designed by J W Brooker in 1891) and rechristened the pub after the great sleuth.

The Northumberland Hotel featured in several stories. It was here that Sir Hugo Baskerville lost his boot before leaving for Dartmoor, while Holmes and Watson frequented the adjacent Turkish baths, the old entrance to which can still be discerned in Craven Passage to the side of the pub.

The pub is strewn with original cartoons, newspaper cuttings, film stills and memorabilia, including Dr Watson's old service revolver and a distinctly tacky but lugubrious stuffed head of the Hound of the Baskervilles. In the restaurant on the upper floor is a complete, if rather dog-eared, replica of Holmes and Watson's sitting room and study set behind a glass partition; all as conceived in 1957. Here is the portrait of General Gordon, although the "veritable gasogene" seems to have vanished. To add to the authenticity, the wall is peppered with revolver shots marking out the royal insignia "VR".

In 1990 the number 221b Baker Street was assigned to the much more convincing Sherlock Holmes Museum in Baker Street which opened in the same year. A year later another opened in the basement of the old English church in Meiringen, Switzerland, the village where Holmes stayed before his fateful encounter with Professor Moriarty at the Reichenbach Falls.

"They still live for all that love them well; in a romantic chamber of the heart, in a nostalgic country of the mind; where it is always 1895." (Vincent Starrett)

Gordon's Wine Bar

47 VILLIERS STREET, WC2N 6NE
UNLISTED

Located in the ground floor, basement and 17th century cellars of a building lying in the shadow of Charing Cross Station, Gordon's is believed to be the oldest wine bar in London, having been established in its present form in 1890.

It was founded by Angus Stafford Gordon, a Free Vintner, in 1890 and has remained in the Gordon family ever since. The extraordinary cavernous interior and atmospheric candlelit cellars seem frozen in time and resonate with a remarkable sense of history. The simple vertical-boarded walls, historical newspaper cuttings and memorabilia lie faded with age and coated with layer upon layer of soot and grime, creating an atmosphere quite unlike anything else in London.

Once the Thames lapped at the very edge of the cellars. The bar stands on the site of York House, the former home of the Duke of Buckingham, who built the nearby York Watergate in 1626 for better access to the Thames. When the estate was mortgaged and subsequently redeveloped by Nicholas Barbon in the 1670s, the new house, which was built in 1687-8, was occupied by the diarist Samuel Pepys, who remained there until 1701. In 1788 that house too was demolished and the site developed with two new buildings – one let out as chambers, and the other as a warehouse for Minier, Minier & Fair, a firm of seedsmen. Minier's improved the building, but between 1864 and 1870 the river was embanked, rendering the warehouse landlocked, so in 1880 the upper floors were converted to a rooming house, and the ground floor used as shops.

In 1889 Rudyard Kipling arrived in London from India and took rooms in the building above. In the parlour over the bar, he wrote his first novel *The Light that Failed*. Villiers Street is the setting for the lodgings of the tragic hero Dick Heldar, who becomes incurably blind from the delayed effects of a war wound received in the Sudan. In despair from both encroaching blindness and unrequited love, he returns to the Sudan, where he charges the enemy and dies in the arms of his best friend; a theme subsequently taken up by A E W Mason in his epic novel *The Four Feathers*. G K Chesterton and Edgar Wallace also drank and wrote from here.

Rather less romantically, in 1923 a tenant, Alfred Frederick Joyce, was convicted of running a brothel at the address, confirming Kipling's view that "Villiers Street was primitive and passionate in its habits and population".

With its proximity to the Players' Theatre, in the 1940s the bar became the haunt of Peter Ustinov, Laurence Olivier, Vivien Leigh and other stars of the West End stage. Today it is a seductive refuge for the oenophile and cognoscenti.

Aldwych
Underground Station

STRAND, WC2R 1EP
LISTED: GRADE II

There is something indefinably eerie about buildings designed for large numbers of people when the crowds have gone home, even more so when they lie disused and forgotten – haunted by echoes of their past lives. For this very reason, with their intangible air of mystery, London's abandoned underground stations have become part of the city's urban folklore.

The station opened as Strand on 30 November 1907 for the Great Northern, Piccadilly and Brompton Railway. To avoid confusion with two other stations of the same name, it was rechristened Aldwych in 1915. Almost from its inception, the Aldwych branch was an oddity, in that it operated a shuttle service between Holborn and Strand. This was because this central stretch of the Piccadilly Line was an amalgamation of a number of different projects which came together in 1906. Various extensions were envisaged, so the station was built, but they never came to fruition, leaving Aldwych as a dead end.

Built on the site of the old Royal Strand Theatre, the new station enjoyed frontages to both Strand and Surrey Street. It was designed by Leslie Green using the familiar ox-blood terracotta blocks so typical of his work. In the expectation of expansion, three large circular lift shafts were completed, but only one was fitted out with trapezium-shaped lifts, which still survive.

As early as 1917, the eastern tunnel and platform were closed, and used as secure wartime storage for pictures from the National Gallery. After the First World War, passenger demand remained low, and closure was mooted as early as 1933. From 1940 to 1946 the station was used as a public air-raid shelter. The tunnels were used to store the Elgin Marbles and other valuable antiquities from the British Museum.

The station finally closed on 3 October 1994. Today it is used for training and as a film location, with old tube stock permanently stationed at the branch for filming.

Reputedly haunted by the spectral figure of an actress from the former theatre on the site, it is appropriate that amongst the many films shot at Aldwych were the macabre London cult classic *Death Line* in 1972, and *Ghost Story* two years later.

2 Temple Place

VICTORIA EMBANKMENT, WC2R 3BD

LISTED: GRADE II*

No 2 Temple Place, the former residence and estate office of the first Viscount Astor, is a Victorian version of the mediaeval fashion for siting grand aristocratic and mercantile residences along the banks of the Thames.

William Waldorf Astor was born in New York City in 1848, the only child of John Jacob Astor III, a family whose original fortunes had been made in the fur and shipping trade. On the death of his father in 1890, he inherited a vast fortune. Overnight he became the richest man in America. In 1891, following a family feud with his aunt, and to reduce the risk of kidnap of his children, he moved to England, where nine years later he became a British citizen. On his arrival he rented Lansdowne House, Berkeley Square, before purchasing the Cliveden estate from the Duke of Westminster, and embarking on a career as a newspaper proprietor, financier and hotelier, opening the Waldorf Hotel in Aldwych in 1908.

No 2 Temple Place was completed in 1895 to the designs of the eminent Victorian architect John Loughborough Pearson. Astor specified that the house should personify and celebrate literature, as well as the other liberal arts, but otherwise Pearson was given free rein unfettered by financial constraints. The result was astonishing – one of the most opulent Victorian houses in London.

Crowned by a gilded copper weathervane of Columbus's caravel, the *Santa Maria*, by J Starkie Gardner, externally the house is an elegant but reticent essay in neo-Elizabethan design, with crenellated parapets and mullioned and transomed oriel windows facing the Thames. But alongside its romantic historical allusions, the house celebrated the technological spirit of the age. Flanking the entrance steps are a pair of fine bronze lamp standards by W S Frith with playful cherubs representing electric light and telephony, the latter speaking into, and listening to, the handset of an early telephone.

The interior is grandiloquence personified. The vestibule opens into the great staircase hall which runs full height through the building to an arcaded gallery top-lit by a huge stained-glass lantern. The walls are panelled in oak, the floor inlaid in geometric patterns by Robert Davison in jasper, porphyry and onyx. The chimneypiece is pavonazzetto marble. The staircase, in solid mahogany, has newel posts carved by Thomas Nicholls depicting the principal characters from Dumas's *The Three Musketeers*, which Astor considered the finest novel ever written. Interchangeable alternative figures from Robin Hood are used today to protect the originals. The arcaded gallery at first floor level is carried on 10 columns of solid ebony, above which are eight carved figures of characters from American literature, including Rip Van Winkle and Uncas from *The Last of the Mohicans*. Beneath the lantern is a relief frieze, also by Nicholls, of 82 characters from Shakespeare's plays.

Extending across the entire riverfront is the Great Hall, with a magnificent hammerbeam roof in Spanish mahogany. It is lined in rare pencil cedar with a frieze of 54 portraits of characters from history and literature carved by Nathaniel Hitch. On each end of the beam are the gilded figures of 12 different characters from *Ivanhoe*, including Robin Hood and Maid Marian. The east and west windows have painted glass by Clayton & Bell of Swiss landscapes featuring *Sunrise* and *Sunset*. At the east end is a fine carved pencil-cedar chimneypiece with a small bronze of Florence Nightingale in the central niche. The corresponding chimneypiece to the west end was lost through war damage. A door at the east end leads to the Council Chamber, also with fine panelling which was partially destroyed by a flying bomb in 1944. The real *tour de force* could easily go unnoticed. The inside of the carved door leading to the Great Hall from the staircase (p183 bottom right) has nine enchanting silver-gilt panels by Sir George Frampton illustrating heroines from Arthurian legend.

Beneath the Great Hall, at ground floor level, the Lower Gallery is oak panelled with a coffered ceiling.

Astor was made a peer in 1916 and raised to a viscountcy for his war work just before his death in 1919. The building then went into commercial use and was later used by the Society of Incorporated Accountants and Auditors and opened by TRH the Duke and Duchess of York. In 1999 it was acquired by the Bulldog Trust, which has plans for greater public access for exhibitions.

King's College Chapel

STRAND, WC2R 2LS
LISTED: GRADE I

King's College was founded in 1828 as an Anglican response to the establishment of the secular University College two years earlier. Located immediately to the east of Somerset House on a long narrow site running perpendicular to the river, the elegant Old Building by Sir Robert Smirke built in 1829-31 is now screened from the Strand by an ugly Brutalist block built in 1966-71 to the designs of Troupe and Steele.

At the centre of the Old Building is an impressive classical entrance hall with unusual side staircases which break back towards the entrance. Beyond lies the colonnaded Great Hall. Above, at first floor level, is the little-known chapel marked by pedimented doorcases and commemorative plaques.

By the mid-19th century Smirke's original chapel was deemed too plain and Low Church, so George Gilbert Scott was invited to create something more impressive. He had clear views. "There can be no doubt that, in a classic building, the best mode of giving ecclesiastical character is the adoption … of the character of an ancient basilica."

Given its elevated location over the Great Hall, the redesign called for considerable structural ingenuity. Scott responded with customary aplomb, using iron rather than stone to ease the load. Double columns of cast iron with brass ornament were used for the arcades and iron frames for the walls. The projecting apse was carried on a massive wrought-iron beam and cast-iron columns down on to a brick arcaded structure in Strand Lane below.

The fine polychrome interior is treated in an Italian Romanesque style. The reredos and wall paintings by Powells are based on cartoons by Clayton & Bell and those in the apex by Antonio Salviati. Opus sectile roundels of prophets and prominent churchmen punctuate the aisle walls above the arcades.

Following the construction of the anatomy lecture theatre above the chapel in the 1930s, Scott's original pitched roof was replaced by a flat ceiling. Further unfortunate alterations were carried out by Stephen Dykes Bower in 1948-9 following wartime blast damage which destroyed the original glass.

In 2000 the chapel was restored with great sensitivity by Inskip & Jenkins, who exposed and reinstated much of its original ornamental detail. The windows were replaced with new stained glass by Joseph Nuttgens, including a fascinating window celebrating the discovery of DNA. Much of the experimental modelling to identify DNA was carried out in the Biophysics Unit at King's by Maurice Wilkins and Rosalind Franklin. To mark the service of thanksgiving for the restoration of the chapel on 2 May 2001, a poem celebrating DNA was written by Dr Christopher Southgate:

> The task of this house is to be a lens
> (In a place where light is categorised)
> To gather up explorations.
> Bless them in humility.

Australian High Commission

AUSTRALIA HOUSE, STRAND, WC2B 4LA
LISTED: GRADE II

Built between 1913 and 1918 on a huge triangular site created by the Holborn to Strand improvement scheme, Australia House was the outcome of an architectural competition won by the Scots architects A Marshal Mackenzie & Son. Judged unanimously to be "a lasting monument to the importance of the Commonwealth and a splendid addition to the architecture of London", the splayed corner was enriched in 1924 with a magnificent bronze sculpture of Phoebus and the horses of the sun by the eminent Australian sculptor Sir Bertram Mackennal. Adjoining the main entrance below are two huge figurative groups by a fellow Australian, Harold Parker; a powerful expression of burgeoning national pride and dominion status.

The sumptuous interior, lined with Australian marble and exotic woods, is configured around a huge central axis culminating in an aisled exhibition hall embellished with the Australian coat of arms, the six states of Australia having become a federation within the British Empire in 1902. Flanking the huge Beaux Arts entrance hall are two superb marble staircases with ironwork by Starkie Gardner, and great entrance gates designed by the Bromsgrove Guild.

At the laying of the foundation stone by King George V on 24 July 1913, "a long-drawn, plaintive cry swelled and died again and again" as the largely Australian crowd shouted, "Coo-ee." Poignantly, by the time the King officially opened the building, five years later in August 1918, over 60,000 Australians lay dead following the carnage of the First World War. A further 156,000 were wounded, gassed or taken prisoner.

Australia House is the oldest Australian diplomatic mission, and the largest continuously occupied foreign mission in London.

Royal Courts of Justice

STRAND, WC2A 2LL
LISTED: GRADE I

The Royal Courts of Justice is widely regarded as the most important secular building of the Gothic Revival after the Palace of Westminster, and the last great public building in London to be built in the style. With its carved stone arcades, elaborate ironwork and spectacular fairy-tale skyline of turrets and spires, it is a paean of praise to the romantic ideals of the High Victorian Gothic movement.

The courts owe their origins to the urgent need for radical reform of the judicial system in the late 19th century. Over time a plethora of different courts had arisen to meet different judicial needs in a welter of different buildings. Prior to 1875 courts were located in Westminster Hall, Lincoln's Inn and countless other locations, but pressure mounted for a single new complex. In 1866 Parliament announced a competition for a new design. Two years later, after much wrangling, a design by George Edmund Street was selected for a seven-acre site crammed with overcrowded slum alleys and courts to the north of the Strand.

Building began in 1874 by Messrs Bull & Son of Southampton, but the project was beset by labour troubles, bad weather and financial problems, which delayed completion until 1882, when it was formally opened by Queen Victoria, by which time Street had died of a stroke brought on by the pressures of the project. Its completion was overseen by his son A E Street and Sir Arthur Blomfield.

Faced in Portland stone and red brick with sandstone and granite dressings, the vast judicial complex contains over 1,000 rooms and 3½ miles of corridors. Above the main entrance are statues of Christ, King Solomon and King Alfred, while Moses the Lawgiver keeps watch over the north door.

Inside, the cavernous rib-vaulted central hall is 238ft long and 82ft high with lancet arches, geometrical tracery, heraldic stained glass and a superb polychromatic mosaic floor by Burke & Co. Gothic arcades lead to the main courts. Within the hall are statues of Street by H H Armstead; Lord Russell by Thomas Brock; and Sir William Blackstone, author of *Commentaries on the Laws of England*, by P W Field. Eight huge spiral stairs provide access to the upper floors, while a corridor around the first floor leads to the oak-panelled courtrooms, each one treated differently, two with full timber rib-vaults. Few realise that the famous projecting clock on the great south-eastern tower was erected in 1883 as a memorial to Street.

In 1909 various alterations were carried out to the circulation areas by Sir Henry Tanner, who also designed the West Green building, very much in the style of Street, on an open area to the west.

The Royal Courts of Justice is one of London's most beguiling buildings. Its serrated skyline, delicate flèche spire, turrets, tourelles and gables coalesce to form a truly magical silhouette, either in long views across the rooftops from Lincoln's Inn, or in oblique, progressively revealed, dynamic views from the Strand.

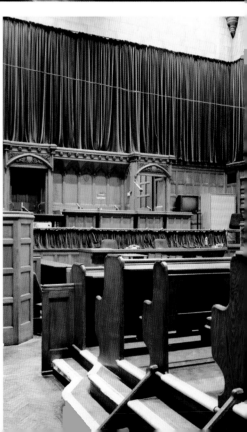

Lloyds Bank

222 STRAND, WC2R 1BB
LISTED: GRADE II

Today it is commonplace for the grand interiors of redundant banks to be converted into restaurants, but over 120 years ago the exact reverse occurred at the Law Courts branch of Lloyds Bank.

Since 1612 the site had been occupied by the Palsgrave Tavern, a favourite haunt of the playwright Ben Jonson. It took its name from Frederick Palsgrave, later the King of Bohemia, who married Princess Elizabeth, the daughter of James I, but in 1883 the Jacobean tavern was demolished for the "Royal Courts of Justice Restaurant" designed by Goymour Gilmour and William Wimble, the architect of the Baltic Exchange. Three years later, having failed to attract lawyers and their clients from the Royal Courts directly opposite, it closed. It was then followed by the Palsgrave Restaurant, but that too was short-lived, and the building remained unoccupied until 1895, when it was taken over and converted from a restaurant into Lloyds Bank.

The branch was the result of an amalgamation of Lloyds Ltd with bankers Messrs Praed & Co of Truro in 1891, and the subsequent merger of the two with R Twining & Co in 1895. Pistols used to protect coachmen on the long journey from Truro to London can still be seen in the senior manager's office.

Described on its opening in the *Penny Illustrated Paper* as "the handsomest and most elegant bank in London", the original restaurant interior survives. The tour de force is the lustrous entrance lobby, which can be seen from the street – a cornucopia of brown, blue and green tiles with ornamental fountains forming a centrepiece at each end. Beyond is a short lobby lined with carved American walnut and sequoia wood with capitals in the form of inscrutable owls. The roof lantern above is decorated with hand-painted tiles depicting the Palsgrave arms.

Within, the highlight of the main banking hall is a series of hand-painted Doulton tile panels depicting characters and scenes from the plays of Ben Jonson, and tile pictures of chrysanthemums, flowers and plants from the Temple Gardens show of 1892.

For all its antiquarian references, the building incorporated the latest technological advances. Fresh water was drawn from an artesian well 238ft below ground. Electric light was supplied with the assistance of steam-driven dynamos, and the whole building was air-conditioned using an ingenious system based on the ventilation of ships' holds.

There is a suggestion that the original dining room was ventilated by a pair of women riding a tandem bicycle in the basement to power a giant pair of bellows, which forced air into the ground floor. Whilst apocryphal, it may just be true. During refurbishment, a piece of equipment resembling a bicycle was found in the basement alongside a mass of ducting, which appears to be the remains of the original system.

Law Society

110-113 CHANCERY LANE, WC2A 1PL
LISTED: GRADE II*

The London Law Institution was founded by London solicitors in 1823 to regulate the profession, set standards and ensure good practice. In 1825 it became the Law Society. Six years later it received the first of its three royal charters, others following in 1845 and 1903.

A handsome new building was erected for the society between 1829 and 1832 by Lewis Vulliamy, with a chaste Ionic portico and an order invented by the architect. With the rapid growth of the profession in the 19th century, the building was extended repeatedly, initially by P C Hardwick in 1856-7, again in 1868-70, and finally by Charles Holden in 1902-4, who produced a splendid neo-mannerist block at the junction with Carey Street, marked by a giant Venetian window and opulent interior.

Behind Vulliamy's portico is an octagonal vestibule and transverse hall, which was extended by Hardwick to provide a sweeping staircase, with later round-headed windows containing heraldic stained glass from the 17th to 19th centuries from Serjeants' Inn (left). At first floor level along the front the imposing library is treated with giant Corinthian columns in green scagliola. At ground floor level on axis with the portico is the original Reading Room with a carved ceiling 30ft high; sedate rather than grand, with red scagliola colonnades by Brown & Co and galleries with balconies to the sides. Closing the vista in a niche at the west end is a fine Second World War memorial in the form of a figure of Pallas Athene by Gilbert Bayes. On the side walls the memorials to the First World War, also by Bayes, take the form of reliefs of children.

Holden's annexe is the most interesting component (left and opposite below), with a grand staircase leading off the northern end of the hall to an opulent Common Room at first floor level. Holden interspersed Arts and Crafts details with full-blown classicism. A primary order of Corinthian pilasters in green cipollino marble with bronze and gilt trim divides the room into bays, between which is rich mahogany panelling carved by William Aumonier with fluted Ionic pilasters. The rich peacock-blue tiles in the fireplaces are by William de Morgan. Squeezed into the frieze over the panelling (and against Holden's advice) is a series of beautiful Della Robbia-style plaques by Conrad Dressler (1904) depicting human and divine justice framed by coloured swags. The Venetian window facing Chancery Lane has more historic stained glass.

Outside Holden's annexe are railings with gilded lion finials by Alfred Stevens, once at the British Museum.

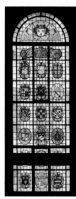

Pathology Museum
St Bartholomew's Hospital

West Smithfield, ec1m 6bq
Listed: Grade II

The Pathology Museum at St Bartholomew's Hospital may be familiar to medical students and cognoscenti, but it is little-known to the public at large; yet this astonishing repository of medical specimens provides a fascinating insight into the physical effects of diseases upon the human body, and the medical and social history of generations of Londoners.

Located west of James Gibbs's great courtyard of the 1730s, the hospital library and museum lie behind an elegant façade erected in 1877-79 to the design of Edward l'Anson. From the outside it resembles a gentlemen's club with a well-stocked medical reference library occupying the lower floors, but above, hidden behind the blind upper storey, is a remarkable top-lit gallery full of extraordinary exhibits.

A museum existed at the hospital as early as 1726, and it was later expanded when the surgeon-lecturer John Abernethy and his assistant Edward Stanley donated their private anatomical exhibits in 1828. However, the teaching collection proper was founded in 1844, when detailed coloured drawings of diseased organs were prepared regularly by William Alfred Delamotte, the eponymous son of the landscape artist. Later photography was employed to both teach and alert staff and students to the signs of particular diseases.

The 5,000 anatomical specimens show in detail the effects of the common and more unusual diseases prevalent in Victorian and Edwardian London, such as tuberculosis, rickets, smallpox, cholera, syphilis, typhoid and elephantiasis. The famous skeleton of Joseph Merrick, the "Elephant Man", is held in the Doniach Gallery of the museum's sister collection at the Royal London Hospital. The Barts museum specialises in cardiovascular, obstetrics, oncology and forensic medicine. Indeed, it was in a chemical laboratory at Barts that Dr Watson was introduced to Sherlock Holmes in Conan Doyle's first novel *A Study in Scarlet*, published in 1887.

By the 1890s attempts were made to collate the drawings, images and specimens into cross-referenced medical notes relating to individual patients, but unfortunately many of the notes and all of the plaster casts were destroyed in the 1940s, although about one-third of the cases depicted in the images have been identified, providing a valuable educational archive of clinical information.

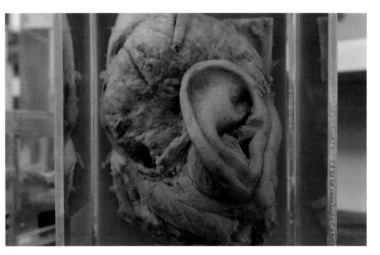

Great Hall
St Bartholomew's Hospital

West Smithfield, EC1A 7BE
Listed: Grade I

Barts, as St Bartholomew's Hospital is popularly known, is London's oldest hospital. It was founded in 1123 by Rahere, who is buried close by in the Church of St Bartholomew-the-Great, but refounded post-Reformation in 1546 by Henry VIII.

The hospital is contained within an outer screen wall designed by P C Hardwick in the 1840s. This replaced a series of tall tenement houses which originally screened the hospital from West Smithfield, an early place of public execution. The plaque commemorating the site of the execution of William Wallace in 1305 was installed in 1956.

The entrance to the hospital is through a striking gatehouse erected in 1702 with a central niche containing the only public statue of Henry VIII in London. Architecturally, the most distinctive feature is the courtyard designed by James Gibbs and built in separate blocks between 1730 and 1768 to reduce the risk of infection and fire.

The interior of the North Block contains the spectacular Great Hall, which is approached via a grand cantilevered staircase around a broad well. The walls are painted with two huge canvases by William Hogarth from 1735-7 symbolically representing *The Pool of Bethesda* and *The Good Samaritan*. At the base are scenes in grisaille showing the founding of the hospital, probably painted by a pupil. In the latter painting, the group of sick people to the left are brutally realistic depictions of patients at Barts who were used as living models by Hogarth. The cripple recalls the insane Rake from his *Rake's Progress* of 1723. The paintings are the most outstanding example of the Baroque fashion for decorative painting and *trompe-l'oeil* initiated by Verrio in the reign of Charles II. Hogarth had studied under his father-in-law, Sir James Thornhill, and was an accomplished painter of historical and allegorical scenes, although his collaborator George Lambert, the principal scene-painter at Covent Garden Theatre, was responsible for the landscape backdrops.

At first floor level is the Great Hall, completed in 1783 as a triple cube, double-height space. The plasterwork ceiling is by the little-known Jean Baptiste San Michele to Gibb's design. In the centre of the north wall is a Palladian-style chimneypiece with a pedimented overmantel flanked by two carved and painted wooden 17th century figures of a wounded soldier and sailor. Opposite is a stained-glass window of 1743 representing Henry VIII giving the hospital its charter. At the west end is a portrait of Henry VIII after Holbein in a pedimented surround "properly framed and fixed with decent respectfull Ornaments" by Gibbs and Hogarth.

However, the most striking feature of the interior is the collection of framed donor boards with gold lettering which adorn the walls. Busts by Lough, Behnes, Sievier and others, and paintings on movable screens, provide sparse relief to the cavernous space.

The murals and Great Hall express 18th century philanthropic ideas, where all sections of society came together to act for the relief of the poor and sick. Mural painting and iconography were deployed for charitable purposes (see p140). Accordingly both Gibbs and Hogarth donated their services to the hospital free of charge.

Prudential Assurance Company Offices

Holborn Bars, ec1n 2nq
Listed: Grade II*

The romantic serrated skyline of the former Prudential Assurance Company offices in Holborn stands as a glorious reproach to the staggeringly inept post-war buildings which surround it. The soaring complex of red brick and terracotta set around a central courtyard (now known as Waterhouse Square) resembles a university quadrangle and was built in stages over a 25-year period.

The company was founded in Hatton Garden by Edgar Horne on 30 May 1848 as the Prudential Mutual Assurance Investment and Loan Association, pioneering the sale of one-penny insurance policies to the working classes. These were collected by door-to-door salesmen – the origin of the stereotypical figure, the Man from the Pru. In 1879 it resolved to move its headquarters from Ludgate Hill to a new building at Holborn Bars.

Alfred Waterhouse was chosen for the task. His characteristic use of red brick and terracotta and romantic Gothic Revival style set a precedent for over 20 regional Prudential offices around the country. The building progressively replaced the old legal precinct of Furnival's Inn and The Old Bell Tavern, one of London's last coaching inns.

The first phase, at the junction of Brooke Street and Holborn, was completed in 1876-9. Further ranges were added in 1885-8, 1895, and 1897-1901. In 1932 the original 1879 range was rebuilt by E M Joseph in a similar style externally, but with distinctive 1930s interior including a sleek directors' washroom in a modish Art Deco style.

The front of the 1897-1901 range contains a series of lustrous interiors sheathed in Burmantoft's terracotta in a brightly coloured mixture of brown, green and yellow hues. The magnificent vaulted directors' staircase is richly embellished with Gothic trefoils and terrazzo floors in intricate geometrical patterns. The principal offices are panelled throughout with original and replicated light fittings. The galleried library with its Gothic arcaded chimneypiece, moulded plaster ceilings and original bookcases remains in library use.

The basement of the E M Joseph building included a muniment room for the safe storage of deeds and securities, entry to which was via two gigantic steel doors and a drawbridge. The two Chubb doors are preserved in their original position, although the room itself has now gone.

In the north-west corner of the courtyard is one of the most beautiful war memorials in London, dedicated to the 786 employees who died in the Great War. Sculpted in bronze by F V Blundstone in 1922, it depicts a dying soldier cradled in the arms of two winged angels. Originally sited on the central axis beneath the huge carriage entrance, it was relocated in 1993 as part of a major refurbishment which opened up the courtyard to public access for the first time. Bronze memorial panels commemorating the fallen of the Second World War were relocated at the same time to frame the entrance from Leather Lane.

Part of the interior is occupied by the headquarters of English Heritage.

Charterhouse

Charterhouse Square, ec1m 6an
Listed: Grade I

Closeted away behind high walls, and approached through a 15th century archway under an early 18th century house, the Charterhouse is a remarkable complex of mediaeval and later buildings. Little known to Londoners, it remains an introverted enclave of private almshouses for gentlemen pensioners.

In 1348-9 the site was bought by Sir Walter de Manny, who gave it to the City as a burial ground for victims of the Black Death, the cataclysmic pandemic which wiped out over half of Europe's population. In 1370 Manny founded a Carthusian monastery on the site, which became renowned as a refuge for spiritual retreat and contemplation. Between 1499 and 1503, Sir Thomas More prayed here wearing a hair shirt as a penance, but in 1535 it was ruthlessly suppressed by Thomas Cromwell following a dispute over the Oath of Supremacy. The Prior, John Houghton, was hanged at Tyburn, and then, while still alive, drawn and quartered. Subsequently it was occupied by Thomas Howard, the 4th Duke of Norfolk, who transformed it into a great ducal mansion from where he plotted against Elizabeth I, prompting his execution. In 1611 Norfolk's second son, Lord Suffolk, sold Howard House, as it was then known, to Thomas Sutton, "the richest commoner in England", for use as a school and almshouses. In 1870 the eponymous school moved away. Part was then redeveloped for Merchant Taylor's School, and later the Medical College of St Bartholomew's Hospital. Badly damaged in the Blitz, it still contains some magnificent historic interiors.

The Entrance Court leads to the Master's Court, which is faced in Kentish ragstone with mullioned windows under hood moulds. This incorporates the Great Hall, which lies off axis with the entrance gateway. Although much restored after the war by Seely & Paget, the interior is still an impressive historic space indicative of a late mediaeval hall in a private residence (opposite above right). The 16th century oriel window has carved spandrels and panelled jambs with the 16th and 17th century heraldic arms of Somerset and Sutton. The splendid screen (restored after the war) was installed by Norfolk in 1571 (opposite below). The gallery on the north wall with arcades and tapering pilasters was added by Sutton, as was the fireplace of 1614 designed by Edmund Kinsman. The original hammerbeam roof, burned in the war, was reinstated by Seely & Paget.

Adjoining the hall to the north is the Library with a range from the 1540s. A line of timber columns at ground level (p210 bottom left) supports the Great Chamber (left middle), above where both Elizabeth I and James I both once held court. Before war damage, it was regarded as the finest Elizabethan room in England, and it is still astonishingly atmospheric. Approached by a plain post-war oak staircase, it comprises a single large chamber with late 16th century decoration, including a fine timber and plaster chimneypiece with depictions of the Evangelists and Apostles, the Annunciation and the Last Supper carved into the columns and strapwork with a central panel repainted in 1626.

East of Master's Court, Chapel Court stands on the site of the original Carthusian chapel. Chapel Cloister (1613-4) (p210 top right) contains some fine early fragments including a 14th century tomb canopy and two 17th century figures of Moses and Aaron.

Beyond lies the present chapel (p210 top left), converted in the early 17th century from the early 14th century Chapter House. The north aisle of 1612-4 has Tuscan columns by Francis Carter, who was Chief Clerk of the King's Works under Inigo Jones. The upper stage of the tower and timber cupola were added in 1613. Within the chapel are some notable historic furnishings including a 17th century carved oak communion table, an organ gallery with tapering piers embellished with musical instruments and firearms, and a pulpit of 1613 with carving by Blunt. The excellent funerary monuments (p210 middle) include a recumbent Thomas Sutton (1615), a tablet and bust to John Law (1614) and another to Francis Beaumont (1624) alongside a legacy of 18th century memorials by Flaxman and Chantrey.

To the north of the Library, only half of the Norfolk Cloister (1571) survives including some entrances to monastic cells and the Priory Garden door.

Elsewhere, Washhouse Court is a highly evocative Tudor quadrangle of red-brick monastic outbuildings and lay brothers' accommodation inscribed with the initials of the unfortunate dismembered Prior Houghton. Pensioners Court to the north is from the 1830s by Blore. Preachers Court was reinstated following war damage with the Admiral Ashmore building, a well-considered new red-brick block by Michael Hopkins & Partners, completed in 2000.

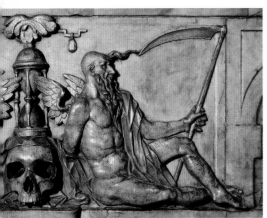

St Etheldreda's Church

ELY PLACE, EC1N 6RY
LISTED: GRADE I

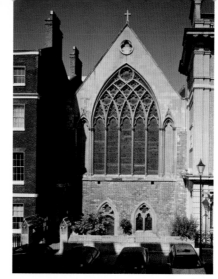

St Etheldreda's is a rare surviving remnant of the mediaeval town house of the Bishops of Ely. It was commenced in 1290 by John de Kirkeby as a two-storey domestic chapel with an undercroft. It took over a century to complete, but by 1327 Ely Place was habitable enough for the 14-year-old Philippa of Hainault to spend Christmas there, prior to her marriage to Edward III. After the sack of the Palace of the Savoy by Wat Tyler in 1381, John of Gaunt lived in the house until his death in 1399. At the behest of Queen Elizabeth, in 1576 Bishop Cox was compelled to lease the house to her favourite Sir Christopher Hatton, who was determined to build a house in the garden, which was renowned for its strawberries. When the bishop demurred, the Queen is supposed to have written angrily: "Proud Prelate, I would have you know that I, who made you what you are, can unmake you, and if you do not forthwith fulfil your engagement, by God! I will immediately unfrock you."

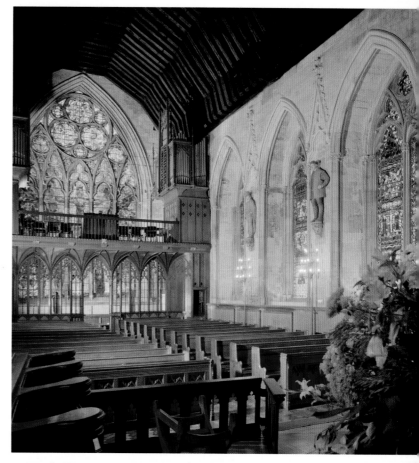

After service as a hospital and prison during the Civil War, the house reverted to the See of Ely, until in 1772 it was sold to the Crown. The dilapidated mediaeval mansion was demolished and a cul-de-sac constructed by Charles Cole lined with two terraces of town houses, but retaining the chapel. After a period as a Welsh chapel, in 1873 the chapel was acquired by the Catholic Order of Rosminian Fathers, and restored with great sensitivity by John Young and Bernard Whelan. It was restored again by Giles Gilbert Scott in 1935, but tragically the old mediaeval roof was lost in the Blitz, together with the Victorian glass.

The east and west windows have fine "geometrical decorated" tracery, a rare hybrid combination of intersecting arches and top circle. Mediaeval corbels with modern statues of the English martyrs by Mary Blakeman (1962-4) march along the walls in painted resin and fibreglass; a spiritual theme continued in the glass of the west window by Charles Blakeman (1964). The east window of *Christ in Majesty* is by Joseph Nuttgens (1952).

The atmospheric crypt, reordered by Blakeman in 1968-70, retains a powerful aura of sanctity.

St Etheldreda, the sister of St Ethelburga, was a 7th century Abbess of Ely and the daughter of Anna, King of the West Angles. The modern corruption of her name is Audrey, and the talismans sold in her name at fairs in the later Middle Ages, through which one could earn her protection, gave rise to the word "tawdry". A small portion of her uncorrupt hand is kept in a reliquary in the church.

Ely Place remains a quaint anomaly. In 1842 commissioners were established for the paving, lighting, watching and cleansing of the street and its environs. Although subsequently most of those responsibilities were transferred to the local authority, it still enjoys a unique status as a private enclave. A beadle keeps watch from the gatehouse at the entrance, and the police may enter only with his permission.

St John's Gate

St John's Lane, ec1m 4da
Listed: Grade I

Once the south gateway to the Priory of Clerkenwell, St John's Gate was built by Prior Thomas Docwra in 1504, since when it has undergone a succession of uses, which ensured its survival.

After passing through various offices of the Crown, in the mid-1660s it was occupied by Sir Richard Levett, later Lord Mayor and a director of the Bank of England, after which it passed to the Presbyterian luminary Matthew Poole, who wrote his biblical commentary *Synopsis* here. By 1703 the east tower had become Hogarth's Coffee Shop run by the artist's father, Richard, which later became The Old Jerusalem Tavern. Edward Cave, who founded the celebrated *Gentleman's Magazine* in 1731, lived at the Gate, where he gave Samuel Johnson a garret of his own from which to work.

By the 1840s the Gate's various incarnations and structural adaptations had left it in such a serious state of disrepair that demolition was mooted, but an energetic campaign by W P Griffith led to its rescue and partial restoration before acquisition by Sir Edmund Lechmere in 1873 secured its long-term future as the headquarters of the modern Order of St John.

A first phase of restoration of the first floor room in the west tower as a chancery was carried out by Norman Shaw in 1874-7, but in 1885 Lechmere employed John Oldrid Scott, the son of Sir George Gilbert Scott, to undertake a 10-year programme of repairs and restoration. Much of the external fabric visible today is the result of Scott's interventions, criticised by some at the time for its "Tower-bridgy ...sort of look", the result of extensive refacing in Chilmark and Bath stone between 1892 and 1895.

In 1885-6 Scott remodelled the Great Hall over the Gateway into the Council Chamber, retaining a fireplace of c1700 but reworking the interior with dado memorial panels, two huge royal portraits and, eventually, heraldic glass by Powell's of Whitefriars, installed in 1910-11. Wherever possible, older fabric was retained, most notably the 16th century staircase (above right) in the west tower, ceiling ribs, window and door surrounds, and a superb carved stone mantelpiece of c1570 taken from the house of Sir Thomas Forster in St John's Lane, later The Old Baptist's Head (opposite below left).

Scott's work was completed by an extension which included an exuberant new hall for receptions and meetings of the Grand Order. The Chapter Hall boasts a great fan-vaulted oak ceiling lit by a raised central lantern suffused with stained glass. The walls are faced in stained oak panelling, heraldic shields and armorial bearings punctuated by five large Perpendicular windows.

Today the Gateway functions as a museum and meeting place for the Order of St John.

Crypt of St John's Priory

St John's Square,
Listed: Grade I / SAM

The Order of the Hospital of St John of Jerusalem was founded to care for the sick irrespective of race, creed or colour after the capture of the Holy City during the first Crusade in 1099. Later it adopted a military role.

In 1140 the Priory in Clerkenwell was established as the headquarters of the English arm of the order, with a circular chapel modelled on the Church of the Holy Sepulchre in Jerusalem. This was later replaced by a more conventional church with an aisle and nave, but in 1381 it was sacked during the Peasants Revolt. After the Dissolution the nave and tower of the replacement church were blown up by Protector Somerset and the material used for Somerset House in the Strand.

The turbulent history of the Priory and the church makes it all the more surprising that the 12th century crypt survives beneath the rather plain Georgian parish church of 1721-3, which was ravaged by fire in the Second World War.

The crypt is one of London's greatest hidden mediaeval treasures, with remnants of the curved wall of the original circular chapel still discernible. The main unaisled section has three bays of rib vaults and plain transverse arches of mid-12th century date. The ribs were decorated with applied plaster chevron ornament. To the east are two further bays from the late 12th century which form an asymmetrical transept with elaborate mouldings and triple rolled ribs.

In the north chapel of the west transept are the remains of the early 12th century external wall, and a superb mid-16th century funeral effigy of Sir William Weston, the prior who died on the very day of Dissolution in May 1540. The monument is in the form of a gruesome cadaver tomb with Weston depicted as an emaciated corpse on a winding sheet. It is the remnant of a much larger canopied structure originally in St James's Church, Clerkenwell Close, but broken up in 1788 and finally placed in its current position in 1931.

Nearby is the alabaster tomb of Don Juan Ruiz de Vergara (c1580), a Castilian Hospitaller who died fighting the Turks near Marseilles. Formerly in Vallodolid Cathedral, it is attributed to Esteban Jordan, the court sculptor to Philip II of Spain, and widely regarded as the finest example of its kind in England. It was donated to the order by the Keeper of the London Museum in 1915. The tomb-chest on which the recumbent figure lies is by C M O Scott from 1916.

The stained-glass east window by Archibald Nicholson (1914) shows the order's role as a protector of pilgrims.

After the Second World War the area to the south of the church was laid out as a secluded memorial garden with a delightful cloister arcade and at its centre a fine relief sculpture of the crucifixion by Cecil Thomas (1957).

Marx
Memorial Library

37A CLERKENWELL GREEN, EC1R 0DU
LISTED: GRADE II

It is ironic that the capital of the greatest empire the world has ever seen offered a liberal haven from persecution for generations of political exiles and foreign radicals. In the early 20th century London acted as the midwife to the birth of Soviet Communism. A generation earlier Karl Marx lived and died here, his tomb in Highgate Cemetery later becoming a site of international veneration.

Between 1902 and 1903 Lenin was exiled in London, and over the next eight years he revisited periodically, devouring books in the Reading Room of the British Museum. A quixotic group of Bolsheviks and other radicals gravitated around him under the watchful eye of Special Branch. Litvinov, Kropotkin, Gorky, Trotsky and Stalin all congregated in the capital, much to the fascination of the British press. "History is being made in London … they are a most picturesque crowd," trilled the *Daily Mirror*. It was in London that Stalin, bank robber, assassin and thug, first met Trotsky, the articulate orator, and loathed him on sight.

No 37a Clerkenwell Green was a former Welsh Charity School built in 1738 by James Steere. For 20 years from 1892 it was used for meetings of the London Patriotic Society, a radical reform club which publicly supported the Paris Commune and the Fenians, before becoming the home of the socialist Twentieth Century Press between 1892 and 1922. Between April 1902 and May 1903 Lenin shared an office with Harry Quelch, the director of the press, from where he edited and printed the journal *ISKRA* (The Spark), which was then smuggled into Russia. His office has been carefully preserved.

In 1933, on the 50th anniversary of the death of Karl Marx, the Marx Memorial Library and Workers School was established in the building. A year later Viscount Hastings completed a large fresco on the wall of the reading room depicting *The Worker of the Future Clearing Away the Chaos of Capitalism*. Hastings had studied under the influential Mexican artist Diego Rivera and produced what has been described as "possibly the most explicitly revolutionary public painting in England of its time". Complete with portraits of Marx and Lenin, it shows a stylised Palace of Westminster and other great buildings being reduced to rubble by an iron-jawed Stakhanovite hero of the proletariat bathed in a corona of sunlight. Today it all seems as quaint and distant as a mediaeval wall painting.

During his exile in London, Lenin took his Bolshevik friends on jaunts around the city – picnics in Hyde Park, and fish and chips at his favourite restaurant near King's Cross Station. At his favourite pub, the nearby Crown and Woolpack in Finsbury, a hapless Special Branch detective once hid in a cupboard to eavesdrop on the dissidents, but when firmly ensconced he suddenly realised he didn't speak any Russian, at which point things took a turn for the worse as he was unable to get out without major assistance.

In 1956 Khrushchev and Bulganin visited the Library, as did Gorbachev and his wife Raisa in 1985. It contains a fine collection of early radical books, tracts and pamphlets, the archive of the International Brigade, the Bernal Peace Library and a collection of over 40,000 photographs.

During refurbishment in 1986, barrel-vaulted tunnels were discovered in the basement which pre-date the building and which may form part of the 12th century nunnery which once stood on the site. A short distance around the corner in the rather unprepossessing surroundings of 16 Farringdon Lane is the eponymous Clerks Well, rediscovered in 1924, which conferred its name on the entire district.

Middlesex House of Detention

CLERKENWELL CLOSE
LISTED: GRADE II

Concealed beneath the handsome brick and terracotta walls of the former Hugh Myddelton School in Clerkenwell Close lie the subterranean vaults of the old Middlesex House of Detention, a melancholic remnant of a much wider complex erected in 1846-7 to the designs of the county surveyor, William Moseley.

The House of Detention stood on the site of two earlier prisons – the Clerkenwell Bridewell, which closed in 1794 to be replaced by the nearby Coldbath Fields Prison at Mount Pleasant, and the New Prison, which was sacked in the Gordon Riots of 1780 and rebuilt in 1816.

By the 1840s the New Prison held 30 to 40 prisoners to a room, with lines on the floors to delineate areas for particular categories of inmate. To relieve this chronic overcrowding, a new short-stay prison was erected for those awaiting trial for petty crime. Conditions were strict, but not as fearsome as in the long-term correctional establishments. Although communication between prisoners was forbidden, they were allowed to wear their own clothes and to receive food and work materials from friends and relatives.

The new prison was modelled on Pentonville, which had been completed recently with long wings of cells radiating out from an octagonal central hall. Each cell had its own WC and basin and single small window. Ventilation and heating followed the same principle as Pentonville, with fresh air heated in the basement, circulated to the cells, then drawn off in flues and expelled by means of a central funnel over the octagon.

On 13 December 1867 the prison was the scene of the "the Clerkenwell Outrage" – the first Fenian bomb attack on London. A barrel of gunpowder was exploded beneath the exercise yard in a failed attempt to free Richard O'Sullivan Burke, an Irish arms dealer. The blast killed six bystanders and injured 50 others, damaging the houses in Corporation Lane (now Row) beyond repair. The incident triggered a huge backlash against the Irish cause amongst the British working classes. Karl Marx wrote: "One cannot expect the London proletariat to allow themselves to be blown up in honour of Fenian emissaries." The ringleader Michael Barrett was hanged outside Newgate Prison, the last person to be executed publicly in England.

After further enlargement, the surface buildings were levelled in 1890 for the Hugh Myddelton School, now converted to flats and offices. The basement of the cental octagon survives under the school, together with a grim range of vaults which once lay under the female wing, said to be haunted by the sound of a young girl sobbing, and which can be accessed from a narrow staircase and door off Clerkenwell Close.

During the Second World War the vaults were adapted and strengthened for use as an air-raid shelter. Wartime graffiti can still be seen on the walls.

Finsbury Town Hall

Rosebery Avenue, EC1R 4RP
Listed: Grade II

With the reorganisation of London's civic government following the London Government Act 1899, the parishes of Clerkenwell, Charterhouse, Glasshouse Yard, St Luke's and St Sepulchre were all merged to form the new Metropolitan Borough of Finsbury.

The eclectic character of the town hall is as much a reflection of its phased development as its free Flemish Renaissance style. It was designed by Charles Evans-Vaughan, who won an architectural competition in 1893, and built in two stages. The first phase, completed in 1895, faced the newly formed Rosebery Avenue. The second, beneath an elaborate pediment carved with figures of Peace and Plenty, followed on five years later in a more florid Baroque style to replace an earlier parish watch house at the rear of the site, built in 1814 and enlarged in 1855.

Evans-Vaughan was commissioned to design the interior decoration. Whilst much of this is fairly conventional – glazed tiled dados and marble columns to the entrance halls and staircases – the Large Hall has a wide barrel-vaulted ceiling divided by plaster strapwork terminated by an apsidal west end decorated with plaster figures representing music and poetry. However the real highlights are the "Clerkenwell Angels". Sexy, draped winged female figures adorn the Ionic pillars bearing sprays of foliage with light-bulbs as flowers. The figures, modelled by Jackson & Co, and the elaborate brachiated light fittings, by Vaughan and Brown of Hatton Garden, impart a strong sensual Art Nouveau flavour to the entire hall, and are one of London's hidden delights.

The building is now the home of the Urdang Dance Academy.

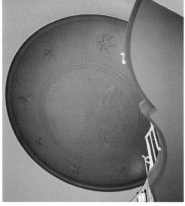

Metropolitan Water Board Offices & Testing Laboratory

New River Head, Rosebery Avenue
Listed: Grade II

From the 13th century onwards the supply of fresh drinking water to London was a recurrent problem. Conduits were built to carry water from wells in outlying fields in Holborn, Hackney, Hampstead and even Muswell Hill to the City of London, but after a particularly violent outbreak of plague in 1603, James I granted a charter to Captain Edmund Colthurst to allow him to bring sweet spring water from Hertfordshire to London. The result was the New River – an audacious feat of engineering involving the construction of a 40-mile canal following the natural contours of the river, 10ft wide and 4ft deep with a fall of just 5 inches in the mile. Fresh water was then fed to large areas of the City through hollowed elm logs. It was opened by Sir Hugh Myddelton amidst scenes of public rejoicing on Michaelmas Day 1613 to "drummes and trumpets sounding in a triumphal manner".

After repeated scandals and public health disasters throughout the 19th century, in 1904 the Metropolitan Water Board took over the private water companies. Following an architectural competition, between 1915 and 1920 a splendid new headquarters building was erected at the New River Head to the designs of H A Hall with a gracious Board Room and Revenue Hall in English neo-Georgian style. The entrance hall is enriched with friezes containing the seals of the private water companies taken over by the board.

In an enlightened early exercise in the preservation of an historic interior, the brief provided for the reconstruction of the resplendent Oak Room of 1696-7, which had graced the previous offices on the site. Attributed to Grinling Gibbons, but more probably by another, the walls are fully panelled in dark oak with richly carved frieze panels and a superb overmantel framed by Corinthian half-columns bearing the arms of William III surrounded by carved fishing and hunting themes. The ceiling bears the arms of Sir Hugh Myddelton and John Grene, the first clerk between 1667 and 1705, along with various playful relief panels on the theme of water including a mermaid, Neptune, a swan and dolphins and a large oval painting of William III carried by the Virtues. Another room contains the ceiling from the east loggia of the old Water House.

Adjacent is the former Water Testing Laboratory (now converted to flats) designed by John Murray Easton and built in 1936-8 along striking modernist lines. Faced in brown-red Himley brick with stone dressings, it is one of the most elegant compositions of its time, with a gentle curved elevation terminated by a semi-circular staircase tower. Soaring vertical glass-brick windows light a fine cantilevered staircase, above which incised in gilt is the figure of Aquarius the water carrier by F P Morton.

THE VENERABLE

John Wesley's Chapel
Gentlemen's Public Conveniences

49 CITY ROAD, EC1Y 1AU
LISTED: GRADE I

"While matters are always to be found of which it is not usual to speak of in aesthetic society, there are some to which attention must occasionally be drawn, even at the risk of offending our prude propriety."

(The *Metropolitan*, 1882)

Hidden beneath the sacred portals of John Wesley's chapel beside his house in City Road lie London's most magnificent public conveniences – a hymn of praise to the glories of Victorian sanitation and the pioneering work of George Jennings.

Jennings and his compatriots – Joseph Bramah, Thomas Twyford and John Shanks – were among the great unsung heroes of Victorian sanitary reform, responsible for transforming standards of public health and saving countless lives.

Little-known today, Jennings was the greatest of all the enlightened innovators in the heroic age of sanitary engineering. Encouraged by the award of the Medal of the Society of Arts in 1847, and the enthusiastic support of the Prince Consort, Jennings invented the first public convenience and, later, the forerunner of the modern lavatory. The opening of the first public convenience outside the Royal Exchange was put to verse:

> I' front the Royal Exchange and Underground,
> Down Gleaming walls of porc'lain flows the sluice
> That out of sight decants the Kidney Juice,
> Thus pleasuring those Gents for miles around …

The great chamber at Wesley's chapel is approached unobtrusively from within the building. Beneath a frieze of green and brown tiles, the walls are clad in plain white encaustic tiles, which provide the perfect foil for the ranks of sumptuous urinals which lie beneath. Each is divided by tall grey marble privacy screens to avert the unwanted glance of the competitive or merely curious, while the original Jennings ceramic urinals are inset into pink marble surrounds carrying the company's royal crest. The terrazzo floor, decorated with a Greek key border, has a pink edge to delineate the optimum range for those using the facilities.

Opposite are individual mahogany stalls with brass fittings. Each boasts a Thomas Crapper Valveless Water Cistern carried on ornamental cast-iron brackets bearing the company's TC monogram – complete with their original porcelain pulls and chains. Beneath lie the original "Venerable" Crapper throne, with ceramic bowls inscribed with ornate lettering and mahogany seats. Outside lie the washbasins, each inset into massive pink marble surrounds with their original brass taps.

John Wesley died in the adjacent house in 1791 and is buried in the secluded graveyard behind the chapel.

Quality Chop House

94 FARRINGDON ROAD, EC1R 3EA
LISTED: GRADE II

The Quality Chop House is a unique survival of an early 20th century working class restaurant of a type which was once commonplace.

Outside, the canted shopfront has twelve square lights to each side with central three light strips boasting "Quick Service", "London's Noted Cup of Tea", "Civility, Snacks", "Progressive Working Class Caterer" and "Best Quality".

But it is the interior that is remarkable with nine bays of oak benches and tables with cast-iron legs set in two lines around a central aisle. Around the walls is simple linenfold panelling with shelf brackets, a frieze of steleorite decorative tin panels and a pendant central gasolier.

At the rear the kitchen is reached through an oak screen with a carved door and sliding glazed hatch.

After a period standing empty and vulnerable, it is now under new management and recently has been restored sensitively.

Armoury House

BUNHILL ROW/CITY ROAD, EC1Y 2BQ
LISTED: GRADE II*

Armoury House is the headquarters of the Honourable Artillery Company, the oldest regiment in the British Army, with the peculiar distinction of having fought for both sides during the English Civil War. It was founded in 1537 when the Fraternity or Guild of St George received a charter of incorporation from King Henry VIII intended for "the better increase of the Defence of this our Realm and maintenance of the Science and Feat of shooting Long Bows, Cross Bows and Hand Gonnes". In 1658 the Company moved from the old Artillery Garden in Spitalfields to its present site adjacent to Bunhill Fields.

The entrance is approached discreetly through gates by George Dance (1793) alongside a romantic, rough-hewn, castellated gatehouse designed as a barracks by J J Jennings in 1857.

Beyond the gates, Armoury House faces south across the huge 6-acre parade ground, the product of at least five different phases of work. The centrepiece is the oldest part and was funded by George I. It comprises a five-bay block designed by the Company carpenter Thomas Stibbs, and completed in 1736 with a Doric portico. The parapet above is embellished with five stone finials in the form of exploding cannonballs. Further modifications took place in 1787, 1802 (when the distinctive flag tower was added), 1843, 1862 (when the iron-trussed drill hall was completed at the rear) and again in 1900.

The interior bears witness to this extensive remodelling and to the august history and tradition of the regiment. The entrance hall, remodelled with a barrel vault in the 1930s, leads to the Great Stairway, a handsome, broad dog-leg staircase. Beneath are iron gates, the gift of the Lord Mayor of London, Sir Richard Hoare, c1740. Behind is a fine South Africa War memorial designed by Walter Crane. The stained glass in the Victorian windows commemorates the Company's losses in South Africa and two World Wars.

The Long Room is the main dining room. Although the panelling was installed as a war memorial in 1919, there are several earlier features, including 18th century pedimented doorcases and two chimneypieces; over that to the east is the Company arms, and over the west the royal arms. The musicians' gallery with its delicate cast-lead balustrades is from 1787.

To the north-west is the Court Room with painted friezes of *trompe-l'oeil* trophies by Francis Holman, a fine double-faced clock (1748), a relief of George I (1753) and a carved pine mantelpiece (1778) alongside Company silver and a rare suite of Elizabethan tilting armour. In the West Wing is the Drum Room, containing a brass drum used as a coffee table, and pictures depicting the first balloon ascent from English soil in 1784, which took place on the parade ground at the front of the building.

Ceremonially, the regiment provides guards of honour for royal and state visits in the City of London. Operationally, it is part of the Allied Command Europe Rapid Reaction Corps.

When toasting another member of the Company, members give "Regimental Fire" – a ninefold shout of the word "Zay" accompanied by sideways movements of the right hand culminating in an upward movement on the last and loudest shout; a tradition which might stem from the movements required to light an 18th century grenade.

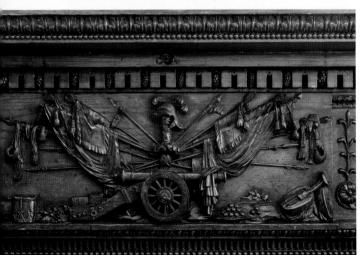

21 Holywell Row

EC2A 4JB
UNLISTED

Many of the historic streets and roads of inner London are lined with terraces of 18th and 19th century buildings which still contain unexplored, hidden interiors. In ancient inner London neighbourhoods, and along old highways like Old Kent Road, Clapham High Street, Mile End Road and Kingsland Road, previously undiscovered interiors are being unearthed above ground floor shops, where the upper floors have been used for dead storage, or simply just abandoned for generations.

No 21 Holywell Row in Shoreditch is a typical example. The house was refronted in 1924, and for many years the ground floor has been used as a café. However, as is so often the case, the older brick rear elevation offered a tantalising clue that a much earlier building lay inside, a hunch which was borne out on closer inspection.

The interior is a rare surviving example of a one-room-deep London Georgian house, probably built in the 1780s or thereabouts. The upper floors, deserted for decades, lie frozen in time – preserved as a remarkable time-capsule of a long-vanished past.

A narrow winder staircase in its own panelled compartment leads to the upper floors. With the exception of this, the first floor room occupies the entire footprint of the house. On the floor above, what was once a single room has been divided by a panelled partition with a narrow door, probably reused elements relocated from elsewhere in the original building.

The brown paintwork, early 20th century fireplace, fingerplates with embossed peacocks and decaying floral linoleum on the garret staircase suggest that nothing has happened to the interior for almost a century. Throwbacks like these exude a very palpable sense of history, from which much can be learned, and an aura of romantic decay which will be lost when it is brought back to use once again.

Masonic Temple
Andaz Liverpool Street Hotel

40 LIVERPOOL STREET, EC2M 7QN
LISTED: GRADE II

Situated on the site of the first Bethlehem Hospital founded in 1247, the former Great Eastern Hotel was a late addition to the Liverpool Street Station complex and completed in two stages – the original range by Charles and Charles Edward Barry in 1880-4, and a later extension by Colonel R W Edis between 1898 and 1901. Originally the hotel had 160 bedrooms, but only 12 bathrooms. A set of dedicated railway tracks into the station regularly supplied provisions and salt water from Harwich for the hotel baths.

Externally it is a rather rambling, red-brick, gabled affair with mullioned and transomed windows in a vaguely French idiom, but internally some fine spaces can be found.

The dining room has an impressive central dome of coloured glass surrounded by elaborate plasterwork. During the Second World War it was swathed in mattresses and blankets to protect it from blast damage, which proved surprisingly effective. Only one small piece needed renewal, now marked in red glass. The former Abercorn Bar (now The George) resembles an Elizabethan coach house with a heavily embossed ceiling and dark oak panelled walls. A painting of Bishopsgate in the 17th century hangs over the bar. The former Hamilton Hall has rich plasterwork and painted scenes in rococo frames modelled on an apartment in the Palais Soubise in Paris. However, the real highlight of the interior lies hidden upstairs.

Up a fine marble staircase (by Edis) and through a maze of corridors is the mysterious Masonic Temple designed by Brown & Burrow in Greek style and completed in 1912 at a cost of £50,000 – equivalent to £4m today. A wood panelled antechamber leads through double doors into the Temple, which is set at a lower level and lined with 12 different varieties of Italian marble beneath a blue and gold ceiling decorated with the signs of the zodiac. At the centre is a gold sunburst with an illuminated central star. Around the perimeter is seating with two thrones set in mahogany aedicules adorned with Masonic symbolism. A bronze bust of the Duke of Connaught, the Grand Master, guards the entrance.

There is no truth in the assertion that the Temple was rediscovered by builders behind a false wall during the hotel's renovation in 1997. It is an urban myth, no doubt generated by the arcane nature of the room itself. A second temple in an Egyptian style in the basement by Edis was in poor condition and converted to a gym. Only the pilasters remain.

Gibson Hall

13 BISHOPSGATE, EC2N 3BA
LISTED: GRADE I

Situated at the junction of Bishopsgate and Threadneedle Street, Gibson Hall is the former banking hall of the National Provincial, later National Westminster, Bank.

In 1862 the directors of the National Provincial Bank resolved to build their new headquarters in Bishopsgate. The architect John Gibson was approached to prepare designs which would encapsulate the wealth, security and durability of his client's institution. He succeeded brilliantly. Gibson Hall is the finest Victorian banking hall in the City of London.

On the Bishopsgate frontage, the single-storey banking hall is treated as a pavilion articulated by six huge bays with arched windows set between fluted Corinthian columns. The corner to Threadneedle Street culminates in a great curve to the main entrance. Above each bay are wonderful Pre-Raphaelite reliefs by John Hancock, each with a guardian angel presiding over scenes of human endeavour – the arts, commerce, science, manufacture, agriculture, navigation and shipbuilding. Crowning the parapet are statues representing England and Wales, London, Manchester and the great cities of England. In 1878-9, Gibson added two further bays at the north end.

Inside, what was once the main banking hall was cleared of its counters and fittings in 1980-2 to create an assembly hall as the final part of a wider 10-year development of the site for the National Westminster Tower (now Tower 42) by Richard Seifert & Partners. The hall is lit by three huge glazed saucer domes hung with modern chandeliers. Around the walls is a swaggering array of red Devonshire marble columns with gilded Corinthian capitals carrying a deeply carved, latticework ceiling. At each end are triple arcades. At one end four panels of putti represent the production of gold, coinage and the association with banking, and at the other, three more depict smelting, coins and banking.

Unbelievably, in 1959 proposals were advanced for its demolition. Ten years later pressure was applied once again in connection with the wider redevelopment, but this too was resisted. Today it remains inconceivable that a building of such quality should ever have been threatened.

The hall now operates as a stylish venue for conferences, receptions and gala dinners.

Drapers' Hall

THROGMORTON AVENUE, EC2N 2DQ
LISTED: GRADE II*

The Drapers' Company, which received its first royal charter in 1364, was the earliest corporate body in England to receive a grant of arms in 1439. Its first hall was in St Swithin's Lane, but in 1543 the company acquired its present site from Henry VIII, who had sequestered the original house and site from Thomas Cromwell following his execution. Successive buildings were ravaged in the Great Fire of 1666, and again in 1772, after which the rebuilt Hall was altered in 1868-70 by Herbert Williams, and again in 1898-9 by Sir Thomas Graham Jackson.

One might be forgiven for expecting the end result to be rather a dog's dinner, but nothing could be further from the truth. The interior is the finest Victorian livery hall with a grandiloquent suite of rooms which make Buckingham Palace seem homely. Indeed the Hall and Drawing Room have been used as alternatives to the Palace in various films, including *The King's Speech*.

Entered via a long oak panelled corridor lit by stained glass containing the arms of Drake, Nelson, Earl St Vincent and Raleigh, a grand marble and alabaster staircase in Quattrocento style rises to a spacious first floor landing under an elliptical ceiling. The walls are lined with Greek cipollino marble, the arcades of Ionic columns in Breccia marble and the doorcases in Emperor's Red marble. Between the Ionic columns are busts of Queen Victoria, Prince Albert and Frederick, Duke of York, together with Egyptian-style bronzes. Beyond is the Court Room, renovated by Herbert Williams in the 1860s but incorporating earlier 18th century work with magnificent Gobelin tapestries and portraits of Wellington and Nelson (opposite below left).

The Livery Hall (overleaf), enlarged by Williams, is a vision of breathtaking opulence. Marble Corinthian columns march around the entire room, paired in the apse, with each bay containing full-length royal portraits. The columns support a gallery and lunettes painted in a rather lurid purple hue. The vast ceiling, painted by the artist Herbert Draper, depicts scenes from *The Tempest* and *A Midsummer Night's Dream* with allegorical depictions of history, science, ethics and literature at each end. At the buffet end are two niches with 19th century statues of Hypatia by Richard Belt and Venus by John Gibson.

From the apse an oak panelled corridor leads to the plush Drawing Room (opposite above), designed by Herbert Williams and decorated by John G Crace in green and gold with a massive Victorian marble chimneypiece crowned by a segmental pediment and clock within a ram's head garland. On the wall is Herbert Draper's *The Gates of Dawn*, painted to mark the dawn of the 20th century.

Finally comes the Court Dining Room (opposite below right), a remnant of the 1667-71 reconstruction by Edward Jerman following the Great Fire, but comprehensively renovated in 1869 with a ceiling painting of *Jason and the Golden Fleece* by Barrias and a great coved cornice with the coats of arms of members of the Court. Two more Louis XV Gobelin tapestries depict the legend of the Golden Fleece.

Chartered Accountants' Hall

Moorgate Place, ec2r 6ea
Listed: Grade II*

With the growth of manufacturing industry, commerce and limited liability companies in 19th century Britain, demand increased for proficient accountants who could deal with the increasing complexity of financial transactions. In 1880 the Institute of Chartered Accountants was established to address the issue and maintain professional standards and probity.

Chartered Accountants' Hall is one of the most flamboyant examples of late Victorian neo-Baroque and more than a match for many of the City's older livery company halls. Completed in 1890, and extended in 1930, it was designed by John Belcher following an architectural competition.

Externally it is lavishly decorated with figurative sculpture. The figure frieze and sculpture of *Justice* is by Sir Hamo Thornycroft, and the entrances, termini and corner oriel by Harry Bates, their melancholic androgynous forms tinged with Art Nouveau nuances. The later extension, completed by Belcher's partner J J Joass, has a figure frieze by J A Stevenson in the same vein, with caryatids carved with modish hairstyles of the period.

Inside, beyond the vestibule (p240 below), which has two fine war memorials, is a narrow coffered, barrel-vaulted entrance hall reminiscent of the Palazzo Cambiaso in Genoa (opposite below right middle). To one side at ground floor level the Members' Room, now a library, has an extraordinary balustraded gallery which leaps across the room as a bridge link.

The staircase leads to a first floor landing overseen by the imperious gaze of Queen Victoria, in the form of a bust by Onslow Ford. All this is but a prelude to the architectural climax of the interior – the handsome former Council Chamber, a basilica with apsidal ends crowned by a handsome dome and glazed lantern with a gallery beneath. The two walls are filled with massive wall paintings by George Murray completed in 1913-14: over the door the triumph of law with an exquisitely detailed clock sitting on the doorcase, and opposite, science bringing order to commerce. Next door in the small reception room, the door handles are deliberately set low as a visual illusion to suggest that the room is larger. The ceiling is in the manner of Inigo Jones with a bronze chimneypiece by Alfred Stevens.

In 1978 William Whitfield extended the building to provide a Great Hall for receptions. Hailed at the time as an effective marriage of new and old, today the juxtaposition seems rather uncomfortable.

Bank of England

THREADNEEDLE STREET, EC2R 8AH

LISTED: GRADE I

The Bank of England was born out of strategic necessity. In the late 17th century the need to rebuild a powerful navy dictated a revolution in national finances. A loan was raised and the subscribers were incorporated as the Governor and Company of the Bank of England with exclusive control of the government's balances, and the ability to issue banknotes. After its foundation in the Mercers' Company Hall, and a period at Grocers' Hall, in 1734 the Bank moved to Threadneedle Street where it expanded in stages with additions by Sir Robert Taylor in 1765-70, and then by Sir John Soane between 1788 and 1827, but by this time the distinctive blind screen walls, secure internal courts and top-lit banking halls were already established features.

During the First World War, the Court of Directors resolved to rebuild and expand the Bank within Soane's perimeter screen wall. Between 1923 and 1939 the Bank was reconstructed and extended upwards by Sir Herbert Baker. Plans to retain Taylor's and Soane's interiors proved impractical, although Baker's new top-lit perimeter banking halls closely follow Soane's original models. Taylor's Court Room and Committee Room were moved from the ground floor to the first, where they remain today.

Castigated by many for demolishing Soane's work and for reducing his noble perimeter wall to "a footstool for his work", for a long period Baker's reputation has been tarnished, the rebuilding condemned by Pevsner as "the worst individual loss suffered by London's architecture in the 20th century". In fact, Baker's work is a highly accomplished essay in the imperial classical style incorporating the very best materials and craftsmanship available.

Beyond a set of superb bronze doors by Charles Wheeler, the entrance vestibule has monolithic columns of black Belgian marble beneath a shallow vaulted stone dome. Below, on the floor, the central mosaic of St George slaying the dragon, taken from the reverse of the gold sovereign, is based on a design by Benedetto Pistrucci. Fine symbolic polychrome mosaics by Boris Anrep provide a continuous theme along the floors of the corridors. Beyond the vestibule is a double-height hall and gallery off which rises a magnificent open-well cantilever staircase leading to a colonnaded landing and the principal historic rooms. At the centre of the building the Garden Court was once the churchyard of St Christopher-le-Stocks, demolished for the Bank's expansion in 1782.

The Governor's Room and Ante Room contain fine paintings and furniture, the latter lined in red and gold damask with a Chinese Chippendale mirror (c1760) and oval desk (left and p244 below middle). The lavishly carved alabaster chimneypiece of Apollo and the Muses (c1791) attributed to Sir Richard Westmacott is from Uxbridge House in Burlington Street, once the Bank's West End branch.

Taylor's relocated octagonal Committee Room is the economic nerve centre of the United Kingdom. It is in this room that the Bank's Monetary Policy Committee meets to set the Bank rate and national fiscal and monetary policy. The exquisite sage-green Court Room, terminated at each end by triple arcades, is the meeting place of the Court of Directors, full of allegory and symbolism: the winged head of Mercury representing trade, and over the Committee Room doors griffons guarding the mythical pile of gold at the earth's centre. The three marble chimneypieces are by Taylor, and the wind dial is a replica of the 1805 original which was used to forecast the arrival of shipping into the Pool of London and thereby anticipate its effect on commodity prices.

The Dining Room beyond, entirely by Baker, is in similar style and contains a fine set of glassware of 1855 by Daniel Maclise engraved with Britannia, the gift of the National Bank of Poland in 1946.

Goldsmiths' Hall

FOSTER LANE, EC2V 6BN

LISTED: GRADE 1 / SAM

Goldsmiths' Hall is one of London's oldest and richest livery companies. Although the Goldsmiths' Company received its royal charter from Edward II in 1327 with St Dunstan as its patron saint, a fraternity of goldsmiths had been trading in and around Cheapside since the late 12th century. It acquired its present site – originally a merchant's house – in Foster Lane in 1339.

Concerned at the flood of counterfeit coins in circulation, in 1478 Edward IV established the Assay Office at the Hall, requiring the king's mark – the leopard – to be applied to all new gold and silver wares. The "hallmark" is alleged to be the oldest form of consumer protection in existence. In 1588 the company was appointed as one of the keepers of the Troy Weight, used for measuring gold and silver. A nest of standard weights remains in the collection and an annual Trial of the Pyx is still carried out to test the authenticity of British coinage.

The present building was erected in 1832 by Philip Hardwick on the site of an earlier hall built by Nicholas Stone in 1635-8, which in turn replaced the original merchant's house. Elements of the Stone interior were incorporated by Hardwick into a magnificent new Baroque building, which overtly expressed the astonishing wealth of the company. The exterior is palatial, with a grand order of Corinthian columns on a plinth of Haytor granite crowned by capitals modelled on the Temple of Mars Ultor in Rome, and arms, emblems and trophies carved by Samuel Nixon.

Inside is a vision of staggering opulence. Restored carefully after war damage, the double-height entrance hall and gallery boasts a rich variety of purple, green and grey marble designed by R Hesketh from 1871. The staircase is bifurcated at landing level and enriched with statues of the four seasons, also by Nixon. On the upper landing is a huge bust of Edward III by Armstead.

Hardwick's main livery hall, embellished by Aitchison in 1892 and redecorated by Donald Insall in 1990, was designed to overwhelm and impress. It succeeds.

Resplendent in crimson and gold with huge pier glasses, an applied order of Corinthian columns in yellow scagliola leads the eye to an apsed central alcove for the ceremonial display of the company's collection of plate. The superb crystal chandeliers of 1835 are by Perry & Co, while the windows are filled with armorial glass.

Across the landing in the Court Room, Hardwick incorporated elements of the earlier building including superbly carved panelling with scrolls, swags and unicorns, and a central fireplace of 1735 with bearded herms by Cheere (p249 top left). To one side is a second century Roman altar found beneath the hall during its reconstruction in 1830.

The Drawing Room (left) was restored after war damage by Fernand Billerey for the Festival of Britain in 1951.

Midland Bank

27 POULTRY, EC2
LISTED: GRADE I

Midland Bank was founded by Charles Geach in Birmingham in 1836. Over the next 20 years, by financing the expansion of its iron foundries, engineering companies and railways, it helped to transform the city into the workshop of the world. After a series of shrewd acquisitions, in 1891 it expanded its interests to London. By 1918, under its managing director and later chairman Sir Edward Holden, it had become the largest bank in the world, with deposits of over £335m and over 650 corresponding banks across the globe.

Holden was a firm believer in a corporate design policy. At the last general meeting before his death in 1919 he declared: "I have to report again that in modern days it is absolutely necessary to have good premises." Holden's successor as chairman was Reginald McKenna, the husband of Gertrude Jekyll's favourite niece, for whom Sir Edwin Lutyens had designed a house in Smith Square. In 1924 Lutyens was appointed to design the new bank headquarters in Poultry, working with Gotch and Saunders, who had designed many previous banks for the Midland. The vast pile which arose was one of the finest bank buildings in England.

Situated adjacent to the Bank of England and diagonally opposite the Royal Exchange, Lutyens produced a magnificent new building worthy of its wider setting and the pre-eminent status of the bank.

Externally it is Italian Mannerist in style, with giant austere elevations which rely for effect on subtle changes of surface modulation, including Lutyens' characteristic disappearing pilasters. Recessed behind the central aedicule is a shallow, saucer-shaped dome typical of Lutyens' work.

Internally it is gigantic. The double-height banking hall is divided into two intersecting axes by massive square Corinthian columns in green African verdite with white marble walls. The two axes meet at a circular marble light well (later converted to a reception desk) inset into the floor to light the safe deposit rooms below.

The lower level is reached by a giant Imperial staircase with a central niche and bronze statue of the *Boy with Goose* by Cecioni echoing the two on the front elevation by Sir William Reid Dick. There is a range of secure rooms with simple grilles for depositors to examine their safe deposit boxes in privacy. The safe deposit with its 25-ton door was built by the Chatwood Safe Company and displayed at the British Empire Exhibition in 1924. More recently it doubled as the setting for Fort Knox in the film *Goldfinger*.

High above at fifth floor level is the lush double-height Board Room surrounded by tapestries, the Directors' Dining Room and a superb range of oak panelled offices complete with purpose-designed furniture by Lutyens, including individual hat and umbrella cupboards for senior staff.

Currently vacant, the building is earmarked for conversion into a grandiloquent, seven-star hotel.

Bevis Marks
Synagogue

Bevis Marks, ec3a 5dq
Listed: Grade I

Tucked away in a discreet alley in the City of London is Britain's oldest purpose-built synagogue. Even in England, with its long tradition of religious tolerance, for many years Jews were not permitted to build on public thoroughfares, with the result that synagogues, like Non-conformist chapels, tend to be located away from the public eye in courts, alleys and backland areas.

A synagogue for Spanish and Portuguese Jews (Sephardim) was established in Creechurch Lane in 1657, and enlarged less than 20 years later, but it soon outgrew the building, and in 1699 the present site was acquired for a new building designed by a Quaker, Joseph Avis. Strongly influenced by the design of the Amsterdam synagogue of 1675, it also bears a striking resemblance to various City churches. This is not surprising as Avis, a carpenter, worked for Wren on St Bride's, Fleet Street, and St James's Piccadilly, and he brought with him a team of skilled English craftsmen including bricklayers, masons, plumbers, plasterers and painters.

Externally, it resembles a Non-conformist chapel – a plain brick box with stone dressings, and a central doorway at the west end crowned by a segmental pediment bearing the Hebrew inscription "Sanctified to the Lord, Holy Congregation, Gate of Heaven, New Year 5462". Given the need for discretion and architectural reticence, all the ornament was concentrated on the interior, which remains practically unaltered complete with all its original fittings. The roof is alleged to incorporate a beam from a royal ship presented by the then Princess, later Queen Anne.

Internally 12 Doric columns symbolising the 12 tribes of Israel support a women's gallery with latticework fronts. This encloses three sides leading the eye to the echal, containing the Torah ark. Similar in form to a colossal reredos, this is divided by fluted Corinthian pilasters into three bays. Above the central bay is a raised pedimented centrepiece with round-headed panels with the Ten Commandments painted by Cordoueiro, and the Hebrew inscription "Know before whom thou standest". Seven pendant brass lamps in the central space symbolise the seven days of the week, the largest a gift from the Amsterdam synagogue representing the Sabbath. Inward-facing oak benches running parallel to the sides provide seating for the congregation with a number reserved for senior members of the community. The backless benches at the rear date from 1657 and were relocated from Creechurch Lane.

As the only synagogue in Europe to survive substantially unaltered in its original form with over 300 years of unbroken worship, it is of great historical and cultural significance. Architecturally, its dual identity draws on the Jewish traditions of the western Sephardim and the Amsterdam synagogue, but expressed by an English architect using English craftsmen steeped in the construction of ecclesiastical buildings. It offers a fascinating glimpse of the cross-currents of multi-cultural London over 300 years ago.

Lloyd's Register of Shipping

71 Fenchurch Street, EC3 4BS
Listed: Grade II*

Although both can trace their origins back to Edward Lloyd's 18th century coffee house, the Lloyd's Register of Shipping should not be confused with Lloyd's the international insurance agency. The Register of Shipping operates internationally as a risk management organisation, providing quality assurance and certification for ships and equipment, a role recently extended to embrace manufacturing, rail, oil, gas and nuclear facilities.

The register was established in 1760, but in 1901 it took possession of a magnificent new purpose-built headquarters which overtly expressed Britain's maritime and commercial pre-eminence. Designed by Thomas Collcutt in an exuberant Arts and Crafts Baroque style, it resembles an opulent Italian palazzo, incorporating some of the finest architectural sculpture of its time.

Across the façade are carved allegorical friezes of trade, and bronze figures personifying steam and sail, by Sir George Frampton; a theme continued on the copper gilt weathervanes crowning the corner tourelles.

Inside is a spectacular sequence of richly decorated processional spaces rising from the entrance hall, which is lined in grey-and-red veined Torquay marble, to a huge vaulted first floor landing with stencilled decoration by Gerald Moira. Around three sides of the landing is a ribbon of exotic bronze relief by Frank Lynn Jenkins depicting the development of shipping from Viking longboats to 19th century steamships, interspersed with elegant maidens enriched with turquoise, ivory and mother-of-pearl.

At the head of the staircase is the superb figure of *The Spirit of British Maritime Commerce*, also by Jenkins. A maiden carved in white Carrara marble with nacreous bronze wings rides the seas on a barge with a lion's-head prow, surging through the water borne aloft by sinuous sea nymphs. It is one of the finest Art Nouveau sculptures in Britain. All this, however, is simply a foretaste of the spaces that lie beyond.

The former Classification Committee Room, now restored as the chairman's office, boasts panelling of seasoned Essex oak, stencilled ceilings and a fine overmantle painting of the visit of Queen Elizabeth to Sir Francis Drake at Deptford by Sir Frank Brangwyn. Beyond the reconstructed Board Room is the architectural climax of the entire interior – the General Committee Room, one of the finest architectural spaces in the capital. Blood-red Ionic columns of Numidian marble carry a huge barrel-vaulted ceiling modelled on the Sistine Chapel, decorated by Gerald Moira with the four elements flanked by the signs of the zodiac. At the west end beneath a semi-circular pediment is a huge red marble chimneypiece with panels of bronze repoussé work and exotic blue William de Morgan tiles set into the fireplace beneath. Inset above is a white marble relief sculpture by Bertram Pegram, covered over for decades but now revealed once again in its full glory in a recent restoration of the interior, part of a massive redevelopment of the entire complex by the Richard Rogers Partnership completed in 2000.

The Lloyd's Register of Shipping is a superb testament to British architectural craftsmanship and sculpture at its zenith.

Lloyds of London

1 LIME STREET, EC3M 7DQ
LISTED: GRADE I

The Lloyds building belies Oscar Wilde's famous dictum that nothing ages so fast as the truly modern. Thirty years after its completion in 1986, it remains as revolutionary and futuristic as when it first appeared. With its soaring vertiginous mass of pipes and services snaking up the outside of the building, its in-built flexibility and glistening, stainless steel carapace, it resembles some vast space age machine humming with the arcane world of high finance. Loved and loathed in equal measure when opened, it is now widely regarded as the ultimate exemplar of the High Tech style in Britain, and is one of only a handful of modern buildings to be listed Grade I.

Lloyds takes its name from Edward Lloyd's coffee house, which began in Tower Street in 1686. It rapidly became the haunt of ship-owners and seafarers as well as the first underwriters who insured the ships and their cargoes. After moving to Pope's Head Alley in 1769, it relocated to the Royal Exchange in 1774 where it remained until 1928 when it moved to purpose-built offices designed by Sir Edwin Cooper with a vast new underwriters "Room" located behind a huge triumphal entrance arch.

Following an architectural competition, in 1978 the Richard Rogers Partnership secured the commission and produced one of the most innovative buildings of the late 20th century using the English members of the team that had overseen the Pompidou Centre in Paris.

Externally the concrete frame is articulated by six strongly-expressed service towers. Stainless steel round-ended staircase towers resembling giant ring binders soar upwards, while lines of replaceable stainless steel toilet cabins with porthole windows sit within their own concrete frame.

Inside, a huge, awe-inspiring central atrium rises 197ft skywards, culminating in a great barrel-vaulted glass roof executed with all the swagger and confidence of Joseph Paxton's Crystal Palace and the great mediaeval cathedrals.

On the ground floor is the Underwriting Room and famous Lutine Bell, traditionally rung once for the loss of a ship, and twice for her return. The first four levels of galleries are open to the atrium with banks of escalators rising through the centre, above which are enclosed floors reached via outside lifts, the first installed in the UK.

Bizarrely, for all its High Tech bravura, the ninth floor Board Room is a complete 18th century dining room by Robert Adam, which was removed from Bowood House in Wiltshire to an earlier 1950s Lloyds building, and then reconstructed once again within the new building. The delicate plasterwork details and pastel colour scheme forms a surreal counterpoint to the High Tech building in which it sits, but it epitomises the City's ability to retain tradition alongside cutting-edge modernity.

Port of London Authority Offices

10 Trinity Square, ec3p 3ax
Listed: Grade II*

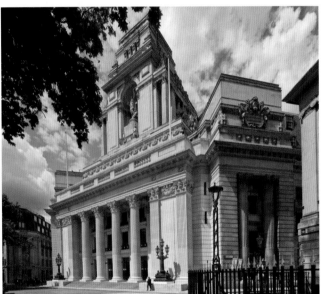

By 1899 the Port of London was in severe difficulties. Beset by internecine rivalries and ruthless price-cutting, many of the private dock companies faced imminent financial collapse. Huge investment was required to dredge the river to allow passage for new deep-draught ships. Following a royal commission in 1909, the dock companies were effectively nationalised and the Port of London Authority (PLA) was created to oversee the management and improvement of the port. It was a huge success. It regulated dock labour, extended the docks and dredged the river, triggering a new era of prosperity that sustained London as the world's greatest port for a further 50 years.

The PLA immediately launched an architectural competition for a new headquarters building. In 1912 an exuberant Beaux Arts design by Sir Edwin Cooper was selected. Conceived on an imperial scale, it reflected the ebullience and self-confidence of Edwardian England, but with the hiatus of the First World War it would be 10 years before it was completed. Its construction involved the clearance of an entire street block of 18th century houses and alleys on the eastern edge of the City of London.

The main entrance facing Tower Gardens is a huge Corinthian portico in antis, above which rises a gigantic Portland stone tower, at the centre of which is a triumphal arch containing a statue of Father Thames by Albert Hodge and executed by C L J Doman. On each flank of the tower are splendid allegorical sculptures of *Exportation* (a galleon with sea horses) and *Produce* (a chariot driven by oxen). Adjoining the main entrance at an angle with the five-storey side ranges are two more sculptural groups of *Commerce* and *Navigation*, also by Doman.

The interior is luxuriously appointed, with a huge double-height entrance hall with giant pilasters lined in Subiaco marble, which originally led into a domed central rotunda, destroyed in the Second World War. At second floor level is a series of lavishly panelled committee rooms in oak and walnut with limewood trophies of English worthies by George Haughton (opposite top row).

Behind the portico is the colossal former Board Room (opposite below) with walls divided into bays by paired Corinthian pilasters. Exquisite polished walnut panelling and carved trophies depict navigation, commerce and the territories and dominions of the British Empire. Such is the scale and magnificence of the room that in 1946 the inaugural meeting of the General Assembly of the United Nations was held here.

The PLA moved to Tilbury in 1970, after which the building was occupied by Willis Corroon. No 10 Trinity Square is now being converted into 41 private residences, a luxury 120-bedroom hotel, a spa, restaurant and private members' club for completion in 2014.

College of Arms

QUEEN VICTORIA STREET, EC4V 4BT
LISTED: GRADE I

The College of Arms owes its inception to a royal charter of incorporation granted by Richard III in 1424 to consolidate the work and records of his various heralds. Until 1555 they lived in a mansion in Coldharbour off Upper Thames Street, but following a royal charter of re-incorporation, in the same year they were granted Derby Place, close to St Paul's Cathedral, which is the site of their present home.

Heralds performed a variety of roles in the great households of Europe, especially diplomatic, ceremonial and military duties, and in particular the ability to identify the heraldic devices of different army commanders and knights on the battlefield from their banners, shields and surcoats. Heralds also organised tournaments and became experts in formal state ceremonies, a function which continues to this day. Under the direction of the Earl Marshal, the Duke of Norfolk, the college oversees coronations, state funerals, the State Opening of Parliament and the annual Garter ceremony at Windsor, alongside researching the rights of individuals to bear family arms.

When Derby Place was destroyed in the Great Fire, the current building was erected in stages on the same site. Begun in 1671-3, the centrepiece was designed by Maurice Emmett and Francis Sandford, the Lancaster Herald. The wings followed in a similar vein between 1682 and 1688 – the west wing by John Hodge, a carpenter, and the east by Ephraim Beauchamp.

Originally there were two short return wings with a terrace between, echoing the older quadrangular plan of its 15th century predecessor, but these were swept away in 1867 for the construction of Queen Victoria Street, at which point the entrance was remodelled, leaving the east wing one bay longer than the west.

In spite of extensive alterations, the college is a remarkable, if idiosyncratic, survival in the heart of the City. The handsome entrance steps lead directly into the double-height, panelled Court Room, which is dominated by the Earl Marshal's throne with fluted Corinthian pilasters crowned by two putti bearing the Earl Marshal's baton and a ducal coronet, all contained within a railed enclosure. Immediately adjacent is the Public Office (below) in dark-stained oak with a delicately carved overmantel of intertwined garlands by William Emmett, the architect's brother. Beyond is the galleried Record Room (right and opposite above), lit by a large Venetian window added by Robert Abraham in 1842-4. Elsewhere are two staircases with massive handrails, one with turned, and the other with twisted, balusters. The plainly detailed Heralds' Rooms, lined with ancient volumes (p265 below left), are enriched with armorial devices and escutcheons.

The superb wrought-iron entrance gates enclosing the forecourt came from Goodrich Court, Herefordshire, in 1956, the gift of Mr Blevins Davis, an American citizen, to mark the close associations between the college and the United States after the originals were requisitioned in 1942.

Library and Geometrical Staircase
St Paul's Cathedral

EC4M 8AD

LISTED: GRADE I

Hidden from the public gaze in the south-west tower of St Paul's Cathedral is one of London's most awe-inspiring spaces – the Geometrical Staircase, which serves the Cathedral Library.

Andrea Palladio had illustrated various forms of spiral staircases in the first book of his *Quattro Libri*. Between 1629 and 1635 Inigo Jones introduced the first stone cantilevered staircase in England – the Tulip Stair – at the Queen's House in Greenwich, but for its colossal scale, structural ingenuity and sheer audacity Wren's Geometrical Staircase stands in a league of its own. It was built by the master mason William Kempster with delicate wrought-ironwork by Jean Tijou. Spiralling to the heavens, it swirls around the stone walls in two great revolutions up to the Cathedral Library, which is a veritable time capsule, virtually untouched since its completion over 300 hundred years ago.

The Library is contained in a huge stone chamber; the corresponding room on the north side of the cathedral, the Trophy Room, contains the famous Great Model of St Paul's. The chamber is lined with the original bookcases and dark oak panelling constructed under the watchful eye of Wren's master joiner, Sir Charles Hopson. Below the gallery, with its peculiar open balustrade, is an impressive sequence of timber console brackets intricately carved in 1709 by Jonathan Maine. Above, the stone mullions to the windows are also handsomely carved by Kempster with garlands of fruit and flowers playfully entwined around open books, inkwells and quills – an explicit reference to its function.

The Great Fire destroyed tens of thousands of volumes and much of the cathedral's original collections, but in 1713 Henry Compton, Bishop of London, bequeathed his collection to St Paul's, which accounts for his portrait hanging in pride of place over the original bolection – moulded marble chimneypiece. The Library has been added to ever since and now contains 16,000 books on theology. In 1710 Humfrey Warley, librarian to the Earl of Oxford, offered his collection of biblical editions to the cathedral, including one of only three priceless surviving copies of the first edition of Tyndale's New Testament, believed to have been printed in Worms in 1526. It is the Library's greatest treasure.

In 1710 the German bibliophile Zacharias Conrad von Uffenbach visited the Library and recorded what he saw: "The room is of moderate size, but very high, so that many books can be housed there. For in the upper part there is one shelf above another, which can be reached by a gallery … The Keeper of the Library is an Englishman, that is to say a person who concerns himself little about it … This place was somewhat dark for a library."

Today the librarian is both scholarly and diligent, but the room remains virtually exactly the same as when Uffenbach visited over 300 years ago: a place of great serenity haunted by the ethereal sound of the cathedral choir singing far below.

Cutlers' Hall

WARWICK LANE, EC4M 7BR
LISTED: GRADE II

Unlike the majority of City livery companies, which are renowned for their urbane reticence, Cutlers' Hall in Warwick Lane boasts a striking red-brick and sandstone frontage with a fine terracotta frieze by the Sheffield sculptor Benjamin Creswick (1853-1946), explicitly showing cutlers at work, alongside a large elaborate neo-Jacobean entrance doorcase.

The Cutlers, whose work embraced the making of swords, cutlery and surgical instruments, are mentioned as early as 1285. They were granted a charter in 1416, and their arms 60 years later. For over 400 years they were based in Cloak Lane, but in 1882 the Metropolitan and District Railway Company acquired most of their site for a new underground railway, and they moved to a new hall in Warwick Lane, which was completed on 7 March 1888 to the design of the company surveyor, T Tayler Smith.

The neo-Jacobean treatment continues inside and pervades the entire building. The screen to the staircase has columns resting on carved elephants (the company's emblem), which recur playfully throughout the interior. The small Committee Room (left) has early 17th century pilastered panelling, originally from a house in Yarmouth, whilst the Victorian Court Room, restored after war damage, is hung with portraits of past Masters.

On the staircase is a fine oak panel of the company's coat of arms dated 1569, which was one of the few relics to survive the Great Fire of 1666. The elongated stairwell is suffused with dappled light from 17th and 18th century stained glass which was relocated from the old hall prior to its demolition.

On the walls are display cases of presentation swords, including the personal sword of King Edward VIII and a set made for Tipu Sultan, the Tiger of Mysore.

The *tour de force* is the Dining Hall with its steeply pitched, hammerbeam roof and paired hammer posts carved with elephants' heads, their trunks raised in perpetual salute to the assembled throng beneath. Mounted high across the entire end wall is a barge banner used in the Lord Mayor's Procession of 1763 depicting the company arms, Britannia, the wand of Mercury, Roman fasces and the wand of Aesculapius. Around the walls are shields carried by members in the Lord Mayor's Procession of 1834.

Beneath the banner is a wooden canopy carrying the Stuart coat of arms. Adjoining the Hall in the Old Smoking Room is a superb collection of cutlery, from Stone Age tools and Roman utensils to contemporary pieces.

Central Criminal Court

Old Bailey, EC47EF
Listed: Grade II*

Inscribed over the entrance to the legendary Central Criminal Court are the words "Defend the Children of the Poor and Punish the Wrongdoer". Commonly known as the Old Bailey, the court is one of London's great landmark buildings, its distinctive dome modelled on the Royal Naval College, Greenwich. Crowning the dome, the gilt bronze sculpture of Lady Justice by F W Pomeroy has become a London icon – erroneously assumed to be blindfolded, and bearing the sword of punishment in her right hand and the scales of justice in her left. In the segmental pediment over the entrance are allegorical figures of Truth, Fortitude and the Recording Angel, also by Pomeroy.

The court originated as the sessions house of the Lord Mayor and Sheriffs of the City of London and Middlesex and was rebuilt several times. By the 19th century, the Old Bailey was a small courtyard adjacent to Newgate Prison, which was demolished amid great controversy to make way for a magnificent new building, the outcome of a limited architectural competition won by E W Mountford.

Erected between 1900 and 1907, it is a superb Edwardian Baroque composition, but because of restricted public access, its interior is relatively little known.

Behind the original entrance is a huge tripartite hall with double-aisled spaces framing an Imperial staircase in cream, green and white marble. The Grand Hall on the first floor with its huge domed centrepiece echoes St Paul's, with carved pendentives of the Virtues by Pomeroy. Friezes inscribed with elevating references run around the space, including "The law of the wise is a fountain of life" and "London shall have all its ancient rights". Severely damaged by a bomb in 1941, the paintings in the lunettes are post-war replacements by Gerald Moira depicting the emergency services, as are the rather lacklustre painted figures in the main dome and spandrels. The four original courtrooms open off this space. Around the halls are statues of Charles I, Charles II and Sir Thomas Gresham taken from the tower of the second Royal Exchange, as well as a series of eminent Victorian and Edwardian figures including the prison reformer Elizabeth Fry by Alfred Drury (1913).

Some of the most famous trials in British legal history have taken place at the Old Bailey. Dr Crippen, Lord Haw-Haw, the Kray Twins, Ruth Ellis, Dennis Nilsen and the Yorkshire Ripper were all called to account here.

Adjacent is a contextual extension by Donald McMorran and George Whitby completed in 1972, beneath which is a short section of Roman city wall and an even earlier cemetery which contained some fine funerary ware. A year after the completion of the extension, the Provisional IRA exploded a car bomb in the street outside. A glass shard remains embedded in the wall at the top of the stairs as a reminder of the incident.

Apothecaries' Hall

10-18 Black Friars Lane, EC4V 6EJ

Listed: Grade I / SAM

The Worshipful Society of Apothecaries is the oldest extant livery company hall in the City, boasting a fine Great Hall, Court Room and Parlour which survive largely unaltered from their construction in 1668-70.

The society can trace its origins back to the "Gild of Pepperers" in 1180, which was responsible for importing, inspecting, cleansing and compounding spices and peppers. In 1373 it assumed the title of the Grocers' Company on account of its members importing goods in bulk, or *en gros*, and in 1429 it gained its first charter.

Some members of the company were "apothecaries" who handled medicinal preparations, as well as confectionery, perfumes, cosmetics, special wines and other products. In 1614 Gideon de Laune, the apothecary to Anne of Denmark, the consort of James I, successfully petitioned for a charter to form an independent company; the King commented "grocers are but merchants, the business of an apothecary is a mystery, wherefore I think it fitting that they be a corporation of themselves". Decades of rivalry with the College of Physicians ensued. As a practical knowledge of botany was essential for the apothecary, with the help of Sir Hans Sloane in 1673 the society established the Chelsea Physic Garden, one of the oldest botanical gardens in Europe. In 1815 the Apothecaries' Act gave the society the power to license and regulate practitioners of medicine throughout England and Wales.

In 1632 the society acquired Cobham House, which included the guest house of the Old Dominican or Black Friars Priory, and parts of a covered way over the Fleet River built by Henry VIII to connect his palace at Bridewell to the frater of the priory. Although most of the old buildings were destroyed in the Great Fire, some of the surviving fabric was incorporated into the rebuilding by Thomas Lock, which echoed the layout of the previous buildings.

Approached through an archway off Black Friars Lane, the central courtyard is marked by a large lamp standard raised on a plinth which stands on the site of a 13th century well. In the north-east corner is the doorway to the entrance hall, which was enlarged in 1928. The massive timber staircase complete with twisted balusters carried on urns was built in 1671.

The Great Hall is panelled throughout in dark stained Irish oak by the craftsmen Robert Burges and Roger Davies (1673), resplendent with a carved screen crowned by a broken pediment carried on paired Corinthian columns. At the centre is a bust of Gideon de Laune by Nicholas Young (1671) beneath an elaborately carved royal coat of arms by Henry Philips. When modifications were carried out to the hall in 1793, the screen was moved back against the wall, a small minstrels' gallery was added to the north end and the fluted oval ceiling installed. Above the panelling are the society's old barge banners and streamers, last used for the funeral of Lord Nelson in 1805.

The adjacent panelled Court Room (right and opposite far left) is dominated by two stained-glass windows with the Stuart royal arms and the arms of the society by Carl Edwards (1967) to commemorate the 350th anniversary of the grant of the Society's charter.

In the Parlour, which has a mid-18th century fireplace from West Harling House, Norfolk, is a fascinating collection of decorated and glazed jars and pill tiles juxtaposed with portraits of former masters.

On the night of 11-12 October 1940 the Hall narrowly escaped destruction when a 500lb delayed-action German bomb fell behind the north wall of the Parlour. It was defused by the Royal Engineers.

The Viaduct Tavern

126 NEWGATE STREET, EC1A 7AA
LISTED: GRADE II

Embedded in the railings of the churchyard of St Sepulchre, Snow Hill, is the first drinking fountain to be erected by the Metropolitan Drinking Fountain and Cattle Trough Association in 1859. The association pledged to provide free fresh drinking water to the poor as a viable alternative to polluted communal pumps, or adulterated beer and gin. Ironically, directly opposite is The Viaduct Tavern, with one of the finest pub interiors in London.

The pub was completed in 1869 on a quadrant corner site at the same time as the newly opened Holborn Viaduct, and it was later altered in 1899 by Arthur Dixon. Externally, the elegant curved façade is a fairly conventional Italianate design common in the mid-19th century, but internally it is a riot, with many of the original fittings including cut-and etched-glass mirrors, a Jacobean-style bar with an arcaded counter, and a lincrusta ceiling decorated with ornate strapwork designs. Around the walls is a moulded-plaster frieze interspersed with cherubs' heads beneath a shell-coved cornice.

At the rear of the bar is a semi-circular arched hood and doorway carved with relief panels which forms part of a rare surviving cashier's office from which the landlord sold tokens to buy beer, thereby removing the need for bar staff to handle cash. However, the most stunning feature of the interior is the east wall, which contains three large paintings depicting agriculture, banking and arts, in full-blown romantic Pre-Raphaelite style set in green and orange marble architraves and signed "Hal". Arts still bears the scars of a shot fired at her bottom, allegedly by an over-exuberant soldier celebrating the end of the First World War.

In the cellars beneath the pub are what are alleged to be cells from Newgate Prison. Unfortunately this is an urban myth. They are simply wine cellars.

Daily Express Building

120-129 FLEET STREET, EC4A 2BE
LISTED: GRADE II*

The former *Daily Express* building (now Goldman Sachs) was the first curtain-walled building in London; a revolutionary exercise in uncompromising modernism described at its opening in 1932 as "Britain's most modern building for Britain's most modern newspaper".

Commissioned by its Canadian proprietor, Lord Beaverbrook, the architect was Sir Owen Williams (1890-1969), who took over the work from Ellis and Clarke, who had proposed a more conventional, masonry structure. Williams was originally an aircraft designer and engineer by training, who made his name with a series of bold concrete buildings for the British Empire Exhibition at Wembley in 1924, including the famous Empire Pool, and later the iconic Boots factory in Nottingham. His final work in the late 1950s was the design of the M1 motorway.

By providing a concrete basement box, Williams doubled the unobstructed width of the printing hall and clad the entire structure in sleek black Vitrolite with streamlined chromium-stripped horizontal fenestration, its glowing ribbons of light symbolising a newspaper that never sleeps.

The result was described anthropomorphically by the influential modernist Serge Chermayeff as "frankly elegant in tight-fitting dress of good cut which tells with frankness and without prudery the well-made figure wearing it".

In complete contrast to the smooth functional exterior, the entrance foyer is a complete riot – a full-blooded Art Deco romp inspired by Hollywood and the architecture of the American cinema. It was designed by Robert Atkinson (1863-1952) and is, quite simply, one of the finest surviving examples of its style in Britain.

At the centre, hanging over the entire hall, is a huge Expressionist-style pendant lantern surrounded by zig-zag, back-lit coving set in a silver and gilt

starburst ceiling. The walls are lined with travertine above a rosewood dado with a black marble plinth and stainless-steel fittings. The floor is inlaid with serpentine patterns resembling waves of the sea. Beyond is a wonderful sinuous spiral staircase.

As if this was not enough, the highlight of the hall are the fantastic plaster reliefs designed by Eric Aumonier (1899-1974) representing industry. At each end are large relief panels in silver and gilt. One depicts Britain as the great workshop of the world, complete with a steam locomotive and liner. Opposite is *Empire* – a superb evocation of the people, flora and fauna from a community of nations on which the sun never set – complete with stylised elephants, writhing snakes, ostriches and kangaroos.

In 1961 the interior featured in the science fiction film *The Day the Earth Caught Fire*.

Prince Henry's Room

INNER TEMPLE GATEWAY, 17 FLEET STREET, EC4Y 1AA
LISTED: GRADE II*

Historic buildings generate urban myths, and Prince Henry's Room in the Inner Temple Gateway is a textbook example. In the late 19th century the entire façade of 17 Fleet Street was covered with boards proclaiming that it was "formerly the palace of Henry VIII and Cardinal Wolsey". It was no such thing. However, the building was of such exceptional significance that in 1900 it was the first to be acquired by the London County Council for its antiquarian interest, after which it was carefully restored by W E Riley with advice from the South Kensington Museum.

The site was once owned by the Knights Templar and, after their dissolution in 1312, it passed to the Knights Hospitallers of the Order of St John of Jerusalem, who leased it to various tenants. By the early 16th century the eastern half of No 17 was a tavern called The Hand and the rooms over the archway known as The Prince's Arms. In 1610-11 the property was rebuilt as a tavern perpetuating the name of The Prince's Arms, which later changed to The Fountain. Between 1795 and 1816 the front part was occupied by Mrs Salmon's Waxworks, which had relocated from the other side of the street.

Although extensively restored, the Gateway is one of the best surviving timber-framed houses in London to pre-date the Great Fire of 1666. Internally, the principal feature of interest is Prince Henry's Room at first floor level. Once panelled throughout in oak, only the west wall with its original Ionic pilasters and strapwork survives, the remaining walls and chimneypiece being later Georgian interventions. However, the heavy Jacobean strapwork ceiling with a central star and emblem of Prince of Wales feathers is original and one of the best examples of its kind in London. The stained-glass windows, detailed in the Stuart manner, add to the atmosphere, but are much later interventions by Burlison & Grylls in 1906.

The alleged association with Prince Henry might be attributed to the Council of the Duchy of Cornwall, which met regularly in Fleet Street at the time, and it is reputed that the room was set aside for their use after Prince Henry became Prince of Wales in 1610. There is no evidence at all for this. It is much more likely that the Prince of Wales emblem is commemorative and referred to the name of the tavern – The Prince's Arms. Nonetheless the interior is a fine and rare survival of the period, and currently houses an exhibition on Samuel Pepys.

Ye Olde Cheshire Cheese

WINE OFFICE COURT, 145 FLEET STREET, EC4A 2BU
LISTED: GRADE II

Unlike so many London pubs, which have been ruined by unthinking modernisation, Ye Olde Cheshire Cheese enjoys layer upon layer of history which confer a timeless sense of antiquity. William Sawyer, a late 19th century regular, wrote of it: "No new-fangled notions, no new usages, new customs, or new customers for us. We have our history, our traditions and our observances, all sacred and inviolable."

Built in 1667, directly after the Great Fire, the rambling, labyrinthine interior offers a rare glimpse of the atmosphere of a late 18th century chop house and tavern. Marked by an old circular 19th century lantern, the entrance, off Wine Office Court, is through a late 18th century shopfront. To the right of the door is a list of the 15 monarchs who have reigned during the pub's lifetime. Another celebrates its distinguished visitors, which reads like a roll-call of the giants of English literature: "Here came Johnson's friends, Reynolds, Gibbon, Garrick, Dr Burney, Boswell and others of his circle. In the 19th century came Carlyle, Macaulay, Tennyson, Dickens, Forster, Hood, Thackeray, Cruikshank, Leech and Wilkie Collins. More recently came Mark Twain, Theodore Roosevelt, Conan Doyle, Beerbohm, Chesterton, Dawson, le Gallienne, Symons, Yeats and a host of others ... "

The interior is wonderfully evocative. On entering, to the right is the Gentlemen's Bar, a dark-stained early 18th century room with an open fire, next to which Charles Dickens used to sit beneath a full-length 1829 portrait of William Simpson, a former waiter, which was commissioned by the clientele of the time as a measure of the esteem in which the old retainer was held. Dickens was a frequent visitor, and in *A Tale of Two Cities* it is the model for the pub to which Sydney Carton takes Charles Darnay after his acquittal for treason.

To the left is the Chop Room with booths of high-backed oak settles; its once-renowned 80lb meat puddings stuffed with beef, kidneys, oysters, larks, mushrooms and spices being mentioned in Galsworthy's *Forsyte Saga*. Here are Dr Johnson's chair and *Dictionary*. Although there is no documentary evidence Johnson ever visited, it is highly unlikely he did not, as the pub adjoins one of the approaches to his house beyond in Gough Square. In 1923 the eminent Soviet writer Boris Pilnyak visited and wrote a story in Russian *Staryi syr* or *Old Cheese*, which is set in the pub.

A fine late 18th century staircase leads to a series of panelled upper floor rooms which are used for private dining. Downstairs in the basements is a warren of vaulted cellars which predate the pub and are believed to originate from an earlier 13th century Carmelite monastery which stood on the site.

For many years the Cheese was the home of Polly, a foul-mouthed parrot, now forever mute, who sits stuffed perched serenely in the ground floor bar (opposite centre). On Armistice Night 1918 she imitated the popping of champagne corks over 400 times before promptly keeling over and fainting. Polly's death in 1926, aged 40, was announced to a distraught public on BBC Radio and in over 200 newspaper obituaries around the world.

The Saturday Review launched a competition to mark her passing. The winning epitaph read :
Enough! No maudlin tear be shed
Not all of Polly shall be dead.
Though silent: here upon the shelf
I stand in memory of myself,
A special prize was awarded for:
Our talking parrot, native of the East
Has now gone West.

Middle Temple Hall

MIDDLE TEMPLE LANE, EC4Y 9AT
LISTED: GRADE I /SAM

Middle Temple forms the western quarter of the precinct known as The Temple, which, until their dissolution in 1312, was once the headquarters of the Knights Templar. It is one of a number of surviving liberties, which are not governed by the Corporation of the City of London, and which also lie outside the jurisdiction of the Bishop of London.

Situated on Fountain Court, the Hall pre-dates the Spanish Armada. It is the finest surviving Elizabethan building in central London. Elizabeth I dined here frequently, and the first performance of Shakespeare's *Twelfth Night* took place in the Hall at Candlemas 1602.

The Hall was begun in 1562 by Edmund Plowden, the Treasurer of the Inn. Its architect was probably John Lewis, the master carpenter from Longleat in Wiltshire, who was summoned to London by Plowden. The building was completed c1570, five years after Lewis returned to Longleat, but there are unmistakable similarities in both works. Over the centuries it has undergone various modifications, including extensive restoration by Sir Edward Maufe following bomb damage in World War II, but it remains a remarkable survival of Elizabethan London, and a direct link to the heroic days of Drake and Raleigh.

It is spanned by a huge double hammerbeam roof – one of the finest in England, the great curved braces enhancing the sense of rhythm and height. Ornamental urns decorate the lower hammerbeams. The posts above the collarbeams are treated as miniature classical columns.

The highlight of the entire Hall is the stunning two-storey screen created c1570, the round-headed doorways embellished with elaborately carved caryatids and figures of Hercules on the pedestals. The carved foliated doors were added a century later in 1671 as a security measure after some young members occupied the Hall and "kept Christmas" for several weeks. On the arcaded pierced parapet are small carved figures set in niches. At the centre of the screen is a white marble Victorian bust of Edward Plowden. The screen was severely damaged in the Second World War, but subsequently restored with painstaking sensitivity reusing much of the original fabric.

The Hall is panelled to cill height and enriched with the painted arms of the Readers from 1579 to 1899. Fine armorial glass survives from the 1570s onwards.

The High Table comprises three 29ft planks from a single oak from Windsor Forest, allegedly a gift from Elizabeth I, the timber being floated down the Thames before the building was completed. In August 1586 Sir Francis Drake was given a rapturous welcome here by the Benchers and Members on his return from his exploits in the Spanish West Indies and North America. The "cupboard", or table, which stands below the High Table and is the centre of ceremonies, was crafted from the hatchcover of his ship *The Golden Hind*. On it is laid the book which members sign when they are called to the Bar.

In a similar manner to the Oxbridge colleges, the Hall remains the centre of the social life of Middle Temple. Students are required to dine in Hall for a minimum of 12 qualifying sessions. Today the Inn provides education and support for newly qualified barristers and training in ethics and advocacy for pupil barristers.

The nearby Middle Temple Library contains a pair of Emery Molyneux's priceless Elizabethan terrestrial and celestial globes, the first to be made in England.

City of London School

Victoria Embankment, EC4Y 0JP
Listed: Grade II

The City of London School owes its origins to a bequest of property by John Carpenter, Town Clerk of London, who on his death in 1442 left a legacy "for the finding and bringing up of four poor men's children with meat, drink, apparel, learning … until they be preferred, and then others in their places forever". The boys became known as Carpenter's Children.

By the early 19th century, under the enlightened guidance of Warren Stormes Hale, the first chairman of the School Committee and later Lord Mayor, the bequest was used to establish a new day school for boys. A site was selected in Milk Street, and in 1835 the foundation stone was laid by Lord Brougham for a new school building in a handsome Elizabethan Gothic style designed by J B Bunning.

The school was ground-breaking for its time in being open to all religious persuasions, including Non-conformists and Jews. It was the first in England to include science on the curriculum alongside classics and mathematics.

Given its immense popularity, the school rapidly outgrew its site in Milk Street, and in 1883 it relocated to a splendid new building on Victoria Embankment at Blackfriars. Designed by Davis & Emmanuel, it is radically different from the conventional London Board schools then in the course of construction across the capital. With its steeply pitched Westmoreland slate roof and great lantern, corner turrets and cupolas, and French Neo-Renaissance style, it resembles a vast opulent riverside residence rather more than a hothouse of learning.

Internally, a marble-lined imperial staircase with elaborate plasterwork leads to a colonnaded lobby, but the real *tour de force* is the double-height hall lit by five huge arched windows facing the river. Above is an open roof structure of tie beams supporting clusters of columns from which spring longitudinal and transverse arches. The stained glass, by Heaton, Butler and Bayne, is original.

Standing sentinel along the river frontage are statues of Shakespeare, Milton, Bacon, Newton and Thomas More, symbolic affirmations of the school's literary and scientific traditions. Past Old Citizens include Prime Minister Herbert Asquith, the writers Kingsley Amis, Julian Barnes and James Leasor, the actor Daniel Radcliffe, the physicist Peter Higgs and the mathematician Max Newman, the creator with Alan Turing of Colossus, the world's first digital electronic computer, at Bletchley Park.

In 1987 the school relocated to an uninspiring new brick building in the shadow of St Paul's, adjacent to the Millennium Bridge. The former school building is now occupied by J P Morgan.

The Black Friar

174 Queen Victoria Street, EC4 4EG
Listed: Grade II*

Built near the site of a Dominican friary established in 1279, which subsequently conferred the name Blackfriars on the entire area, the eponymous Black Friar now stands isolated on a wedge-shaped site at the junction of Queen Victoria Street and New Bridge Street.

The original pub was a fairly conventional affair, built in 1875, but in 1905 the interior was remodelled in high Arts and Crafts style for a publican by the name of Petit by H Fuller Clark with the sculptors Henry Poole and Frederick Callcott to create a riotous mediaeval fantasy of "Merrie England". Poole was master of the Art Workers Guild. Here craftsmanship was deployed in the service of fun and as a secular parody of the rich ecclesiastical interiors of the time. Jolly fat friars cavort and carouse in a range of worldly pursuits interspersed with life-enhancing homilies.

The lush interior is clad in pink, green and cream marble with ornamental friezes and panels of jovial friars in copper, bronze, timber and mosaic. Over the fireplace with its corner seats is a bas-relief of singing friars entitled *Carols*. A stained-glass window shows a friar in a sunlit garden. Above the bar another frieze – *Tomorrow will be Friday* – shows monks catching trout and eels.

Beyond is the Grotto, built in 1917 by Clark as an extension into the adjacent railway arch, over which is another frieze – *Saturday Afternoon* – portraying monks gardening, enriched with lustrous coloured enamels.

Beneath the mosaic vaults and mirrors of the Grotto are mottoes of wisdom – "Finery is Folly" and "Don't advertise, tell a gossip" – the latter with monks doing their weekly washing. Elsewhere, *A Good Thing is Soon Snatched Up*, is a vignette of a pig trussed up in a wheelbarrow, while beneath the cornice are devilish imps representing music, drama, painting and literature. Quotes from Aesop's *Fables* and nursery rhymes were executed in elaborate gilt lettering by the Birmingham Guild, while the lamps hang from fittings of carved wooden monks carrying yokes on their shoulders.

Today it seems inconceivable that such a magnificent testament to British craftsmanship and creative imagination should have been threatened, but in the 1960s demolition was seriously mooted and only averted following a public campaign led by Sir John Betjeman. It is yet another example of a superb historic building only saved through the efforts of a handful of enlightened individuals who were prepared to challenge established orthodoxy.

Sion College

56 Victoria Embankment, EC4Y 0DZ
Listed: Grade II

Sion College, situated close to Blackfriars Bridge, was established in 1624 under the will of Thomas White, the vicar of St Dunstan's in the West, as a college, guild of parochial clergy and almshouses at a site on London Wall. It was soon augmented with a library donated by Dr John Simson, one of White's executors. Ten years after receiving its royal charter in 1630, it had become a stronghold of London Presbyterianism.

After various vicissitudes, including extensive damage in the Great Fire, in the 1850s the college expanded its membership and took on the examination of boys in the City's Ward and National Schools, triggering its relocation to a new site on the Victoria Embankment at Blackfriars Bridge.

The new building was designed in a Perpendicular Collegiate Gothic style by Sir Arthur Blomfield, the son of the Bishop of London from 1828 to 1856 and a former Fellow and Visitor of the College. It was opened by the Prince and Princess of Wales on 15 December 1886. The most innovative feature of the new complex was a large two-storey porch and forecourt which were carried over the District Line beneath on an elliptical brick arch. Unfortunately the porch was demolished in 1965 for the Blackfriars Underpass, and replaced by a low, slit-windowed extension by Ronald Ward & Partners.

Internally, the galleried and clerestoried library sits beneath a deal hammerbeam roof. The great south window overlooking the Thames has post-war stained glass of historical figures designed by Cox & Barnard in 1951. In 1944 the City Livery Club co-located and shared the premises, but in 1996 the college was dissolved and its collections relocated to Lambeth Palace Library and the Maughan Library, King's College, London. It is now in use as private offices.

Guy's Hospital Chapel

ST THOMAS'S STREET, SE1 9RT

LISTED: GRADE II*

Few are aware that behind the elegant elevations of Guy's Hospital lies a unique Georgian gem – the only 18th century hospital chapel in England.

Guy's Hospital was founded in 1724 by Thomas Guy, the son of a wharfinger who made a fortune speculating in South Sea stock. On his death, aged 80, the bulk of his estate was left as an endowment for the hospital that continues to bear his name for the "reception of four hundred poor persons or upwards, labouring under any distempers, infirmities, or disorders, thought capable of relief by physick or surgery; but who ... are, or may be judged ... Incurable".

Approached through a fine set of wrought-iron entrance gates of 1741 bearing the hospital motto "Dare quam Accipere", at the centre of the hospital courtyard is a modest statue of the eponymous benefactor by Peter Scheemakers, completed in 1734 with panels depicting the Good Samaritan and Christ healing the sick. Enclosing the three sides of the courtyard are classical wings erected in stages between 1721 and 1777, that to the east a facsimile of the original following destruction in the Second World War.

Through a narrow vestibule inside the west wing is the chapel, a simple chaste design by Richard Jupp c1779. Square on plan, the body of the chapel is six bays long with groin-vaulted galleries on three sides carried on slender wood Ionic columns. Overhead groined semi-vaults springing from the columns at gallery level lead the eye to a circular fan motif in the centre of a flat plaster ceiling.

The chapel contains a stunning series of memorials. At the rear, set in a semi-circular green marble surround, is a magnificent Baroque white marble 1779 memorial by John Bacon to Thomas Guy, who rests in a plain coffin-shaped tomb in the crypt below. It is widely regarded as one of the noblest and most masterly of its period in England. Beneath the galleries are beautiful Victorian mosaic panels of scriptural figures alternating with oak memorial panels commemorating men and women who died in the service of the hospital.

The sanctuary was remodelled in 1956. Over the altarpiece are three stained-glass windows in memory of William Hunt, a former governor, who died in 1829.

Old Operating Theatre and Herb Garret

9A St Thomas Street, London se1 9ry
Listed: Grade II*

One of London's most intriguing historic interiors lay undiscovered for almost a century in the roof of St Thomas's Church, Southwark. In 1957 an intrepid researcher, Raymond Russell, climbed into the sealed roofspace and uncovered a remarkable relic swathed in cobwebs – the remnants of the oldest surviving operating theatre in the country, once part of St Thomas's Hospital.

The church was built as part of the wider hospital complex by Sir Robert Clayton, president of the hospital and a former Lord Mayor of London. Its architect was Thomas Cartwright, who had worked with Sir Christopher Wren on three of his City churches, including St Mary-le-Bow. Completed in 1703, the church was constructed with a garret in the form of a large, aisled, barn-like structure, which appears to have been used by the hospital's apothecary for the storage of medicinal herbs. During its restoration, a drying rack was found, together with the dead heads of opium poppies in the rafters.

In 1822 the garret was converted into a new purpose-built operating theatre for female patients from the adjacent Dorcas Ward, which abutted the garret. A skylight was installed over the Operating Theatre, and windows added to the garret, probably for use as a recovery ward. In 1859 Florence Nightingale established her famous nursing school at St Thomas's. Three years later, the hospital moved to its present site in Lambeth to facilitate the development of London Bridge Station, at which point the garret was sealed up and forgotten.

Ether was introduced as an anaesthetic in 1846, and chloroform a year later, but it was not until 1865 that antiseptic procedures adopted by Sir Joseph Lister became widespread. Until then, surgeons wore frock coats to operate, their aprons "stiff and stinking with pus and blood". Speed and swift techniques were essential. The patients were all poor, respectable women, but in spite of all the limitations, amputations, lithotomy and trepanning were carried out regularly and successfully, witnessed for training purposes by dressers (apprentice surgeons).

Beneath the central skylight is an early 19th century wooden operating table, complete with cut marks, brought from University College Medical School, with a sawdust box beneath to catch the blood. To one side is a cabinet with a bandage winder and an illustration of the amputation of a toe by means of a mallet and chisel calculated to make even the most iron-souled wince.

The pupils stood in semi-circular rows of standings rising one above the other, "packed like herrings in a barrel, but not so quiet, as those behind were continually pressing on those before … and had not infrequently to be got out exhausted. There was also a continual calling out of 'Heads, Heads' to those about the table whose heads interfered with the sightseers."

Amongst the herbs is a later metal operating table for children dating from 1905 taken from the Evelina Children's Hospital. In the display cases is a gruesome collection of surgical instruments – amputation saws, knives, sputum cups and stomach pumps; specimens of bladder stones, brains, kidneys and other treats; and, not least, the label from a packet of Concentrated Maggot Wash.

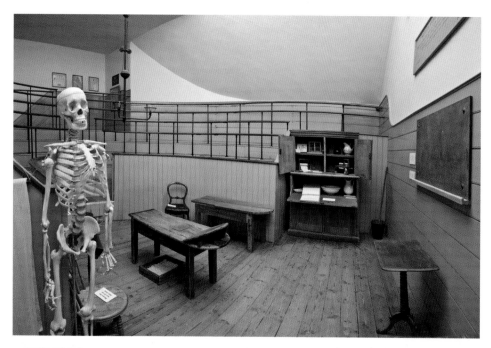

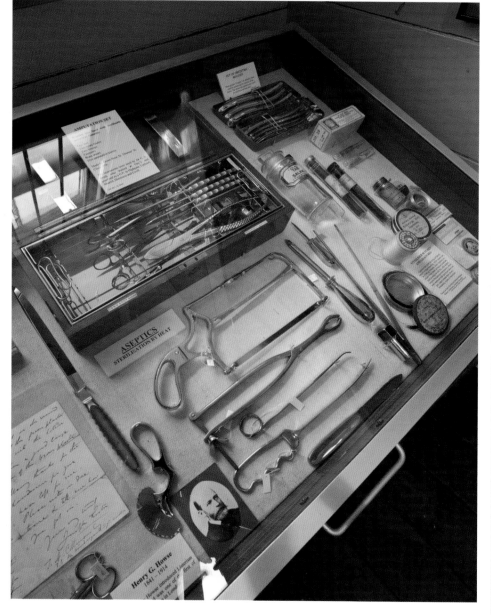

Octagon Library
Queen Mary College

MILE END ROAD, E1 4NS
LISTED: GRADE II

The Octagon Library at Queen Mary College is the most important surviving remnant of the original People's Palace, which was built to provide "intellectual improvement and rational recreation and amusement" for the people of the East End.

By the late 1880s south London boasted the Crystal Palace, north London Alexandra Palace, and plans were afoot for large new exhibition halls at Olympia and Earl's Court. In 1882 the historian and novelist Walter Besant argued persuasively in *All Sorts and Conditions of Men* for a "People's Palace of Delights" for East Enders. "Two millions of people, or thereabouts, live in the East End of London … They have no institution of their own to speak of, no public buildings of any importance … no picture-galleries, no theatres, no operas … they have nothing."

Unknown to Besant, a group of Unitarian philanthropists and trustees of the Beaumont Trust, led by Sir Edmund Hay Currie, had advanced proposals for the mental and moral improvement of the neighbourhood. J T Baxter Beaumont was a miniaturist and insurance magnate who had founded the New Philosophic Institute in Mile End. On his death in 1841 he had left a legacy to build a centre for higher education in the area. Capitalising on fears of social unrest in the festering slums of the area, Currie secured private donations and support from the Drapers' Company to bring Beaumont's vision to fruition some 40 years after his death, and to give tangible expression to Ruskin's belief that "perhaps … the final outcome and consummation of all wealth is in producing as many as possible fully-breathed, bright-eyed and happy-hearted human creatures".

Designed by E R Robson, the architect to the London School Board, a vast new complex was built on the site of Bancroft's School and the Drapers' Company Almshouses. The Queen's Hall was a colossal concert hall with a magnificent organ beneath a sweeping barrel-vaulted roof enriched with coloured glass and elaborate plasterwork lined with tiers of balconies adorned with the Queens of England. On its opening by Queen Victoria in 1887, *The Times* noted that this "happy experiment in practical Socialism" aspired "to sow the seeds of a higher and more humane civilisation among dwellers and toilers in [that] unlovely district".

Initially the palace was hugely popular, with 26,000 visitors on a single Bank Holiday in 1888 and over 1.5 million in its first year, but gradually its popularity waned. Like its counterparts at Crystal Palace and Alexandra Palace, in 1931 it suffered a disastrous fire. Only the frontage building and Octagon Library survived, and in 1934 both were incorporated into the adjacent Technical Schools, which became Queen Mary College of the University of London.

The Octagon drew its inspiration from Smirke's famous Reading Room at the British Museum; a huge cross-vaulted octagonal drum flooded with light from a central lantern and surrounded by two tiers of neo-Grecian iron galleries with niches containing busts of some of the great figures of English literature – Chaucer, Shakespeare, Dryden, Milton, Johnson, Wordsworth, Scott and Byron. Originally staffed entirely by women, once it was used by over 1,000 local people every day, who came in search of opportunities for education and self-improvement. Today it is a multi-purpose hall of the university and a thriving conference venue.

Adjacent, the new People's Palace, designed in stripped classical style by Campbell Jones, Sons & Smithers, was opened in 1937 by King George VI. The frontage is embellished with stylish Moderne low-relief panels by the sculptor Eric Gill. It too is now part of the university campus.

Blizard Institute of Cell and Molecular Science

4 Newark Street, e1 2at
Unlisted

The Blizard Institute is named after the surgeon Sir William Blizard, who founded the London Hospital Medical College in 1785. Blizard was described by John Abernethy, who later established the St Bartholomew Medical School, as "the beau ideal of the medical character", who would say: "Let your search after truth be eager and constant … Should you perceive truths to be important make them the motives of action, let them serve as springs to your conduct". Abernethy commented: "I cannot readily tell you how splendid and brilliant he made it appear, and then he cautioned us never to tarnish its lustre by any disingenuous conduct, by anything that wore even the semblance of dishonour."

These qualities are as relevant today, as the quest for scientific truth lies at the heart of the Blizard Institute. However there is nothing remotely traditional about the eponymous building with its sleek lines of curtain walling incorporating coloured glass artwork by Bruce McLean. The architect, Will Alsop, one of Britain's most original and idiosyncratic architects, allowed his creative imagination full rein, symbolically treating the inside of the building as an organism. His characteristic trademark pods occur in wildly different forms housing seminar rooms and meeting spaces within the atrium. The Cloud Pod resembles a large eyeball, while a large orange cluster – the Centre of the Cell – is a public exhibition space entered via a bridge with views into the laboratories beyond. The 400-seat lecture theatre has light fittings resembling illuminated platelets.

Intended to open up medical research and engage the public in the process, the £45m building is one of London's most striking new architectural landmarks, housing a world-class centre for interdisciplinary collaborative medical research.

Wilton's Music Hall

GRACE'S ALLEY, E1 8JB
LISTED: GRADE II*

Wilton's Music Hall is the oldest of its kind in the world – the only remaining example of a first-generation grand music hall. It is hauntingly atmospheric, with a pervading aura of romantic decay, which presents a real conservation challenge. It requires a very light touch if the fabric and distressed finishes are to be saved, and its existing fragile, character preserved.

Like many buildings of its kind, its history is accretive. Its nucleus was the "small, and not very respectably conducted" Prince of Denmark public house, believed to be the first in London to boast mahogany bars and fittings – hence its nickname the Old Mahogany Bar. The first concert room – the Albion Saloon – existed behind the pub, licensed in 1843 to a Matthew Eltham.

In 1850 John Wilton, the manager of the well-known Canterbury Arms music hall in Lambeth, acquired the building, and, according to contemporary accounts, "rid the house of the irreclaimable. Quiet has superseded riot, and order disorder." Soon after he bought the neighbouring properties, behind which he constructed a much larger hall to the designs of Jacob Maggs. After various changes of ownership, and a disastrous fire in 1877, it was rebuilt by J Buckley Wilson of Wilson, Wilcox and Wilson of Swansea with a raked floor and proscenium arch, reopening briefly as Frederick's Palace of Varieties. However, its new incarnation was short-lived. In 1888 it became a mission hall, and later a rag-sorting depot and warehouse before it was acquired in 1963 in an enlightened intervention by the Greater London Council. It is now owned by Wilton's Music Hall Trust.

The entrance hall is simply the enclosed paved yard of the original tavern. A narrow staircase leads to a warren of small supper rooms tainted with the aura of scandalous liaisons. Given its proximity to the docks, prostitution was rife and music halls were notorious for soliciting. Traces of the original painted plasterwork remain. Ad hoc development hid a multitude of gimcrack structural solutions, including the use of salvaged railway tracks as girders to support the floors.

The main hall is one of London's hidden wonders – a long, thin apsidal-ended auditorium with an elliptical barrel-vaulted ceiling. Around three sides is a gallery carried on barley-sugar columns with the balcony fronts decorated with carton pierre, or papier maché, decoration by White & Parlby. The faded plaster walls have paired recesses which once held a glittering array of mirrors. At one end the high stage is framed by a proscenium arch, whilst in the centre of the auditorium space for supper tables was surrounded by promenades for standing customers. Other than some charred ceiling joists, alas nothing now remains of the colossal sunburner chandelier once brilliantly illuminated by over 300 gas jets and 27,000 crystals. The burner, built by Defries & Son, was renowned as "a solid mass of richly-cut glass in prismatic feathers, spangles and spires".

Wilton's attracted the usual mixture of the entertaining, the exotic and the bizarre. Particular highlights included M Rotae, the Hungarian contortionist, the Brothers Ridley, celebrated acrobats, and Herr Whautkins, a flamboyant Anglo-German who "wound up his feats of dexterity by juggling with flaming torches". One critic avidly awaited "a dissolving diorama of the Ascent of Mt Blanc" which was to be added to the programme that week. George Leybourne, the original Champagne Charlie, performed here, and it is alleged that Wilton's was the scene of the first London display of the can-can after which it was immediately banned.

Wilton's is of immense social, historical and cultural significance. Every effort should be made to preserve it for future generations.

Wapping Hydraulic Power Station

WAPPING WALL, E1W 3SG
LISTED: GRADE II*

Before the widespread use of cheap electricity, hydraulic power was one of the principal sources of energy for raising and lowering machinery across the capital. Cheap, reliable and sustainable, it powered everything from the famous revolving stage at the London Palladium to dockside cranes and lifts in countless mansion blocks, offices and department stores. Until their modernisation in 1974, the huge bascules of Tower Bridge were raised by this system before being replaced by new electro-hydraulic machinery using oil rather than water.

Each week over 33 million gallons of Thames Water was pumped through 186 miles of cast-iron underground pipes to drive key parts of London's infrastructure quickly and efficiently.

Cheek by jowl with the river and dockside warehouses it was built to serve, the Wapping Hydraulic Power Station was one of five built by the London Hydraulic Power Company. Constructed between 1889 and 1893 to the design of E B Ellington, the engineer to the Hydraulic Engineering Company of Chester, it provided a pioneering prototype for other systems across the world – in Europe, the United States, Australia and Argentina.

Initially the pumping station was steam-powered, with six steam boilers and engines fired by coal delivered by barge to the adjacent Shadwell Basin. In 1923 two electric turbines were added before the entire station was converted to electricity in the 1950s. However, as electricity became cheaper and new electronic sources of power were developed, the use of hydraulic power waned. Gradually the remaining hydraulic power stations were closed. By 1977 only Wapping remained – the last working example of its kind in the world – before it too finally shut down.

After standing empty for years, the fabric was repaired by the London Docklands Development Corporation to secure its long-term preservation. In 2000 it was converted by Shed 54 to provide dramatic exhibition and performance space as an arts centre and restaurant. The atmospheric interior with its original redundant machinery demonstrates how industrial buildings can be adapted and converted into stylish and innovative new venues for cultural activities without losing their quintessential qualities.

The Boiler and Filter Houses have been stripped back to their original form, with contemporary interventions of self-rusting materials designed to reinforce the pervasive atmosphere of romantic decay.

St George's German Lutheran Church

ALIE STREET, E1 8EB
LISTED: GRADE II*

Tucked away in the backstreets of Whitechapel, St George's is the oldest surviving German Lutheran church in Britain, with a beautifully preserved 18th century interior, now the headquarters of the Historic Chapels Trust which was responsible for its salvation.

The church was founded in 1763 to provide a place of worship for the émigré German merchants who dominated the sugar industry of east London, having brought their expertise to the capital from the Baltic Hanseatic towns in the mid-16th century. At its height there were around 16,000 German Lutherans in Whitechapel alone. Its principal benefactor was Dederich Beckman (c1702-66), a wealthy sugar refiner, who donated the huge sum of £650 towards the total of £1,802 needed to build the church. Beckman is believed to be buried beneath the communion table. His son-in-law, Gustavus Anthony Wachsel, was the first pastor. Shortly after his appointment, Wachsel was responsible for assisting over 600 Germans who were abandoned in London in 1763 en route to St John and St Croix. Wachsel's appeal raised over £600. The Tower of London gave 200 tents for temporary shelter, and the King intervened directly to enable them to travel instead to Carolina.

The architect was probably Joel Johnson, a local carpenter turned architect who worked with Boulton Mainwaring on the nearby London Hospital and who was responsible for St John's, Wapping. The modest pedimented exterior has a central Venetian window flanked by two doorcases. The original bell tower was demolished in 1934.

The delightful and little-changed interior is filled with rare original grained and numbered box pews surrounded on three sides by timber galleries carried on eight timber Doric columns also with box pews set in raked rows. At the liturgical east end is a high pulpit approached by a short set of stairs with a tester above carrying a gilded dove. Flanking the pulpit are two large commandment boards with German inscriptions in Baroque style carved with scrollwork and cherub heads, probably by Errick Kneller in 1763. Above are the gilded royal arms of King George III. At the opposite end, the organ is by the Walcker family using the earlier organ case. The stained-glass window of the Crucifixion is an early work of Powell & Sons, part of a refurbishment carried out in 1855.

A door at the foot of the vestry staircase leads to a small courtyard that until 1855 was the chapel's cemetery, which was

later enclosed by a German Infants' School by E A Gruning, now converted to flats. Wachsel's successor as pastor, C E A Schwabe, was also chaplain to Queen Victoria's mother, the Duchess of Kent, who was patron of the schools and a regular worshipper.

In 1930 Dr Julius Rieger was appointed pastor. Rieger was an associate of Dietrich Bonhoeffer (1906-45), a theologian and vehement opponent of National Socialism, who served as a pastor elsewhere in London in 1933-5 and preached in the chapel in 1935. The church became a relief centre, providing advice and shelter for German and Jewish refugees in the pre-war period. Bonhoeffer was hanged at Flossenberg concentration camp in April 1945, days before the war ended.

The church was taken into care by the Historic Chapels Trust in 1999, and restored in 2003-4 at a cost of £900,000. Wachsel's collection of over 750 rare books was handed to the British Library for safe keeping.

Whitechapel Bell Foundry

34 WHITECHAPEL ROAD, E1 1DY
LISTED: GRADE II*

With a recorded history spanning the reign of 27 monarchs, Whitechapel Bell Foundry is a site of international importance and the oldest manufacturing company in Britain. It was established in 1570, but can trace its lineage back through a continuous line of master founders to Robert Chamberlain in 1420. Its present buildings were built in 1670, just after the Great Fire, as a coaching inn – The Artichoke – but in 1738 the company relocated from its earlier site on the north side of Whitechapel Road and soon enlarged the buildings.

Architecturally, the foundry is an extraordinary time capsule. A refined early 19th century shopfront leads into a beautifully preserved interior with painted and grained fittings, polite panelled rooms and a wealth of memorabilia. Beyond, facing Plumber's Row, is the workshop where bells are still cast for projects in the UK and all over the world.

Overseas exports began in 1747 when a set of bells was sent to St Petersburg. Other commissions soon followed, notably to Christ Church, Philadelphia, in 1754 and St Michael's, Charleston, South Carolina, 10 years later, but historically its most famous export was the legendary Liberty Bell of Philadelphia, cast in 1752 with the prophetic inscription "Proclaim Liberty Throughout All the Land Unto All Inhabitants Thereof", taken from Leviticus.

In 1858 Big Ben was cast here. At 13½ tons it was the largest bell ever cast in the foundry. The gauge used to make the mould of the bell still hangs behind the entrance doors. When the bell was transported through the streets of London on a trolley drawn by 16 beribboned horses, huge crowds lined the route to cheer the leviathan on its way. Two months after its inauguration, it cracked. After a three-year hiatus, the bell was turned and adjusted, a lighter hammer was fitted, and it was put back into service, the crack subsequently conferring its distinctive world-famous tone.

During the Second World War the foundry switched to manufacturing aluminium castings for submarine parts for the Admiralty. As a result of wartime damage to so many churches and buildings across the world, and the subsequent resurgence of pride in architectural heritage, a steady stream of work has continued to maintain the foundry's extraordinary role in the industrial history of London and the UK.

18 Folgate Street

E1 6BX

LISTED: GRADE II

There is nothing remotely like 18 Folgate Street anywhere else in London. Its dream-like, fantasy interior was the life's work and vision of Dennis Severs (1948-99), an oddball but gifted American collector, who acquired the house as a shell in 1979. Over the next 20 years he painstakingly assembled each room as a sequence of experiences or "spells" reflecting the decoration, furnishings, textures, light, sounds and even smells of different periods of the past from 1724 to 1914. Meticulously researched, many of the finishes were mocked up in the manner of stage scenery using inexpensive materials like discarded timber from the nearby Spitalfields Market to replicate panelling or chimneypieces. All is artifice. Nothing is what it seems, yet it conveys a haunting sense of the past embalmed.

Marked by a bracketed Windsor lantern over the entrance door, externally there is little to distinguish the three-bay-wide house of 1724 from its neighbours, other than the unusual trellis pattern carved into the box frames of the first floor sash windows. However, on entering, the visitor is transported into an atmospheric time warp as though walking through a frame into a painting with a time and life of its own, where he becomes part of a *tableau vivant*, part theatre, part fantasy, part invisible performance art and part still-life drama. The visitor experiences each room in silence, absorbing the moods and ambience of each as a mute witness. Severs's aim was to give visitors "a rare moment in which they become as lost in another time as they appear to be in their own".

Severs invented an entirely fictional silk-weaving family – the Jervises – around which the experiences revolve. Half-eaten food and half-filled wine glasses lie strewn around the rooms amongst bowls of fruit, guttered candles and pungent pomanders as if the family has just left the room as one enters. Recorded sounds of the 18th century city outside and from next-door rooms are used to startling theatrical effect to convey the impression of being a silent observer of everyday household life. Clocks chime. A canary chirps. The stairs creak and whispers can be heard just outside the door.

The smoking room is artfully arranged to reflect the Hogarth picture which hangs within it: the miasma of cigars pervading the air. The drawing room is aggrandised and dressed with garlands of walnut shells (opposite below). The boudoir above is left as though the occupants have just risen, with an unmade bed and unemptied chamber pot. As one rises through the house to the top floor the scene shifts to Dickens's London and abject poverty. Washing is hung across the staircase; the paint is peeling. Cobwebs hang in the corners. A thick layer of dust coats every surface and rags hang at the windows.

For all its artifice, stagecraft and illusion, 18 Folgate Street conveys a much more compelling presentation of past London life than the rather sterile, sanitised approach of the great heritage organisations and museums. The motto of the house is "Aut Visum Aut Non!" – "You either see it or you don't". Totally bonkers and utterly wonderful.

Les Trois Garçons

1 Club Row, E1 6JX

Listed: Grade II

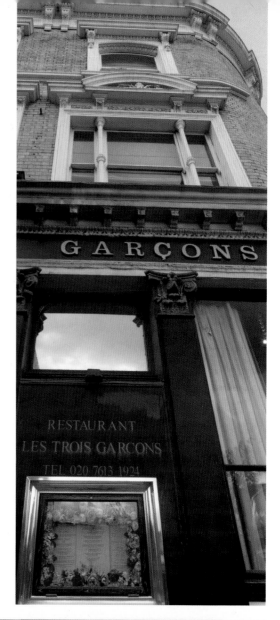

As London's centre of gravity has shifted eastwards over the past 20 years, once unfashionable neighbourhoods have been rediscovered by a new generation of enterprising individuals. As a result peculiar juxtapositions have arisen, and none more peculiar than Les Trois Garçons.

Crafted within the gilt and glass shell of a listed, near derelict, late Victorian public house on the edge of what was once London's most notorious slum, the Old Nichol, is a truly surreal interior.

Les Trois Garçons was founded and designed in 2000 by three business partners with enthusiastic support from Alexander McQueen, Mario Testino and other leading lights of the contemporary arts scene. In a bold reaction against the conventional, minimalist interiors of the time, the restaurant pioneered the theme of camp eclecticism, which has reinforced London's reputation as a creative hotbed of eccentricity.

In homage to the old animal market in Club Row, the partners' collection of taxidermy has been used to adorn the restaurant. Stuffed animals draped in costume jewellery stare balefully at diners from the walls. A stuffed tiger wearing a crystal garland prowls in a corner alongside a chimpanzee smoking a fat cigar and wearing a ducal coronet and iron cross. Lines of handbags hang from the ceiling, interspersed with crystal chandeliers. A gang of china and porcelain animals cavort along the top of the original mahogany bar, a haughty Dalmatian at the centre watched over by two flighty herons.

With its roots in theatre design, and its tongue firmly in cheek, the whole dotty ensemble has been taken up and copied, but never bettered, elsewhere. London remains a wonderfully inventive centre of the creative arts.

Paget Memorial Mission Hall

18-26 Randells Road, n1 0dh
Listed: Grade II

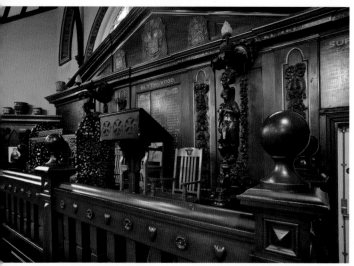

Hidden behind an unprepossessing terrace of late 19th century houses, the Paget Memorial Mission Hall is a poignant tribute to a wife from her grieving husband, and one of London's most bizarre ecclesiastical buildings.

Violet Mary Paget, the daughter of Lord Alfred Paget, was a Mildmay deaconess, who held Bible classes in a temporary iron hut on this site in 1887-9, prior to her marriage to the Reverend Sholto Douglas, later Lord Blythswood. On her death in 1908, her distraught husband was touched to receive a letter of sympathy from one of her pupils and resolved to acquire the site and build a permanent mission hall in her memory. Designed by Beresford Pite, it was opened in the presence of a large number of relatives and friends by HRH the Duchess of Albany on 20 May 1911.

The hall was one of many undenominational missions founded to offer spiritual guidance and social welfare to the deserving poor, but the Paget was unique because it incorporated a wealth of much older 17th and 18th century artefacts, taken from the music room at Sholto Douglas's home at Douglas Support in Lanarkshire following a disastrous fire. While much of the interior can be attributed to Pite, the whole extraordinary melange is quite unlike any other mission in the country.

The pulpit is embellished with two late 17th century Venetian walnut torchères with figures depicting Vice and Virtue beneath a broad oak pediment carrying the arms of Lord Blythswood and memorial panels to his wife's Bible class. Over the lunette window above, and beneath a fine Jacobethan roof, are uplifting evangelical inscriptions, including "The Word of the Lord Endureth For Ever."

Around the perimeter the arcaded panelling is divided by carved cartouches carrying the monogram "VP" by Martin Travers, a pupil of Pite. Running along the cornice above are stencilled gilt violets – a recurrent decorative motif also found carved in the pulpit rails.

A great organ loft bears the organ from Douglas Support carved on four barley-sugar columns with bulbous bases. Adjacent is a simple, pedimented chimneypiece with an overmantel portrait of Violet, but on the south wall are two grotesque chimneypieces, one with a lion rampant in low relief crowned by three statuary figures, the central one of Christ after Thorwaldsen. The other incorporates original Jacobean carving with two massive twisted columns on huge carved bases.

In the Leader's Room is the original Minton breakfast set, a gift to the couple from Queen Victoria.

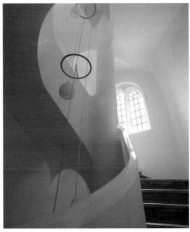

Rudolf Steiner House

35 Park Road, NW1 6XT
Listed: Grade II

Born in Croatia in 1861, Rudolf Steiner – philosopher, architect, mystic and social theorist – was the founder of anthroposophy, a new spiritual movement which attempted to fuse science and mysticism by exploring a union of the rational and the numinous. In later life his ideology was expressed increasingly through art and architecture and "eurythmy", a new art form based on the expression of movement. The little-known London centre, Rudolf Steiner House, is arguably the most important expressionist building in Britain.

For a period in his late 20s, Steiner edited the Goethe archives in Weimar and was influenced strongly by his philosophy. "Just as the eye perceives colour and the ear sounds, so thinking perceives ideas." As leader of the German-Austrian branch of the Theosophical Society, Steiner refined his esoteric and spiritual interests before breaking away in 1912 to form a new group, the Anthroposophical Society. Based at Dornach in Switzerland, Steiner established The Goetheanum, an extraordinary cultural centre built of concrete in an organic expressionist style which was completed in 1928, three years after his death.

A year before he died, Steiner gave his blessing to a new building in London on a site in Park Road, close to Regent's Park. Designed by Montague Wheeler (1874-1937), a pupil of E P Warren, it was built in stages between 1924 and 1938 in cast concrete with granolithic facings. Externally the only hints of expressionist design are in the curved eyebrow hood mould over the shopfront and in the stylised entrance doors, but internally it is remarkable, with sinuous organic staircases reminiscent of the work of Steiner's contemporary Antoni Gaudí in Barcelona, and Erich Mendelsohn's Einstein Tower in Potsdam.

Commenting on his own work, Wheeler wrote: "No forms have been employed for the sake of tradition, and the materials used have been shaped in the manner in which their nature seems to suggest." In his "free and plastic use of concrete", originally modelled in clay, Wheeler closely followed Steiner's principles, to release "its real potentialities". The staircases, restored in 2008, are washed in water-based pastel pigments which enhance the impression of movement and light, and confer an ethereal, spiritual quality on the whole interior.

The main hall, with its expressionistic curves and angles and decoration by Baron Arild Rosencrantz, was designed as a stage for performances of eurythmy, a profound philosophical concept which permeates the form and design of the entire building, including the serpentine patterns on the terrazzo floor, which were revealed as part of a major restoration in 2007-8.

In his advocacy of ethical individualism, Steiner was a prophetic holistic thinker and polymath who anticipated many current issues, including biodynamic agriculture (the precursor of organic farming), complementary medicine, developmental work for those with disabilities, racial tolerance and educational freedom from government control.

Of the 17 buildings designed by Steiner, three have been cited as being amongst the most significant works of modern architecture, yet he remains relatively unknown.

London Central Mosque and Islamic Cultural Centre

146 PARK ROAD, NW8 7RG
UNLISTED

With its burnished copper dome and soaring minaret gracing the skyline, the London Central Mosque and Islamic Cultural Centre adds a touch of Oriental exoticism to the Arcadian views from Regent's Park. However, few are aware that it is also a testament to the close ties of friendship between the UK and the Muslim community. In 1939-40 Lord Lloyd, the Secretary of State for the Colonies, lobbied the government for a site for a London mosque, pointing out that the Empire contained more Muslims than Christians, and that it was anomalous that there was no central place of Muslim worship. In October 1940, at the height of the Battle of Britain, Winston Churchill's War Cabinet authorised £100,000 for the acquisition of the Regent's Park site as a tribute to the thousands of Indian Muslim soldiers who had died defending the British Empire.

The first purpose-built mosque in Britain – the Shah Jahan Mosque – was erected at Woking in 1889, the brainchild of the Jewish Orientalist Dr Gottlieb Wilhelm Leitner, and designed in an Indo-Saracenic style by W I Chambers. In 1941 the East London Mosque was established in three buildings in Commercial Road. Three years later King George VI opened the Islamic Cultural Centre on the current site at Hanover Gate in Regent's Park.

Between 1954 and 1969 a series of designs was commissioned for the mosque, but all failed to receive planning permission. Two years later the Mosque Trust launched an international competition. Over 100 designs were submitted from both Muslim and non-Muslim architects, but the one selected was by the English architect Frederick Gibberd. He produced a mosque with two prayer halls and two three-storey wings containing a library, reading room, study rooms, offices and the minaret, all funded by the Muslim community and donations from King Faisal of Saudi Arabia and Sheikh Zayed bin Sultan Al Nahayan, the ruler of Abu Dhabi.

Externally, compared with the lustrous turquoise tiled domes of the mosques of Central Asia and the Middle East, the London Central Mosque is plain and unadorned, with a simple rhythm of arcades around a central courtyard. This is hardly surprising given Gibberd's modernist background and the sensitive wider townscape context of cream-painted, stucco Regency terraces, but it has worn well with time and does not deserve Pevsner's dismissive comment as "disappointingly banal".

The main prayer hall, designed for 1,800 worshippers, is square in shape with four corner columns and a huge blue central dome resting on a straight drum decorated with bands of Islamic calligraphy and brilliant blue geometric patterns. At the centre is a colossal chandelier. The *mihrab* is a simple niche with an enriched polished brass surround.

In the adjacent wing the elegant modern library has transverse barrel vaults following the shape of the windows.

Blustons

213 Kentish Town Road, NW5 2JU
Listed: Grade II

Blustons was one of eight branches of a family business established by Jane and Samuel Bluston, Jewish Russian émigrés, who arrived in London in the early 20th century. After working in the tailoring business, they set up their first shop in Stoke Newington and opened the branch in Kentish Town in 1931.

Blustons is a rare survival of an inter-war, arcaded shopfront with a central island window display of a type that was once common across London, but which has now virtually disappeared from the high street. In the 1930s arcades and island showcases were used by some West End retailers to entice shoppers off the street and into their premises. The fashion was soon taken up and used by suburban shopkeepers, but subsequently, with pressure to maximise retail floor space, nearly all have vanished. Blustons is exceptional as the window display and arcade occupies virtually half of the entire shop area.

With its black Vitrolite fascia and raised central section framing the legend "Blustons" flanked by diagonal lettering reading "Coats" and "Gowns", it is a throwback to a more refined age. The arcade floor has black and white chequered marble and the display cases have chrome surrounds, those to the side with backs of moulded classical designs and Art Deco sunburst fanlights and mirrors.

Inside, the original counter and shelving have been removed, but the glazed entrance doors with diagonal gilt lettering remain, together with the original pay booth. Portraits of Jane and Samuel hang in a niche at the back of the shop, which remains in family ownership and specialises in frocks and gowns for the older woman.

Highbury Stadium

HIGHBURY SQUARE, AVENELL ROAD, N5 1BU
LISTED: GRADE II (IN PART)

Conservation is about the adaptation of old buildings to new uses. It requires vision, imagination and professional skill of a high order. From 2007 Highbury Stadium was converted into a whole new urban quarter in one of the most unusual conservation projects of recent times under the enlightened direction of the architects Allies & Morrison.

In 1913 Woolwich Arsenal FC arrived in Highbury from the Manor Ground, Plumstead. The club's first stadium, a single stand for 9,000 people with three sides of concrete terracing, was designed by Archibald Leitch, but as the club succeeded on the field, so pressure grew for new facilities. In 1925 it acquired the freehold of the Highbury site, and embarked on an ambitious programme of expansion to emulate the grandeur of Villa Park, the home of Aston Villa FC, which was widely regarded as the most impressive stadium in England.

In 1932 the West Stand was constructed to the designs of Claude Waterlow Ferrier, who worked with the engineer H J Deane to provide covered space for 21,000 people. It was opened by the Prince of Wales to the strains of "For He's a Jolly Good Fellow", the prince waving his bowler hat to a happy multitude of over 60,000 people.

Four years later the magnificent new East Stand was completed in Art Deco style, also by Ferrier but in partnership with Major William Binnie, with an impressively marshalled street elevation to Avenell Road embellished with the club emblem. Within lay the so-called Marble Halls – a fine entrance hall and staircase overlooked by a bronze bust of the manager Herbert Chapman by Epstein, and an opulent Directors' Boardroom (left) and Lounge. The two stands have been described as "the grandest piece of football architecture ever built in Britain with the possible exception of the East Stand at Ibrox Park".

Highbury was the venue for the historic World Heavyweight title boxing match between Henry Cooper and Muhammad Ali in 1966. Arsenal played their last game at Highbury 40 years later in May 2006 before relocating to the new Emirates Stadium at nearby Ashburton Grove.

The adaptation and conservation of the old East and West Stands to flats is the only instance of a listed football stadium being converted to a new use. It is a resounding success. The former pitch is now a new internal London square, transformed into a contemporary garden landscape. New blocks at the north and south ends maintain the original sense of enclosure. The historic East (left middle above) and West Stands have been enclosed by glass curtain wall elevations overlooking the former pitch. The iconic Marble Halls, Directors' Boardroom and Lounge, imbued with the memories of generations of players and fans, have been carefully preserved within the complex of 711 new flats.

W Plumb

493 Hornsey Road, N19 3QL
Listed: Grade II

Until the mid-20th century most high streets were lined with elegant shopfronts in carved timber, bronze or brass which bore testament to British craftsmanship and design. Their interiors were designed to make shopping an aesthetic pleasure, with mahogany fittings, marble counters and encaustic tiles. Today the shops in most high streets have been replaced by identikit aluminium shopfronts bereft of style with hideous plastic fascias and bland interiors devoid of character. Change should never be confused with progress.

As our high streets have been traduced into a repetitive series of clone stores, it is salutary to encounter a survivor from a more elegant age, as it is an indication of just how much has been lost.

W Plumb is a typical local family butcher's shop of a kind which once was familiar, but is now extremely rare. The shop was converted to a butcher's c1900 by Arthur Hancock, who sold it on to Thomas Knowlden in 1911, although it is unclear who specified the elaborate interior. In 1962 the Knowlden family sold the business to an employee, William Plumb, who had worked in the shop for the previous 36 years.

The superb Art Nouveau tiled frieze, dado and wall panels were all manufactured by Burmantofts of Leeds and the fine mosaic floor is by Pilkingtons. Wrought-iron meat racks still hang from the ceiling. At the rear is the original mahogany cashier's booth with etched and frosted glass panels. Unfortunately this was painted in the 1980s for environmental health reasons and the splendid marble and tiled island block removed. The highlights are the beautiful hand-painted tiles depicting pastoral scenes of grazing animals from nearby Hampstead Heath.

Since 2006 the shop has been preserved by a private owner, who lives in the attached flat. On occasion the ghost of a cow is alleged to slam the inner door accompanied by a plaintive "moo".

For those interested to see a similar traditional butcher's shop still in operation, M & R Butchers at the junction of Goswell Road and Chadwell Street lies a couple of miles to the south.

W Martyn

135 Muswell Hill Broadway, N10 3RS
Listed: Grade II

Martyn's is the best-preserved traditional grocer's shop in London. It is virtually unchanged since it was established by the owner's great-grandfather, William Martyn, in 1897. William was born in 1862 in Broad Clyst, Devon, and moved to London in 1890 where he was an apprentice at the Hampstead branch of Walton Hassell and Port before opening his own business seven years later in the new suburb of Muswell Hill, a highly successful piece of town planning laid out by James Edmundson and W J Collins between 1896 and 1914. Martyn's is the only surviving original occupier of the first range of shops to be opened in Queens Parade at the heart of the new suburb.

Externally, the shop was altered twice in the inter-war period, but it retains black Vitrolite stallrisers and a fascia bearing the name W Martyn in crimson raised block capital letters.

Inside is a wonderfully atmospheric grocer's shop from the early 20th century, with produce displayed in the traditional manner. The shop has simple matchboarded linings to the walls with twisted barley-sugar columns and fluted pilasters to the display shelves. Running along one side is a panelled mahogany counter, behind which are semi-circular storage bins with hinged wooden lids and lines of drawers. In front of the counter are old metal biscuit barrels, stacked goods and sacks of coffee. At the rear the hatch to the original cash desk remains.

The shop is currently run by third and fourth generation members of the Martyn family.

Alexandra Palace Theatre

ALEXANDRA PALACE WAY, N22 7AY
LISTED: GRADE II

Sprawling across the heights between Muswell Hill and Wood Green, Alexandra Palace is a great London landmark commanding views across a wide arc of north-east London and Essex.

The global success of the Great Exhibition of 1851 triggered the construction of a wave of similar exhibition buildings worldwide. Originally intended as the Palace of the People, Alexandra Palace was the brainchild of the architect Owen Jones and the engineer Sir Charles Fox, who had both worked on the reconstruction of the Crystal Palace at Sydenham in 1852-4.

The palace was completed in May 1873 by the architects Alfred Meeson and John Johnson using materials salvaged from Captain Francis Fowke's 1862 South Kensington Exhibition building, but it was tragically destroyed by fire just 16 days after its opening. Phoenix-like, it arose again from the ashes, reconstructed once more by Johnson. Two years later it reopened as a huge multi-purpose entertainments complex with a colossal concert hall, incorporating the finest Willis organ in Europe, art galleries, a museum, lecture hall, library and theatre.

Embedded in the north-east corner of the palace complex, the theatre was used for Victorian melodrama and uniquely retains a complete set of Victorian stage machinery designed by Messrs Grieve and Son. The wooden bridges, traps, pulleys and levers used to facilitate scene changes and the projection of props and actors onto the stage is the finest unaltered example in the country. Resembling a large music hall or concert hall, it was never successful as a theatre, and from the early 1900s it was used increasingly for cinema. During the First World War the palace was closed and given over for use as an internment camp for German and Austrian prisoners of war. Prior to its reopening in 1922, the theatre was refurbished by the general manager, W J Macqueen-Pope. Much of the neo-classical decoration dates from this period. A year later it was leased as rehearsal space to Archie Pitt, Gracie Fields' first husband, and it was she who first coined its popular soubriquet "Ally Pally".

On 2 November 1936 the BBC launched the world's first high-definition television service from the palace, and the theatre was consigned to dead storage. During the Second World War the BBC transmitters and iconic mast were used to foil German air raids as part of a network of radio counter-measures assisted by Enigma decrypts from Bletchley Park.

The ill-starred palace suffered another catastrophic fire in 1980, but heroically was restored once again. The theatre has been mothballed with the benefit of grant aid from English Heritage pending a long-term use. Its dark shell still echoes with the voices of those long since passed and the haunting resonance of long-lost dreams.

Underground Reservoir

Claremont Square, N1 9JB
Listed: Grade II

In 1708 a high-level pond was built at the top of Islington Hill above the New River Head to supply the more distant outlying areas of the West End. This Upper Pond was supplied with water pumped from the Round Pond below at the New River Head, initially by a windmill, the circular base of which survives, and later from 1768 by an atmospheric steam engine designed by John Smeaton.

The Upper Pond was progressively embanked to raise the water level. A sizeable reservoir was created, surrounded by a stone-flagged path, of which Thomas Carlyle enthused in 1820: "it was pleasant on fine mornings to take an early promenade".

In 1854-5 the Upper Pond was reconstructed to comply with the Metropolis Water Act 1852 which specified that open reservoirs must be covered over. A huge grid of arcaded brick walls was built within the old pond to carry ranks of segmental arched vaults capable of holding 3.5 million gallons of water. The entire elevated structure was later grassed over to form the raised garden at the centre of Claremont Square.

When the reservoir was drained for cleaning, a rare opportunity was afforded to appreciate the Victorian engineering in all its Piranesian splendour. The reservoir is still used as part of the London Ring Main.

Georgian Orthodox Cathedral Church of the Nativity of Our Lord

Rookwood Road, n16 6ss

Listed: Grade II*

What is now the Georgian Orthodox Cathedral was once the Ark of the Covenant, the spiritual home of the Agapemonites, one of the more colourful Christian sects that emerged in the 19th century.

Known as the Community of the Son of Man, the Agapemonites emerged in the 1840s as followers of Henry Prince, a renegade Anglican minister who established a religious commune – the Agapemone, or Abode of Love – at Spaxton in Somerset. His followers sold their possessions, which funded the development of the commune, and, in 1892-5, an extraordinary church in Clapton for non-resident believers.

The church is a striking composition with a tall Gothic tower, needle spire and four corner turrets each bearing the inscription "God is Love". Four huge apocalyptic bronze winged figures by A G Walker of a lion, an ox, an eagle and an angel taken from the Book of Revelation stand silhouetted against the sky. These are repeated in stone below, trampling underfoot tiny winged human figures representing the trials of earthly life – death, sorrow, crying and pain.

Inside, a great hammerbeam roof covers the entire space. Around the apse is a mosaic band with representations of *The Pelican in her Piety* and *The Phoenix* alongside an inscription from John 11:25: "I am the Resurrection and the Life". The nave benches, fittings and Willis organ are all original, although a later altar has replaced the original throne on which the minister sat. The glory of the interior is the spectacular, semi-opaque stained glass designed by Walter Crane and executed by J S Sparrow depicting Old Testament imagery, symbolic flora and allegorical scenes in a variety of Art Nouveau and Arts and Crafts patterns. The west windows, inspired by the illustrations of William Blake, show a central sun rising over the sea of life with aquatic creatures flanked by windows depicting disease and death and sin and shame with writhing figures tortured by flames and snakes. The whole jolly ensemble encapsulates the eccentric apocalyptic beliefs of the Agapemonites.

In the 1860s Henry Prince achieved notoriety by proclaiming himself the incarnation of the Holy Spirit and practising free love with his harem of attractive women acolytes, but this was nothing compared to the controversy caused by his successor, John Smyth-Pigott, a tall, emaciated figure with glittering black eyes, who on 7 September 1902 suddenly announced from his throne to an astonished congregation: "I who speak to you tonight, I am that Lord Jesus Christ who died and rose again and ascended to heaven. I am that Lord Jesus come again in my own body to save those who come to me from death and judgement."

Smyth-Pigott's blasphemous antics generated "one of the most disgraceful scenes that have ever desecrated an English Sabbath". A full-blown riot ensued, to which police reinforcements were called. Shortly afterwards Smyth-Pigott retreated to the Agapemone, where the "Dear Beloved" consoled himself with his numerous "spiritual brides".

The building later became the Church of the Good Shepherd used by an arm of the Ancient Catholic Church. After lying vacant for several years, it was acquired recently by the Georgian Orthodox Church, which has done excellent work repairing and restoring one of London's more bizarre ecclesiastical buildings.

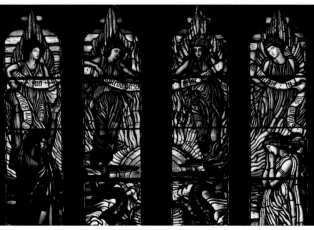

Clapton Park United Reformed Church

LOWER CLAPTON ROAD, E5 0PU
LISTED: GRADE II*

For over 300 years Hackney has had a strong Non-conformist tradition, with a welter of small chapels serving the neighbourhood. Famous Non-conformist figures like Daniel Defoe and Isaac Watts studied and worked at the local academies in Homerton, Hoxton and Newington Green, which were centres of ministerial training.

In 1810, a group of Congregationalists – the Old Gravel Pit community – took the lease on a chapel in Morning Lane. Over the next 40 years the congregation quadrupled. Hackney was changing fast. Between 1841 and 1871 the population rose from 38,000 to 115,000, rising to over 230,000 by 1901. To cater for the spiritual needs of such a rapidly developing area, new churches were built.

By the late 19th century, more progressive Non-conformists were searching for a departure from the traditional plain preaching box in favour of a more distinctive style, one that expressed the more expansive mood of the movement, but that was different from the conventional nave and aisle approach favoured by the Church of England. Innovation and experiment were encouraged.

The Clapton Park United Reformed Church, known as the Round Chapel, is one of the finest Non-conformist churches in London, with a highly distinctive and innovative interior which established a new approach to Non-conformist church design. The architect was Henry Fuller, an established Non-conformist church architect, who had already designed three other chapels in the neighbourhood. Completed in 1891, the interior resembles a huge theatre, with a large unrestricted central auditorium surrounded by a continuous gallery with slender iron columns carrying an arcade of delicate latticework spandrels. Above is deep double coving framing a flat ceiling.

At the east end of the church is a great arch containing the organ case and pulpit, but the design is supremely functional. It enables the entire congregation to see and hear the minister. Behind the main hall are curved ambulatories which facilitate easy access and circulation.

Soon after the completion of the church, a school extension was built adjacent by Fuller's partner James Cubitt in 1873, echoing the Transitional Gothic style of the main building.

With the changing social composition of the area, by the 1980s the congregation had dwindled and the building fell into disrepair. However, in 1991 it was acquired by the Hackney Historic Buildings Trust, which raised over £1m to repair the entire complex using Cazenove Architects. The main chapel is now a flourishing arts and community venue, whilst the Old Schools have been converted to a place of worship. It is a textbook example of how a local community trust can save and adapt a landmark building for the benefit of current and future generations.

L Manze

Eel, pie and mash shops are unique to London and those nearby seaside towns which are frequented by East End families such as Southend. They were started by a small number of families, the Cookes, the Manzes and the Burroughs, all of whom subsequently intermarried.

The Manze family was among the second wave of Italian immigrants who arrived in Britain in the late 19th century and who grew to specialise in popular catering. Michele Manze arrived from Ravello in southern Italy at the age of three in 1878. The family settled in Bermondsey, making a living as ice merchants, and later ice-cream makers. Recognising the need for cheap, nutritious meals catering for the working classes, Michele Manze set up a chain of eel, pie and mash shops. The first shop, established at 87 Tower Bridge Road in 1902, still survives. Thirty years later there were 14 bearing the Manze name, including this one in Walthamstow.

The interior is a superb survival of an early 20th century working-class restaurant. The terrazzo floors are strewn with sawdust. At the entrance is a long marble-topped counter complete with the original cash register. The walls are lined throughout in white ceramic tiles with a dark green and white tiled chequerwork dado divided by rectangular brown edge-tiled panels containing bevelled-edge mirrors. A tiled frieze of green and brown garlands runs in a continuous ribbon around the top of the walls. Below, the tables are set in bays between the original mahogany benches with acorn finials lit by two lines of pendant light fittings above.

Oxford House

DERBYSHIRE STREET, E2 6HG
LISTED: GRADE II

In the late 19th century the East End of London was a foreign country where it was best not to venture. Into this heart of darkness came generations of privileged alumni from England's grandest public schools and universities, who were encouraged to spend time in social and religious work for the church in "settlements" in the poorest urban areas – much as their contemporaries set up Christian missions in the far-flung reaches of the Empire.

Oxford House was established in 1884 by New College and Keble College, Oxford, as an alternative to the more secular Universities Settlement founded by Balliol College at Toynbee Hall, Whitechapel. Seven years later a permanent headquarters was established, designed by (Sir) Arthur Blomfield to accommodate residences for 20 undergraduates, lecture rooms, classrooms, a theatre and a chapel. Its aim was that "The Oxford man ... may learn something of the life of the poor; may try to better the condition of the working classes as regards health and recreation, mental culture and spiritual teaching; and may offer an example, so far as in them lies, of a simple and religious life". Walter Besant described them more bluntly as "lamps in a dark place".

Oxford House was opened by the Duke of Connaught, the Archbishops of Canterbury and York and six other bishops in 1892. The Tudor Revival style of the building was a conscious attempt to evoke the concept of the manor house at the centre of traditional rural society: a deferential hierarchy where benevolent paternalistic gentry supported and moderated the behaviour of the working man; something that was perceived to be totally lacking in the social morass of London's East End. Undergraduates were invited to "Come and be the squires of East London". The more cynical saw them as a refuge for a "surplus of educated gentlemen".

High in the third floor attic is a delightful chapel with a shallow, arched-braced roof and an arcade of octagonal columns along its northern side. At the east end is a timber altar and fine triptych painting from 1914 by Alfred U Soord depicting a grisly Crucifixion embellished with carved doors, tracery and gilding. The inner faces show, to the left, subjects from the Old Testament, and to the right, the Evangelists. At the west end, forming a small narthex, is a neo-Jacobean oak screen with strapwork carving, a wooden cross and obelisk finials. Incised into the panelling are the names of the fallen of the First World War.

This simple chapel offers a compelling view of paternalistic Victorian attitudes to the causes and remedies of poverty in 19th century London, and illuminates the moral fervour and missionary zeal with which practical solutions were pursued.

IN THANKSGIVING TO
ALMIGHTY GOD AND IN
AFFECTIONATE MEMORY
OF HIS TRUE SERVANT
MICHAEL RICHARD
SEYMOUR
Bursar 1913-1922
Head of The Oxford House 1922 until
his death 24th December
1936

He worked devotedly for the Borough
and People of Bethnal Green by
whom he was greatly loved, and by
his Christian example of faithful
worship and loyal service his life
was an inspiration to all who
worked with him.
*Ye know that your Labour is not
in vain in the Lord*

DOUGLAS EYRE
Keble College
Barrister-at-law, Lincoln's Inn
Born 1860 · Died 1933
Resident 1884-1908 · Vice Head 1899-1908
Head 1916-1919

Founder of the Oxford House Club
Webbe Institute and Federation
of Working Men's Clubs
whose Christian humility, ardent
devotion and transparent goodness
were a shining example to generations
of residents and club members.

London Aquatics Centre

OLYMPIC PARK, E20 2ZQ
UNLISTED

Of all the new venues built for the London 2012 Olympics, the most distinctive is the futuristic Aquatics Centre designed by Zaha Hadid. If ever there was a listed building of the future then this is it. Built at a cost of £269m, the building has temporary wings to accommodate 17,500 spectators for the Olympics, after which they will be removed to expose the core complex for use by the local community, with permanent seating for 2,500.

The interior is breathtaking. Two 50m swimming pools and a 25m diving pool holding 10 million gallons of water are contained beneath a vast undulating wave-like roof structure 160m long and 80m wide – larger than Terminal 5 at Heathrow – which both symbolises its function and reflects the surrounding riparian landscape of the Lea Valley and the Olympic Park. Its serpentine silhouette is wholly contemporary, yet echoes the sinuous free forms of Art Nouveau.

Rarely has concrete been modelled with such plasticity and elegance to create such beautiful organic forms. Constructed from 54 tons of concrete, the array of six cantilevered concrete diving boards captures the kinetic energy and movement of the divers for which they were built. The ceiling of the main pool, resembling a rolling wave clad in 30,000 sections of Red Lauro timber, covers arguably the finest new sports building to be erected in Britain for over 50 years.

Much has been written about the legacy of the London 2012 Olympics, but the Aquatics Centre has delivered an important part of it, providing a world-class centre for aquatic sport and a major new architectural icon for the capital.

E Pellicci Café

332 Bethnal Green Road, e2 0ag
Listed: Grade II

London has a long and noble tradition of offering the world's displaced and dispossessed the chance for a new opportunity in life. They, in turn, have added wholly new dimensions to the rich diversity of London's historic neighbourhoods.

In the 1860s the first wave of Italian immigrants arrived as street entertainers, organ grinders and craftsmen, settling in "Little Italy" – the streets around Saffron Hill in Holborn – but later generations of Italians settled more widely and began to specialise in ice cream, cafés and catering.

In 1900 Nevio Pellicci left his poor Tuscan village and headed to London, where he opened an ice-cream parlour. Later, Pellicci's wife Elide commissioned Achille Capocci, an East End Italian carpenter, to craft a fine Art Deco marquetry interior for their premises in Bethnal Green Road. In 1946 the café was refitted with a deep custard-yellow Vitrolite shopfront and fascia with stylised steel letters, and the interior was adapted with the latest stainless steel and Formica fittings.

By the late 1950s the number of cafés in Britain had doubled to 2,000, 500 of which were in London, serving an increasingly affluent new generation of teenagers. This was the golden age of the coffee bar, and Pellicci's is a superb survival from the period.

The steel-topped Formica counter is enriched with a framed panel of sunburst marquetry, while the walls are lined with Capocci's original panelling divided by slender pilasters with Egyptian-style capitals. Each panel has a common central abstract shape, one with a plaque bearing the initials EP. The ceiling is divided by timber astragals into square opaque glazed panels.

The stylish interior is a rare survival which has become an East End institution: the haunt of pop stars, actors from *EastEnders*, diamond geezers and, notably in the 1960s, the Krays.

Royal Foundation of St Katharine

2 BUTCHER ROW, E14 8DS
LISTED: GRADE II*

The Royal Foundation of St Katharine is one of London's oldest and least-known institutions. It was established by Queen Matilda in 1147 as a religious community and hospital for the infirm poor next to the Tower of London on the site now occupied by St Katharine's Dock, and later refounded and re-endowed by the queens consort Eleanor of Castile and Philippa of Hainault. In 1442 it was granted a charter of privileges and became a Liberty with its own prison, officers and court. As a Royal Peculiar, it remained outside the jurisdiction of the City of London. Post-Reformation it was re-established in Protestant form, inhabited by foreign merchants and artisans excluded from the City of London – "English and strangers more in number than some city in England".

In 1825 the entire enclave was demolished for the construction of St Katharine Docks and relocated to a chapel and almshouses in Regent's Park (now the Danish Church) designed by Ambrose Poynter. In 1914 it moved back to the East End to Bromley Hall, Poplar, and finally in 1948 to Limehouse, where it became a spiritual retreat.

Architecturally, it is a rich amalgamation of salvaged artefacts and radical post-war design around the 18th century Master's House, once the home of Matthew Whiting, a sugar refiner and director of the Phoenix Assurance Company, and later the vicarage of St James Ratcliffe.

The house was built in 1795-6, probably by Thomas Leverton, after a disastrous fire destroyed Whiting's earlier home on the site. What makes the house so distinctive is the rare series of late 18th century mural paintings in the ground floor garden rooms. In the drawing room is a classical landscape and a seascape based on Claude's *Arch of Titus* and *Landing of Aeneas* (far left). In the dining room are two more – a seascape by Vernetone showing fortifications against Napoleon (left middle), and an early 19th century painting of Italian subjects by Richard Wilson. The house was badly damaged in the Second World War, but miraculously the murals survived.

A post-war covered cloister (top right) leads from the house to the plain chapel (1951), which contains some remarkable fittings from the original mediaeval site including fragments of richly carved 14th century canopied choir stalls which bear close inspection. They are ranked among the finest of their date in England. Although altered and restored, they date

from the time of Queen Philippa, whose bust, and that of her husband Edward III, appear on the corners, together with an angel with bagpipes and an elephant with castle and rider. A single misericord has the devil seizing two chattering women. Above the west doors filled with stained glass from Poynter's chapel are 17th century carved putti. The 18th century hexagonal marquetry pulpit carries the inscription "Ezra the priest stood upon a pulpit of wood he had made for the preaching". The font in the entrance lobby was a gift from Queen Victoria.

A whole series of fine 17th and 18th century monuments can be found in the chapel and cloister. The altar of dark grey slabs modelled on inscriptions from Roman catacombs is by Ralph Beyer (1954), the crucifixion on the west wall by Michael Groser (1952).

Woolwich Town Hall

WELLINGTON STREET, SE18 6PW
LISTED: GRADE II

Woolwich is believed to take its name from the Anglo-Saxon for "trading place for wool", although there is evidence of earlier Roman and Iron Age settlements. For centuries it was synonymous with England's military-industrial complex, a connection which continues to this day. The Royal Arsenal had already been in place for 40 years when Henry VIII founded the Royal Dockyard in 1512. Given its strategic location on the river commanding the route into London, it soon developed into a garrison town. The Royal Military Academy arrived in 1741, followed by the Royal Artillery Barracks (1776-1802), whose colossal attenuated Georgian façade is the largest continuous elevation in the country.

With the reorganisation of local government, in 1900 Woolwich was amalgamated with Eltham and Plumstead to form the new Metropolitan Borough of Woolwich. A magnificent new town hall was erected which boasts one of the finest civic interiors in London.

Designed between 1903 and 1906 by (Sir) Alfred Brumwell Thomas, the architect of Belfast City Hall, it is a florid essay in the Baroque Revival executed with real panache. The soaring red-brick and stone clock tower is a prominent local landmark, but the real *tour de force* is the interior, which is a self-confident expression of Edwardian civic pride in one of London's poorest neighbourhoods. It was opened on 13 January 1906 by the local Labour MP, Will Crooks.

Victoria Hall, the voluminous, triple-domed and galleried hall, is truly imperial in scale, with a staircase dominated by a fine white marble statue of Queen Victoria by Frederick W Pomeroy embellished with rich ornamental plasterwork, coffered arches and elaborate pendant lights. Stained-glass windows by Geoffrey Webb depict notable local historical events, including the visit of Charles I to the dockyard in 1637 to see his great ship the *Sovereign of the Seas*. The elegant domed council chamber retains its original finely carved joinery.

Crossness Engine House

Belvedere Road, SE2 9AQ
Listed: Grade I

Crossness Sewage Works is a crucial component of the most important public infrastructure project ever built in London. Hailed as a masterpiece of Victorian engineering, the engine house is a veritable cathedral of ironwork.

In the 50 years from 1800, London's population rose from 1.1 million to 2.7 million without any commensurate investment in the sanitary infrastructure required to support such a growth. The concept of environmental health was as alien to most Victorian minds as the connection between dirt and disease. Cholera was believed to be spread by a miasmatic vapour. Urban life was a nightmare for the poor. Cholera, typhoid, the white plague (TB) and typhus stalked the capital. Over 10,000 Londoners died in the cholera epidemic of 1853-4. Four years later, during the long hot summer of 1858, the Great Stink overshadowed the city: a smell so pungent that plans were made to evacuate the House of Commons.

Punch lampooned the city fathers:

> Filthy River, filthy river
> Foul from London to the Nore,
> What art thou but one vast gutter,
> One tremendous common shore.

As a result of public outrage, the Metropolitan Board of Works, which had been founded two years earlier, was empowered to construct a vast new sewerage system for the metropolis under the enlightened direction of its chief engineer, Sir Joseph Bazalgette (1819-91).

Bazalgette devised a visionary engineering solution. Three massive intercepting sewers were built running parallel to the river. Hidden beneath great embankments, these were ovoid in shape to optimise flow and facilitate self-cleaning, diverting foul water from the old sewers and culverted rivers eastwards to great holding tanks at Abbey Mills and Crossness, where it was pumped into the river on the ebbing tide.

Opened in April 1865 by the Prince of Wales, and designed by Bazalgette and the architect Charles Henry Driver, Crossness is a wonderful expression of the exuberance and confidence of the Victorian age. Behind the plain grey gault and red brick exterior, the spectacular engine house is a riot of Victorian ironwork containing four beam engines built by James Watt & Co, named Prince Consort, Victoria, Albert and Alexandra. With 52-ton flywheels and 47-ton beams, they are believed to be the largest rotative beam engines in the world.

In 2003 Prince Consort was restored to working order by the Crossness Engines Trust, which has managed the site since 1987 and is restoring the entire complex to its former glory with the benefit of grant aid from English Heritage and the Heritage Lottery Fund.

A memorial bronze of Bazalgette can be found in central London at the foot of Northumberland Avenue on the Embankment, which he created.

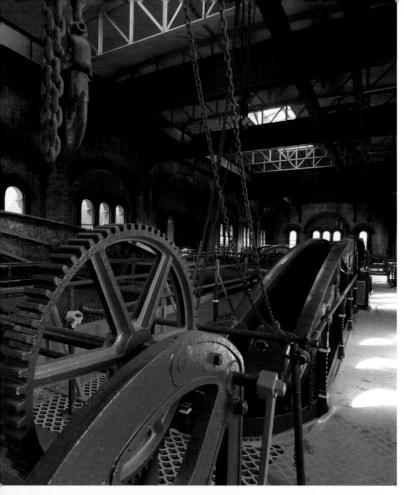

Master Shipwright's House and Office
Old Royal Naval Dockyard

WATERGATE STREET, SE8 3JF
LISTED: GRADE II*

Deptford is an area of immense historic interest. It takes its name from Depeford, after a deep ford across the River Ravensbourne near its influx with the Thames. It was here in 1513 that Henry VIII established the Royal Dockyard, a year after facilities had been completed at Woolwich as part of his huge naval expansion programme, which laid the foundations for England's naval supremacy. By the 1540s King's Yard, as it was known, was the most important royal dockyard in the country, a position it enjoyed for over 100 years before being superseded by Chatham, and later Portsmouth and Plymouth. It was at Deptford that the ships *Resolution* and *Adventure* were equipped for Captain Cook's second voyage to the Pacific, and later *Discovery* for his final voyage. For a while Cook lived across the river in Mile End.

The master shipwright was the senior technical officer in the dockyard, and a house was provided for him on site. In 1705 Joseph Allin petitioned the Navy Board for permission to rebuild his "ancient and decayed quarters" on the site of an older, timber-framed house. It was constructed by dockyard workers, and completed by 1708, probably to Allin's own design. A single-storey brewhouse range was added to the north-east two years later, and by 1720 the adjacent offices had been rebuilt along similar lines. Subsequently the house was remodelled for Sir Henry Peake, the master shipwright in 1803, and the brewhouse range was incorporated, recast as a garden room and entrance hall with a two-storey extension at the east end.

Surviving timber marks from 1809 are the first tangible evidence for the new production and management systems introduced by Sir Samuel Bentham (1757-1831), the Inspector General of Naval Works, in 1796. Bentham rationalised the running of the dockyard, with timber masters charged with the central inspection of all its functions to minimise timber wastage and theft, a concept Bentham had deployed earlier in Russia, where he oversaw naval construction for Prince Potemkin. The principle of central inspection was adopted later by his philosopher brother Jeremy Bentham (see pp 137) for the layout of a 'Panopticon' prison.

Recent research has identified that floor joists in the offices are reused ships' timbers. In the house, the principal staircase from ground to first floor level has a fine open-string staircase with a ramped handrail, twisted balusters and Doric newels, and late Georgian joinery throughout.

With the need to service ever larger ships, and the silting up of the Thames, the yard declined. It was closed finally in 1869, after which it was used as a cattle market. Subsequent redevelopment and massive wartime destruction resulted in the loss of virtually all the surrounding buildings.

Today the house and offices are all that remain of one of Britain's great naval powerhouses. It was here that Sir Francis Drake was knighted and the *Golden Hind* was displayed for over 70 years. It was here for three months in 1698 that Czar Peter the Great arrived to study ship-building. He stayed at Sayes Court, John Evelyn's house, near to which Evelyn discovered the young Grinling Gibbons and launched him on his career as a master carver and sculptor.

A range of early 18th century sea captains' houses survives in nearby Albury Street.

Danson House

DANSON PARK, BEXLEYHEATH, DA6 8HL
LISTED: GRADE I

Once London's most notorious and intractable building at risk, Danson House was saved from dereliction by the direct intervention of English Heritage, which acquired the house in 1995.

Danson is the epitome of the perfect Palladian villa – so chastely detailed and impeccably proportioned that one might be forgiven for thinking it was on the outskirts of Vicenza rather than the more prosaic suburbs of Bexleyheath.

It was designed by Sir Robert Taylor and built between 1764 and 1767 for Sir John Boyd, a West Indian sugar merchant from St Kitts, later deputy chairman of the East India Company. Raised on a hill above the surrounding landscape, it remains a prominent landmark. A 1782 guidebook commented: "The house presents itself to the view of every traveller, between ten and eleven milestones on the Dover Road". Standing in over 600 acres, the estate was landscaped by Nathaniel Richmond in 1761-3 including sweeping lawns and a lake, beyond which was an eyecatcher in the form of a "Gothick" cottage with a thin tapering lead spire, which still survives in Blackfen Road.

After the death of Sir John in 1800, his son demolished the original wings and built a detached stable block to designs attributed to George Dance the Younger, but seven years later the estate was sold to John Johnson, a retired army captain. In turn, in 1863 his son sold the estate to a local railway engineer and developer, Alfred Bean, in whose family it remained until the death of his widow in 1924, at which time it was acquired by Bexley Urban District Council as a public amenity. During the Second World War the house was given over to civil defence duties, after which it went into progressive decline. In February 1991 it reached its nadir when a lessee stripped the interior of its chimneypieces, doorcases, doors and plasterwork. Fortunately the chimneypieces were retrieved by HM Customs, and the remaining artefacts were found a year later in a container in Dagenham.

Between 1996 and 2005 English Heritage carried out an award-winning restoration of the house in three distinct phases, culminating in the restoration of the interiors aided by a set of 1860 watercolours by Sarah Johnson.

At the centre of the house is a magnificent elliptical cantilevered stone staircase rising to an elliptical dome carried on eight Ionic columns surrounded by painted *trompe-l'oeil* stone coffers. The entrance hall has been restored to its original colour scheme, while the octagonal Saloon has been reinstated with real panache with replicated mirrors, based on the Johnson watercolours, and blue chinoiserie wallpaper. In the library the rare surviving domestic chamber organ built by George England has been lovingly restored.

Reopened by the Queen in July 2005, responsibility for the house has been transferred to the Bexley Heritage Trust.

Danson House is a triumph. It demonstrates that even the most dilapidated historic buildings can be saved from ruin through determination and vision, and that expert historical and technical research is essential in striking the right balance between careful conservation and informed restoration.

Eltham Palace

COURT YARD, SE9 2QE

LISTED: GRADE I

Eltham Palace is a rare survival of a mediaeval royal palace, initially given to Edward II by the Bishop of Durham in 1305, and subsequently extended and used as a royal residence. At Christmas 1400 Henry IV entertained Manuel Palaeologus, the Byzantine Emperor, here, and in 1416 Henry V forged an alliance with Sigismund, the Holy Roman Emperor, during a visit to discuss Church affairs. Eltham was also the scene of the meeting between the nine-year-old Prince Henry (later Henry VIII) and the Dutch philosopher Erasmus, who was challenged to write a poem, which he duly did within three days. However, increasingly the palace was eclipsed by Greenwich, and it fell into slow decline, becoming a tenanted farm before a rather intrusive restoration by the Office of Works in 1894-5.

In 1933 Stephen and Virginia Courtauld acquired the building and commissioned the architects Seely & Paget to restore the Great Hall and design a new adjacent home for their collection of art and furniture. The result was a controversial juxtaposition of the mediaeval and modern, which caused outrage in certain circles. The historian G M Young wrote to the *Times* fulminating that "three distinguished architects united their talents and intelligence to destroy one of the most beautiful things remaining in the neighbourhood of London" for "an unfortunately sited cigarette factory". However some of the leading craftsmen and designers of the day – the painters Winifred Knights and Tom Monnington, the Swedish designer Rolf Engstromer and the Italian decorator Peter Malacrida – were employed to produce a series of highly eclectic interiors ranging from the historical to the Moderne, using the best materials including native and exotic woods.

The entrance hall is breathtakingly modern, with light flooding in from above through a perforated concrete and glass dome. The triangular space has rounded corners, the walls lined with Australian blackbean veneer inlaid with marquetry panels of a Roman soldier and a Viking against scenes from Italy and Scandinavia, including the newly completed, iconic Stockholm Town Hall. The Drawing Room by Peter Malacrida has false beams decorated with Hungarian folk art and plaster panels of relief sculpture to the window reveals by Gilbert Ledward. A corridor leads to the monumental Great Hall with its superb hammerbeam roof, after Westminster Hall, the largest of its kind ever built at that time. The minstrels' gallery and armorial stained glass are recent embellishments added by the Courtaulds, who filled the hall with antique furniture.

Upstairs are Stephen Courtauld's Suite, an aspen-lined bedroom and blue vitreous mosaic bathroom, and Virginia's Bedroom, with curved walls lined with maple flexwood and sycamore pilasters inlaid with playful marquetry. Her vaulted bathroom is stunning, with a huge gold mosaic niche containing a statue of the goddess Psyche above a bath resembling a sarcophagus. Further on lie the quarters of the Courtauld's

famous ring-tailed lemur – Mah Jongg. "Jongy's" sleeping quarters enjoyed central heating, walls decorated with bamboo forest scenes and a bamboo ladder which allowed him to roam downstairs to the Flower Room.

The circuit of principal rooms is completed by the Dining Room, also by Malacrida, a famous piece of Moderne design with walls lined with bird's eye maple, and a ceiling with a rectangular central recess entirely covered in aluminium leaf comparable with the Park Lane Hotel (p101). The doors, and the fireplace with its ribbed aluminium sides, are enriched with geometrical fretwork, the doors decorated with delightful ivory-coloured reliefs of animals and birds modelled from London Zoo.

After the Courtaulds left in 1944, the site was occupied by various Army educational units until 1995 when English Heritage assumed responsibility for its management and subsequent impeccable restoration.

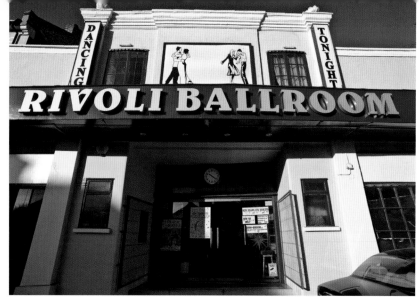

Rivoli Ballroom

346-350 Brockley Road, SE4 2BY
Listed: Grade II

The Rivoli Ballroom is a rare surviving example of a full-blown 1950s conversion of a former cinema to a dance hall catering for the age of jazz, swing and rock and roll.

Designed by Henley Attwater, it opened as the Picture Palace cinema in 1913 opposite Crofton Park Station in the suburbs of Lewisham. After various changes of venue, it was refurbished, extended and reopened in 1931 as the Rivoli Cinema seating 700. For the next 26 years it remained independently operated, until 1957 when it closed in the face of competition from the big cinema chains and television. After two and a half years lying dormant, it was adapted and converted to a ballroom by Leonard Tomlin, a local businessman and enthusiastic dancer, whose relative had been a lessee of the original cinema in 1917.

The plush interior is a creative amalgamation of Art Deco, neo-classical and Oriental motifs to create an exotic venue for the increasingly affluent teenagers of the 1960s. The raked foyer, lined with Deco-style parquetry panels in dark wood inlay with diamond-shaped glazed centres, leads to the spectacular ballroom – a long barrel-vaulted room with a raised viewing dais, proscenium and stage with fixed banquette seating and a purpose-built, sprung Canadian maple dance floor. The lush exuberant décor of red velour padded walls, gilt panels, scallop lights, French chandeliers and Chinese lanterns is wonderfully kitsch and redolent of the period of winkle-pickers and flared skirts.

Along each side are two long narrow bars – one lined with booths and tables in leather upholstery resembling a railway carriage, the other with a front of tiled, interlaced Arabesque patterns. Beyond is a separate late 20th century function room with a ceiling covered in prints of Old Masters.

Now achingly fashionable, many will recognise the offbeat interior as a backdrop for music and fashion shoots, DVDs and television series. There is nothing quite like it anywhere else in London.

Dulwich College

Dulwich Common, se21 7ld
Listed: Grade II*

"The new boy, donning the Dulwich cap for the first time, may well deem himself a potential hero ... for he stands bedazzled in the glory of past years which scintillate with innumerable grand deeds and grander men" (*Westminster Gazette*, 1922).

Dulwich College was founded in 1619 by Edward Alleyn (1556-1626), fêted by Ben Jonson and Christopher Marlow as the most admired actor of his day. Together with his business partner, the entrepreneur Philip Henslowe, he developed a lucrative property portfolio as the owner of theatres, beer gardens and bear-baiting pits in Southwark. As "Chief Master, Ruler and Overseer of ... his majestie's games", he supplied animals to the King for entertainment and baiting across the river at the Tower of London, and as a result amassed a large fortune.

In 1605 he acquired the manorial estate of Dulwich, where he established a hospital for almsfolk and a school for 12 orphan boys. For over 200 years the college struggled financially, until 1857, when it was reformed by the Dulwich College Act. A new Board of Governors was created with twin responsibilities – the educational (for the college) and the eleemosynary (for the charity). Under the enlightened tutelage of Canon Alfred Carver, between 1859 and 1883 Dulwich established itself as one of the great British public schools. To accommodate a rapidly expanding intake of pupils, a whole new range of buildings was developed – the New College.

The architect was Charles Barry Jr, president of the RIBA and the eldest son of Sir Charles Barry, the architect of the Palace of Westminster. He was given a free hand to produce a building "worthy of our aspirations and resources". The result was an eclectic building influenced by numerous references which Barry had assimilated throughout his career and a style which he called North Italian of the 13th century. The ground plan is classical, with a centrepiece and wings linked by cloisters. The main blocks echo the Palazzo Thiene in Vicenza, and the gables on the centre blocks the cathedrals of Orvieto and Siena. However, the main sources of inspiration which permeate the whole composition were the Certosa di Pavia, or Charterhouse, near Milan, and the work of his father at Westminster.

The Great Hall is modelled on Westminster Hall – a great hammerbeam roof and barrel vault with a central lantern and half-wagon wheels inspired by the church of San Fermo in Vicenza. The ends of the hammerbeams are carved as wyverns, the spandrels beneath enriched with the college arms. Built in deal and intended to have a blond finish, in 1911 the timbers were stained dark and the original elaborate Arabesque decoration overpainted with simple stencilling, eroding Barry's original concept. The Great Hall was the spiritual heart of the college, where boys were transformed into Alleynians, as base metal into gold, through music, drama and debate.

Elsewhere, in the Master's Library pride of place is given to a 17th century wooden chimneypiece with two panels of allegorical figures depicting *Pieta* and *Liberalitas*, believed to have been acquired by Alleyn from Queen Elizabeth's state barge. The Governors' Board Room has a deeply coved ceiling divided into hexagonal panels. Pictures of distinguished masters gaze down benignly from pink-papered walls.

The school library has a splendid collection of books and manuscripts, including two of the three volumes of the first folio of Shakespeare, first editions of poetry by John Donne, Edmund Spencer and John Dryden, and a 15th century *Book of Hours*.

Famous alumni include Sir P G Wodehouse, C S Forester, Bob Monkhouse, Sir Ernest Shackleton and Group Captain 'Kit' Lowe, the England rugby international and First World War flying ace, allegedly the inspiration for 'Biggles'.

The *James Caird*, the whaler in which Shackleton made his momentous 800-mile voyage from Elephant Island to South Georgia during the Antarctic winter of 1916, is preserved in the Shackleton Building as an inspiration to pupils and a lasting memorial to his epic feat of endurance and survival against all odds.

Sons of the Mother, forth we go,
'Neath tropic suns, to the Polar snow
(The Edward Alleyn Song, 1911)

Superb!

Christ's Chapel of Alleyn's College of God's Gift

DULWICH COLLEGE, SE21 7AE
LISTED: GRADE II

Christ's Chapel is the core of Edward Alleyn's original endowment, and the heart of the "Old College". It took John Benson, a bricklayer of Westminster, three years to build, but on 1 September 1616 it was consecrated by the Archbishop of Canterbury before an audience which included the Lord Chancellor, Francis Bacon. Ten years later Alleyn was interred here beneath a black stone slab.

The chapel suffered several failures. During the Commonwealth it was occupied by soldiers from Fairfax's army who "committed grave havoc", but under Reverend James Hume, who was chaplain from 1706 to 1728, the foundation was put on a much sounder financial footing. It was Hume who made the gift of the marble font and copper cover designed by James Gibbs which is inscribed with the Greek palindrome "Wash away sin, not the visage only". The organ with its carved case and ornamental pipework (1760) is believed to be the earliest surviving work of George England.

The plain white walls are dominated by two huge paintings – a 16th century copy of Raphael's *Transformation* presented by Thomas Mills in 1769, and a copy of Raphael's *Ansidei Madonna* by Ethel Galer, a local resident.

In 1825 a new south aisle was added, and in the 1850s an oak screen, pulpit and splendid pews carved with figures and animals were installed to enhance the setting of the Founder's Tomb. The improvements culminated in 1911 in the installation of a fine new reredos with painted panels by W D Caroe including a central panel depicting the Epiphany, with two boy attendants wearing the costume of the first Scholars at the school. Beneath the gallery on the south wall is a memorial to the many Old Alleynians who fell in the Great War.

The adjacent Dulwich Picture Gallery (1811-14) by Sir John Soane was Britain's first public art gallery, built to house a large collection of paintings, originally intended to form the nucleus of a collection of the last King of Poland but bequeathed to the college by Sir Francis Bourgeois.

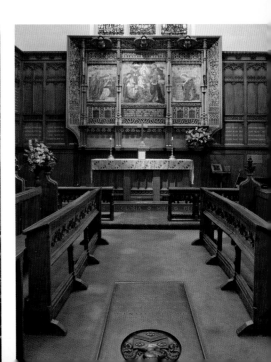

Spirit Collection
Darwin Centre
Natural History Museum

Cromwell Road, SW7 5BD
Listed: Grade I

The majestic central hall and galleries of the Natural History Museum are one of London's greatest public interiors. They house the largest and most important natural history collections in the world – over 70 million specimens from mammoth skeletons to Martian meteorites, including 55 million animals, 9 million fossils, 6 million plants and over 500,000 rocks and minerals.

The famous Romanesque façade and galleries, designed by Alfred Waterhouse between 1873 and 1880, incorporate faience blocks depicting reliefs of both living and extinct species as part of the structural design of the building that offer an insight into the prevailing scientific knowledge of the time.

At the western end of the frontage the new Darwin Centre is a bold, contemporary glass extension (2008) by the Danish practice C F Møller Architects, within which is a breathtaking eight-storey concrete cocoon (the largest sprayed-concrete structure in Europe), which contains the entomology and botanical collections.

The Zoology Spirit Building within the Centre is home to a flabbergasting collection of 22 million preserved specimens stored on 17 miles of shelves. Here you can find a bewildering array of fish, snakes, amphibians, deep sea invertebrates and reptiles in row upon row of exhibits. A highlight of the mollusc collection is Archie, a 28ft giant squid, caught off the Falkland Islands in the South Atlantic in March 2004. Archie is preserved in a large wet storage tank in a formalin and saline solution, and his DNA has been sent for analysis. A year later a juvenile specimen of a colossal squid was caught off South Georgia, and this too is now among the exhibits.

The specimen jars and matchboxes of labels were photographed shortly before the old Spirit building was demolished, after which they were removed to the more modern storage facilities and exhibition areas within the Darwin Centre.

DUMERIL'S GREAVED-TORTOISE
(PODOCNEMIS DUMERILIANA)
NORTHERN S. AMERICA

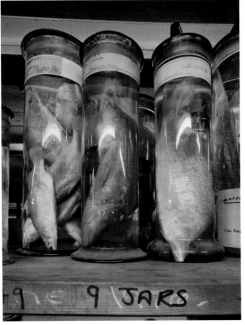

Old Vestry Hall
Chelsea Town Hall

King's Road, SW3 5EE
Listed: Grade II*

The Old Vestry Hall at Chelsea Town Hall, designed by the architect J M Brydon for a competition in 1884-5, is one of the first municipal buildings in the revived English Baroque, or "Wrenaissance" style. At the time the *Builder* purred: "the luxuriance of the style, the freedom and fancy of its ornaments, and the way in which every part seems to laugh at all rule and constraint, make it far more appropriate for a building like a modern 'town hall', to be used, we imagine … for banquets, balls, concerts and such frivolities".

Built as an extension to an earlier building, it is tucked away at the rear of the site, facing Manor Gardens and connected to the later frontage range (1903-4 by Leonard Stokes) by a long, elegant passage with saucer domes and a bust of Leigh Hunt by Joseph Durham. The interior of the Vestry Hall is executed with real panache for its date: richly detailed with grouped pilasters, paired columns of Devonshire marble, circular attic windows with putti and swags, and unusually detailed Baroque doorcases.

However, what makes the space special is the series of murals depicting art, religion, literature, politics, history and science, each portraying eminent Chelsea residents from all periods and painted by Charles Sims, Frank O Salisbury, Mary Sargent and George Woolway. They are of considerable importance in the history of mural paintings, not only because of their didactic purpose in celebrating Chelsea's contribution to the nation and the Empire, but because of their overt symbolism. The female personification of their themes reflected popular sentiments about the rights of women. At the centre of Charles Sims' *History* is Elizabeth I with Nell Gwynne and the wives of Henry VIII alongside. In *Politics*, *History* and *Science* Elizabeth Fry and the religious writer Mary Astell are prominent in the foreground.

With their hidden feminist agenda, the murals were highly controversial at the time, but the row over the feminine iconography was eclipsed by the furore over the inclusion of Oscar Wilde in *Literature*; one councillor complaining that the hall was being turned into an "exhibition of criminals".

Sir Claude Phillips, the director of the National Gallery, referred to the Chelsea murals as "a matter which concerns not only the borough itself, but … the whole of London, nay the whole of the United Kingdom … The art that is destined to adorn the secular temples and palaces of the people … must not only be decorative, satisfying to the eye, but didactic – expressive of great moments in the psychological life of a nation, of great syntheses, of great symbolisms".

Connected to the Vestry Hall by a long corridor is the Small Hall, which is also treated lavishly, with a minstrels' gallery over the entrance and a fine marble chimneypiece incorporating a clock. The ladies' cloakrooms have rather good modern faded classical *trompe-l'oeil* decorations by Rory Ramsden painted by Blaise Designs.

Wandsworth Town Hall

WANDSWORTH HIGH STREET, SW18 2PU
LISTED: GRADE II

Wandsworth Town Hall was built in four separate phases over a 60-year period, but the rather ragged piecemeal complex of buildings was given a clear compositional focus in 1935-7 when a large Moderne-style building was erected as the architectural centrepiece of a wider redevelopment of the town centre.

Located on a triangular corner site with low-hipped pantiled roofs and pavilions topped by tall flagstaffs, the building has a distinctly late-colonial flavour and would not be out of place in Singapore or Rangoon.

It was designed by Edward A Hunt, who was responsible for numerous buildings in the area, with restrained classical elevations of Portland and Corsham stone, the High Street frontage with a bas-relief frieze depicting scenes from local history by David Evans and John Linehan. Beneath the corner entrance a carriageway leads to a small courtyard garden and the principal ceremonial entrance for municipal events.

The entrance hall is a superb period piece and one of the best-preserved town hall interiors of its time. The walls are lined with beautifully patterned African onyx. At the centre a grand Imperial stair with an intricate bronze-scrolled balustrade leads to the upper hall, which has a glazed ceiling from which is suspended a ritzy Art Deco chandelier. The theme is continued in the principal rooms beyond, which are oak panelled with moulded cornices and pink Art Deco light fittings and, in the Mayoral Parlour, a tapestry overmantel. The hexagonal Council Chamber has diagonal-paned top lights and another elaborate chandelier.

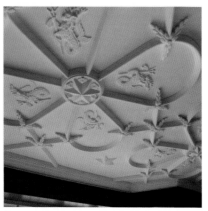

Crosby Hall

DANVERS STREET, SW3 5AZ

LISTED: GRADE II*

History likes patterns. In one of those peculiar chronological resonances that echo through the history of London, a mediaeval City merchant's house is being restored to its full splendour, over 500 years after it was first built, by a modern City financier to form the centrepiece of a phenomenal new riverside home for himself and his family. Quietly but inexorably, a vast new private palace has arisen beside the Thames in Chelsea to provide the perfect setting for Crosby Hall, London's most important surviving domestic mediaeval building. It is the fulfilment of a vision which has inspired its benefactor, Christopher Moran, for his entire adult life.

Crosby Hall was built in Bishopsgate between 1466 and 1475 for Sir John Crosby, a wealthy City merchant, diplomat and ardent Yorkist. It was later occupied by Richard III, as Duke of Gloucester, and Sir Thomas More, after which it enjoyed a chequered existence as an early headquarters of the East India Company, a Dissenters' chapel, a warehouse and latterly a restaurant. Threatened with demolition, it could have been destined for the roof of Selfridge's, but in 1910 it was dismantled and relocated to Chelsea by the LCC under the watchful eye of the architect Walter Godfrey, where it was re-erected on the site of part of Sir Thomas More's old garden for subsequent use by the British Federation of University Women. In 1988 it was acquired by Moran, who embarked on one of the most remarkable post-war building projects London has seen.

Advised by a team of eminent experts, a great neo-Tudor mansion has been crafted painstakingly over the past 15 years as an authentic setting for the original hall and Moran's own spectacular collection of 15th and 16th century furniture and paintings. It is a glorious celebration of British craftsmanship and the full-blown reimagining of a stately Tudor mansion constructed over a period of 150 years, but one accurately modelled on a variety of historical precedents.

The entrance range, inspired by Hampton Court, leads to an Elizabethan garden designed by the Marchioness of Salisbury with an ornamental fountain of Diana by Neil Simmons derived from one at Nonsuch Palace. Beyond, Walter Godfrey's old building has been completely reworked and embellished to form the Council Chamber (p368 bottom and p369), which is approached through a grand Corinthian doorcase. The massive oak door (p368) is embellished with the head of Medusa and inlaid on its inner face with intricate marquetry work.

The room beyond is breathtaking. Over the fireplace is a huge bronze of the owner embellished with his personal motifs – the sea stag and stars. To one side a traditional spyhole hidden in the plasterwork enables the host to time his entrance before his guests to maximum effect. At one end of the chamber is an oak staircase with carved sea stag newel posts leading to a gallery and on into the original great hall; at the other, to an antechamber (the Star Chamber) and on into the huge dining room (below), modelled on Kirby Hall in Northamptonshire, the centrepiece of which is a massive oak dining table hewn from a single 45ft length of timber and lit by heraldic stained glass in the fashion of the late 16th century.

On the upper floors a new long gallery is coming to fruition (right), but it will be several years yet before the whole remarkable vision is fulfilled, including a full-blown chapel beneath the original great hall where, fittingly, the owner will lie for eternity in his private mausoleum in a building which is a monument to his single-minded vision.

Battersea
Power Station

CRINGLE STREET, SW8 4NB
LISTED: GRADE II*

With its sublime external silhouette that has made it one of London's most iconic riverside landmarks, Battersea Power Station is also its most conspicuous listed building at risk, and the largest brick building in Europe.

It was built over a period of 25 years by the London Power Company as two individual power stations side by side. Station A was begun in March 1929, but not completed until 1935, was only complemented by its identical twin, Station B, in 1953-5 when the fourth, south-east chimney was completed. In its heyday the site provided one-fifth of London's entire electricity supply; the most thermally efficient power station in the world had 338ft-high chimneys fitted with water and alkaline scrubbers to minimise sulphur emissions and atmospheric pollution. The waste heat was used to power the Pimlico district heating scheme.

Both stations were designed to form a coherent whole under a design team led by S Leonard Pearce with Henry Allot as consulting engineer, but in order to appease public opinion, exercised at the construction of such a monumental industrial complex on the banks of the Thames, Sir Giles Gilbert Scott was brought in to remodel the exterior with his characteristic use of sparse but subtle ornamental brick detail of brown Blockley brick cladding over a colossal steel frame.

The inside of Control Room A overlooking the original turbine hall, is like a vision from Fritz Lang's *Metropolis*. It is the work of J Theo Halliday in an extraordinary transmutation of Art Deco cinema design to an industrial utility. The quality of the finishes is astonishing. The walls are lined with Ribbon Napoleon marble, with black Belgian marble fluting to the windows. The ceiling is divided into eight huge bays, each coffered and glazed with linear decorative lighting and the original Halophane light fittings. The original L-shaped control panel and walnut veneer furniture all still survive in front of an intriguing array of levers and dials.

The post-war Control Room B (right middle), which opens directly into its own turbine hall, is plainer, but nonetheless impressive, with faience cladding and an arc of stainless steel control panels. Above, the upper control room, added in the 1950s, retains its banks of control desks and panels.

The power station remains one of London's most intractable conservation problems. Since its closure in 1983, it has defeated three major attempts by developers to adapt and convert the building as part of a massive regeneration of the wider area. Its long-term future remains uncertain, but behind its forlorn brick shell lies one of London's most atmospheric and awe-inspiring spaces.

Stockwell Bus Garage

BINFIELD ROAD, SW4 6ST
LISTED: GRADE II*

Given the shortage of steel for major infrastructure projects in post-war Britain, necessity was the mother of invention. A number of highly innovative buildings were erected with futuristic roof structures that were a combination of architectural bravura and cutting-edge engineering.

London Transport had a long tradition of pioneering progressive new architecture and design. In 1937 Oliver Hill designed a bold new bus station for Newbury Park comprising seven semi-circular concrete arches with open ends. As a result of the Second World War it was eventually built 10 years later, and it encouraged a vogue for similar structures.

At the time of its construction in 1952 Stockwell Bus Garage was the largest area under a single roof in Europe. The architects Adie, Button & Partners and the engineer A E Beer used post-war shortages to their advantage and produced an heroic feat of engineering for a utilitarian public purpose.

Formed from ten shallow, double-hinged ribs graduating in depth from 10ft 6in at the ends to 7ft in the centre, the soaring, whale-backed roof spans 159ft across 73,350 square feet of unobstructed floorspace capable of accommodating 200 double-decker buses. Between each pair of ribs, cantilevered barrel vaults filled with a network of glazed rooflights permit bands of light to stream down, flooding the interior. Externally the flowing roofline is supported on angled buttresses enclosed by repetitive bays of vertical lights and double doors.

Stockwell was highly praised at the time. It fostered other innovative roof structures, including the famous hyperbolic paraboloid roof over the Commonwealth Institute in 1962 (by Robert Matthew, Johnson-Marshall & Partners), and the lesser-known shallow elliptical paraboloid dome over the rebuilt Poultry Market at Smithfield (1963 by T P Bennett & Sons), to which it passed the accolade for the largest clear span in Europe.

575 Wandsworth Road

SW8 3JD
LISTED: GRADE II

Khadambi Asalache (1935-2006), the eldest son of a Kenyan chieftain, was responsible for creating one of the most extraordinary interiors ever designed in modern Britain, hidden within an unassuming early 19th century house in Wandsworth Road, Lambeth; an interior so distinctive and individualistic that on his death it was deemed to be of national importance and acquired by the National Trust.

What makes the interior so unusual is that every surface is decorated with Moorish-inspired fretwork, carved by himself using a plasterboard knife and discarded timber from old wine boxes and doors, balanced on his knee in the garden.

Khadambi was born near Kaimosi in western Kenya, and as a youth is said to have read Shakespeare while herding the family goats. Educated in Kenya, he studied architecture at the Royal Technical College, Nairobi, and later fine art in Rome, Geneva and Vienna. Behind his engaging demeanour lay a formidable intellectual and creative talent. A pioneer of Kenyan literature in English, he was the author of the novel *A Calabash of Life* and a collection of highly regarded poems, as well as writing an episode of the BBC series *Danger Man*. After taking an MPhil in the philosophy of mathematics, he became a civil servant at HM Treasury.

In 1981 he spotted the modest house in Wandsworth Road from the top of a No 77 bus, promptly bought it, and proceeded to transform the interior with wonderfully intricate carved fretwork inspired by Moorish architecture from Córdoba, Granada, Istanbul and Zanzibar.

The house retains Khadambi's original furnishings, ornaments, pictures and personal artefacts including his clothes, slippers, dressing case and collections of 19th century lustreware and Ethiopian Coptic crosses – all poignantly remaining as though he had just left the room.

Whilst it was common for British colonial architecture overseas to meld European and local influences, 575 Wandsworth Road is truly remarkable in combining hundreds of motifs from Islamic and African sources within an ordinary London terrace house. It is an important contribution to contemporary British culture and a vibrant and exotic expression of London's standing as a great world city.

HM Prison Wandsworth

Heathfield Road, sw18 3hs
Listed: Grade II (in part)

What happens behind prison walls is beyond most people's direct experience, so the closed world within exerts a peculiar fascination.

Between 1800 and 1840 the crime rate in England quadrupled. New penal measures were introduced to increase prison capacity and to punish the criminal. The model for the new wave of prisons was Pentonville, built in 1840-2 with a radial layout of four separate cell blocks with access galleries to the upper levels around a central hall, an arrangement that allowed for maximum surveillance of each wing by prison staff from the central hall.

Between 1842 and 1879 19 new radial prisons were constructed in England. HMP Wandsworth was typical. It was built in 1851 as the Surrey House of Correction to complement Brixton Prison and designed by the Birmingham architect D R Hill, who was also responsible for HMP Winson Green in his home city. It is a gloomy, forbidding affair, intended to convey an unrelenting regime of harsh punishment. At the entrance is a grim central gatehouse framed by vermiculated stone pilasters flanked by grey gault brick pavilions in an Italianate style.

The utilitarian cell blocks beyond follow the conventional Pentonville plan, with wings radiating from a central tower, based on "humane" principles for the separation of inmates established at Pentonville, and borrowed from American experience. Around the perimeter walls are ranges of houses for prison officers and the governor.

Corporal punishment was commonplace in the penal system until the 1950s, and Wandsworth was the central holding place for the national stock of the birch and cat o' nine tails. Between 1878 and 1961 Wandsworth witnessed 135 executions, including the traitors William Joyce (Lord Haw-Haw), John Avery and Duncan Scott-Ford, the murderer George Chapman (an unlikely Jack the Ripper suspect) and Derek Bentley, who later received a posthumous pardon. Wandsworth was also the scene of the legendary escape by the Great Train Robber Ronnie Biggs on 8 July 1965.

The trapdoor and gallows from the prison were kept in full working order until the 1990s, when they were dismantled and sent to the Prison Service Museum in Rugby. On a more cheerful note, the condemned cells are now the prison officers' tea room.

Gala Bingo Club

50 MITCHAM ROAD, SW17 9NA
LISTED: GRADE I

Better known in its former incarnation as the Granada Cinema, the Gala Bingo Club is the only Grade I listed cinema in England, and one of the most lavish to be found anywhere in Europe.

It opened on 7 September 1931 as the flagship of Sydney Bernstein's Granada empire, featuring Jack Buchanan and Jeanette McDonald in *Monte Carlo*. The architect of the exterior was Cecil Masey (1881-1960), who produced a fairly conventional and rather restrained landmark in an Italianate style covered in white faience with a towering central entrance articulated by four tall Corinthian columns in antis. But in an age of architectural fantasy what set the Granada apart was the astonishing interior, designed by the colourful theatre designer and impresario Theodore Komisarjevsky.

Komisarjevsky (1882-1954) was a director in the Imperial and State Theatres in Moscow. After the Russian Revolution he moved to England in 1919, where he won acclaim as a set designer and modernist producer at the Shakespeare Memorial Theatre, Stratford upon Avon, culminating in a brief marriage to Dame Peggy Ashcroft.

Within is pure fantasy. Five sets of double doors lead into a lobby in quasi-mediaeval style, beyond which is a huge foyer in the form of a baronial hall. At the far end are twin flights of Travertine stairs leading to the balcony. In the void between the rake of the balcony and its soffit is the extraordinary Hall of Mirrors (p380 top right) beneath a barrel-vaulted ceiling encrusted with plaster flowers and lined with long arcades of cusped arches inset with pier glasses.

But the real climax lies beyond: the colossal auditorium, designed to seat 3,000, has an intricate coffered Gothic ceiling, arcaded walls and gabled Gothic canopies suspended over the proscenium arch. To each side are huge Gothic gables decorated with painted murals of troubadours and mediaeval figures including a wimpled maiden and a Negro drummer boy, all executed by the artists Lucien le Blanc and Alex Johnstone.

Under the stage, now converted to a café, is a full-blown 14-rank Wurlitzer organ, which was originally installed in a theatre in Sacramento, California, together with a four manual organ console in the old orchestra pit. The organ was restored in 2007, but damaged by flooding shortly after.

The Granada was equipped for stage shows and variety artists as well as film, and in the 1950s and 60s was the venue for many leading artists of the day including Danny Kaye, Frank Sinatra, the Andrews Sisters, Frankie Laine and Jerry Lee Lewis, but with declining audiences it closed as a cinema on 10 November 1973 with a final showing of *The Good, the Bad and the Ugly*. It remained unused until it reopened as the Gala Bingo Club on 14 October 1976.

Tomb of Sir Richard Burton

CHURCHYARD OF ST MARY MAGDALENE, MORTLAKE, SW14 8PR
LISTED: GRADE II*

Captain Sir Richard Francis Burton (1821-90), soldier, scholar, explorer, geographer, linguist, poet, diplomat and spy, was described in his *Times* obituary with considerable understatement as "one of the most remarkable men of his time".

Renowned for his epic journey in disguise to Medina and Mecca 1851-3, he embarked subsequently on a series of explorations across East Africa. Returning from Harar in Ethiopia in 1854, his head was impaled through both cheeks by a Somali spear, conferring the distinctive scar depicted in later photographs and in his famous portrait by Lord Leighton. In 1856 he began his search for the fabled source of the Nile, reaching Lake Tanganyika with John Hanning Speke in 1858, which triggered their famous feud, culminating in Speke's mysterious accidental death on the eve of a fierce public debate at the Royal Geographical Society.

In January 1861 Burton married Isabel Arundell, a staunch Catholic. "I have undertaken a very peculiar man," she wrote, "I have asked a difficult mission of God, and that is to give me that man's body and soul." After diplomatic postings to West Africa, Brazil and Damascus, Burton was appointed Consul in Trieste, where, fluent in over 40 languages, he translated his most famous and controversial works including *The Kama Sutra of Vatsyayana*, *The Perfumed Garden of the Shaykh Nefzawi* and *The Book of the Thousand Nights and a Night* before his death from heart failure on 20 October 1890.

Recalling his comment that on their death "I should like us to both to lie in a tent, side by side", she designed a wonderfully evocative tomb in the shape of an Arab tent. Standing 18ft high and 12ft square, it is made of Forest of Dean stone modelled to simulate the folds and guy ropes of a tent, crowned by gilded Muslim stars with a crucifix over the door.

Inside is an extraordinary mixture of Christian and Muslim imagery which encapsulates their marriage with an altar at one end and exotic Arab lanterns suspended from the ceiling. Camel bells were placed to catch the wind and tinkle when the door (now sealed) was left open. A small stained-glass window depicting Burton's coat of arms – a white dove of peace flying towards the sun – was intended to let suffused sunlight on to their coffins below. Lady Isabel visited his tomb every Sunday and even held four séances within in the vain hope that the adventurer who had discovered and returned from so many inaccessible places might find some way back home to her from death.

Today the interior can be seen through a glass panel, which has replaced the long-lost stained glass. A mirror, installed as part of the recent restoration, enables visitors to view the altar. Inside, Sir Richard and Lady Isabel lie romantically side by side, united in death as they never were in life: he the charismatic adventurer, and she the devout Catholic.

The tomb was restored with great sensitivity under the aegis of the local Environment Trust in 2010, and is no longer a building at risk.

Little Holland House

40 BEECHES AVENUE, CARSHALTON, SM5 3LW
LISTED: GRADE II

This is the house that Frank built – literally piece by piece over three years between 1902 and 1904.

Frank Dickinson (1874-1961) was a self-taught artist and craftsman, who left school at 13 to work as a shop-boy for an organ builder. His employer encouraged him to develop his innate talent by attending art classes, where he became a lifelong devotee of John Ruskin, William Morris and the Arts and Crafts movement. Recognising that he was unlikely ever to earn enough to buy a house which enshrined such ideals, he resolved to build his own – "a house with beautiful things inside, a house solid-looking and not too showy".

For three years prior to his marriage to his fiancée, Florence, he worked at night in the cellar of his parents' house "sawing up enormous planks of walnut and pine" to make furniture – a coal box, dining table, bedstead and dressing table. Having purchased some land in Carshalton in October 1902, aided by his brothers, a bricklayer and a labourer, he began digging the foundations of his house. Remarkably three months later, the shell of the house was complete. For a further year, he worked during weekends and holidays until the interior had been crafted sufficiently to live there, moving in on his wedding night, 28 March 1904. Florence's savings, intended for her wedding trousseau, were diverted to pay for the green Cumbrian roofing slate. The honeymoon was spent sanding window frames.

Dickinson worked for Royal Doulton, but was a gifted and compulsive creative artist – a painter, metalworker, carpenter, woodcarver and poet, who furnished his entire house in accordance with the ideals of the Arts and Crafts movement. "Our house became a centre for gatherings and festivities, country dancing, play acting, musical evenings and discussion groups," he later wrote.

Externally, the house is unassuming and similar to many suburban houses of the period. Only the ornamental gate posts and gate suggest something more interesting.

Internally, it is delightful. Carved into the great oak beam dividing the living room and the sitting room is the inscription "Serve Humanity the Gods we know not" with a fox intertwined in the tendrils of a vine on the reverse. The polished red pine fireplace in the living room offset with hand-painted tiles has a repoussé copper panel in relief depicting a landscape and setting sun. Above is a painted triptych, a treatment repeated in the sitting room with a moulded plaster panel of dancing nymphs and piping Pans with another triptych painting above. The balusters on the staircase have pierced heart reliefs in typical Arts and Crafts style. Upstairs in the principal bedroom is a painted frieze and fireplace with a winsome plaster panel based on Burne-Jones's picture *The Legend of the Briar Rose*. The bedstead, by Dickinson, is carved "O Sleep it is a gentle Thing".

Dickinson died in 1961, and 11 years later his wife moved into a nursing home. In an astonishingly enlightened move, the house was acquired and restored by Sutton Council and opened to the public in 1974.

Set into the match-boarded dado of the living room is Dickinson's portrait of his hero John Ruskin and the quote: "We will try to make some small piece of English ground beautiful, peaceful and fruitful".

Dickinson succeeded. He dedicated his life to these ideals and with his hands crafted his own very personal English idyll in the sylvan suburbs of Carshalton.

Buddhapadipa Temple

14 CALONNE ROAD, SW19 5HJ
UNLISTED

One of the delights of living in a great world city is the way in which other cultures have enriched London by providing striking new architectural juxtapositions and multi-dimensional perspectives.

Rising high above a conventional Edwardian Arts and Crafts house in the suburbs of Wimbledon is the exotic serrated skyline of the Buddhapadipa Temple. Serenely set in a grove of trees beside a peaceful ornamental lake, it is one of only two similar temples outside Asia, and a centre for the teaching of Theravada Buddhism.

It is conceived entirely in a traditional Thai style, with multiple receding roof tiers and bargeboards decorated with symbolic gilded ornament: the serpentine naga, or snake, and the crowning chofah – a bird's beak – a reference to Garuda, the large mythical bird-like creature in Buddhist and Hindu mythology.

The temple was completed in 1982 to the design of the Thai architect Praves Limparangsri supported by financial donations from the government and people of Thailand.

The Uposatha or Shrine Hall of the temple is sacred. The windows and door frames of gilded teak are inlaid with coloured glass. Around the four walls are stunning mural paintings depicting scenes from the life of the Buddha executed over a four-year period by 27 Thai artists under the direction of three chief artists – Chalermehai Kosipipat, Panya Vijinthanasarn and Pang Chinasai. The panels show both traditional and contemporary references, including depictions of Lady Thatcher, George Bush and other world leaders at the time of the temple's construction.

The hall contains various statues of the Buddha. The Black Buddha from the Sukothai period (1238-1438) was presented by the King of Thailand. The Golden Buddha was the gift of the Committee of the London Buddhist Temple Foundation, whilst the Emerald Buddha is a replica of the original in the monastery of the Grand Palace in Bangkok.

The temple is the home of the Dhammaduta, or resident monks, who are occupied in quiet meditation or teaching. An aura of calm repose pervades the entire complex – a perfect retreat for adherents of the eightfold path to seek enlightenment and to contemplate the transience of all living things with serene compassion.

Kew Bridge
Steam Museum

Green Dragon Lane, Brentford, tw8 0en
Listed: Grade I and II

Kew Bridge Pumping Station is the oldest waterworks in the world containing its original steam pumping engines and the most complete example of its kind in Britain. It is of outstanding importance to both the history of science and industrial archaeology.

Following persistent public outrage at the lamentable quality of London's water in the early 19th century, private water companies invested heavily in new infrastructure. Kew was begun in 1836 to provide a clean and reliable water supply to west London, the third site to be opened by the Grand Junction Water Works Company after Paddington (1811) and Chelsea (1820). Over the next century Kew slowly spread across 25 acres with ancillary engine houses, forges, workshops and filter beds. Six large steam engines plus diesel and electric pumps despatched water to holding reservoirs at Campden Hill and Ealing. After the site became superfluous, in an a far-sighted move, in 1942 the Metropolitan Water Board designated Kew a museum station, to preserve the main engines and concentrate artefacts and objects from other sites at a single location. Forty-one years later, in 1973, the site was taken over by the Kew Bridge Engines Trust.

The elegant 197ft-high Italianate standpipe tower, a west London landmark, announces the site for miles around. It was built in 1867 after the original was damaged by heavy frosts. Encased in brick to protect the cast-iron pipes, provision was made for fires to be lit at the base during cold periods with escape slits for smoke at the top. However, the primary attraction is the world's finest collection of Cornish beam engines which can be found inside.

The oldest engine on the site is the Boulton and Watt "West Cornish" beam engine, built in 1820 and restored in 1975, which was moved to Kew from the Chelsea works in 1840. The Maudslay (opposite above left), the first actually built for Kew in 1838, has been rebuilt extensively. But the real *tour de force* is the magnificent Grand Junction 90" engine (opposite below right) – the largest working beam engine in the world, built by the Copperhouse Foundry in Hayle, Cornwall, in 1846 – and its later synchronised companion, the 100" engine, built by Harvey & Co of Hayle in 1869: the largest surviving single-cylinder beam engine in the world, complete with a cracked beam. Both are beautifully detailed with massive fluted Doric columns over 40ft high, the former described by Charles Dickens as "a monster". After its restoration in 1976, the presenters of the *Blue Peter* television programme climbed into the cylinder through the exhaust valve and held a celebratory tea party beneath the piston.

Close by is the largest known surviving Bull engine (1856), named after the Cornish engineer Edward Bull, the world's only working example. Other delights include an Easton & Amos engine (opposite below left) from Northampton (1863) with a rotary wheel; a triple expansion engine of 1867 from Lord Rothschild's estate at Dancer's End, Tring (opposite above right); a 20ft backshot waterwheel from 1902; and a pumping engine (1910) from Waddon (left).

Strawberry Hill

268 WALDEGRAVE ROAD, TWICKENHAM, TW1 4ST
LISTED: GRADE I

In June 1747 Horace Walpole, the son of Sir Robert Walpole, Britain's first prime minister, acquired a summer residence by the river in Twickenham: "a little plaything-house … the prettiest bauble you ever saw". "Dowagers as plenty as flounders all around, and Pope's ghost … skimming under the window by a most poetical moonlight". Over the next 50 years, he transformed Chopp'd Straw Hall into the first significant house of the Gothic Revival at a time when classicism and Palladianism were all the rage.

Walpole was a gifted dilettante – writer, collector, antiquary, man of letters, essayist, connoisseur and the author of *The Castle of Otranto*, the first gothic novel, which he printed on his own private press. Armed with folios of engravings of mediaeval tombs, rose windows, screens, doorways and Gothic details, he repeatedly added to the original building, helped by a few friends. This Committee on Taste included John Chute, the philosopher Richard Bentley, J H Muntz and later Thomas Pitt, Robert Adam, James Essex and Thomas Gayfere, the master mason from Westminster Abbey.

Walpole intended the interior of the house to be a theatrical experience entered through a gloomy hall, up a grey stone-coloured staircase before bursting out into a spectacular state apartment ornamented with delicate fan vaulting in vibrant crimson and gold. The house has now been restored to reinstate Walpole's original *coup de théâtre*. With the exception of the exterior, the photographs on this spread show the building before restoration. Overleaf the rooms are shown just after the completion of the £9m refurbishment. On the staircase (middle left and p390 top), lit by a gothic lanthorn, Walpole's *trompe-l'oeil* decoration survives beneath later pink paint, the walls once hung with paper painted with Gothic arches from Prince Arthur's tomb in Worcester Cathedral. The stone-grey theme continues into the Great Parlour lit by restored stained glass.

The Library (left, opposite top left and p390 right), the first gothic library in England, has a stunning sequence of elaborately carved bookcases modelled on the side doors to the screens at Old St Paul's, taken from engravings by Wenceslas Hollar. The painted heraldic ceiling above was designed by Walpole himself. The window has restored glass with painted figures representing faith, hope and charity.

After the procession of muted grey spaces, the purple Holbein Chamber with its fantastic ribbed Gothic detail ceiling (opposite bottom left) is a revelation. Copied from the Queen's Dressing Room at Windsor, it is crafted from papier mâché, the extraordinary screen copied by Bentley in 1758 from the gates to the choir at Rouen Cathedral.

The Gallery (p391 top and middle left, opposite middle bottom), according to Thomas Gray in 1763 "all gothicism and gold, crimson and looking glass", is a great architectural climax – the ceiling dripping with exquisitely modelled and recently regilded papier mâché fan vaulting and the walls lined with crimson Norwich damask based on original fragments.

Beyond, the Round Drawing Room in the Round Tower (bottom and middle left), designed by Chute in 1759, has a scagliola chimneypiece (p388 middle right) modelled on the shrine of Edward the Confessor in Westminster Abbey commanding a splendid vista back to the Gallery.

The astonishing Tribune (opposite below right), also to Chute's design in 1762, with "the solemn air of a rich chapel", was Walpole's private sanctum for his prize treasures, viewed by visitors from beyond a grilled door as a precaution against those who "see with their fingers". Quatrefoil in plan, the delicate tracery ceiling rises to a central star of yellow glass. Here Walpole kept his priceless collection of paintings, figures, ceramics, vases and miniatures. Among the eccentricities in the collection were Cardinal Wolsey's hat, William III's spurs from the Battle of the Boyne and Admiral Van Tromp's pipe smoked during his final naval battle.

The Great North Bedchamber, with its excellent Portland stone chimneypiece by Gayfere (opposite bottom left), was once the State Bedroom. In the Beauty Room remnants of panelling from the original house of 1698 can be seen alongside later layers of decoration.

When Walpole died in 1789, the house passed to his cousin's daughter, the sculptress Anne Damer, and then in 1811 to his great-niece Elizabeth Waldegrave. In 1842, in a fit of pique, the 7th Earl of Waldegrave sold Walpole's collection in the Great Sale. In 1856 his widow Frances remarried and extended the house with a whole series of grand rooms for entertainment. In 1923 a Catholic teachers' training college, St Mary's University College, acquired the building. It is now managed by the Strawberry Hill Trust.

Marianne North Gallery

ROYAL BOTANIC GARDENS, KEW, TW9 3AB
LISTED: GRADE II

The Royal Botanic Gardens is one of London's four World Heritage Sites and the repository of some of the capital's most spectacular architecture, including Sir William Chambers's Chinese pagoda (1761) and the famous Palm House (1844-8) – designed by Decimus Burton and the iron founder Richard Turner – the first large-scale use of structural wrought iron outside shipbuilding. The nearby Temperate House is the largest Victorian glasshouse in existence.

Alongside such examples of architectural bravura, the Marianne North Gallery seems unremarkable. Externally it is a simple pedimented red-brick box surrounded by a verandah built by the architectural historian James Fergusson in 1882 to illustrate his theory of how Greek temples were lit by opaions or clerestories. Inside are two linked spaces with a low dado panelled with displays of different woods. Above is a simple cast-iron balcony at clerestory level stencilled with Greek motifs. However, elegant though this is, it is not the architecture which is significant, but the staggering collection of 848 flower paintings covering the entire wall space, painted between 1872 and 1885 by the English naturalist and botanical artist Marianne North (1830-90).

Marianne North, the eldest daughter of a prosperous landowning family, was brought up as a Victorian gentlewoman, well versed in singing, writing, drawing and keeping house. On the death of her father in 1869 she embarked upon a lifelong commitment to paint the flora of the world. Beginning in 1871-2 she travelled to Canada, the United States and Jamaica followed by a year living in a hut in the depths of the Brazilian rain forest. After a brief sojourn on Tenerife, she continued to California, Japan, Borneo, Java and Ceylon before spending an entire year in India where she was "quite dumb-founded by the strangeness of the old Temple of Madura" and delighted at "the squirrels in the roof" of her bungalow and "one of the tiny creatures playing close to me with its child".

On her return to Britain she offered her collection to the Royal Botanic Gardens and the money to erect a gallery to house them. Prompted by Charles Darwin, in 1880 she then travelled to Australia and New Zealand. After a visit to South Africa, an additional room was added to the gallery in 1883, followed by tours of the Seychelles and Chile. She died at Alderly, Gloucestershire, in 1890, one of Britain's greatest female naturalists and artists and, to this day, the only female artist in Britain to have a permanent solo exhibition. A number of plant species were named in her honour.

Normansfield Hospital Theatre

2A LANGDON PARK, TEDDINGTON, TW11 9PS
LISTED: GRADE II*

In 1868 Dr John Haydon Langdon-Down acquired The White House, an unfinished building in Teddington, as a private sanatorium for children suffering from congenital mental conditions, which later became known as Down's Syndrome. As passionate enthusiasts for the theatre, both he and his wife believed that through social interaction and personal expression drama could be used therapeutically to stimulate intelligence.

In 1877 the architect Rowland Plumbe was commissioned to design a multi-purpose entertainments hall and theatre for 300 people. Externally unremarkable, the interior is not only a delightful surprise, but also nationally important as a virtually complete unaltered survival of a theatre of the 1870s.

The theatre resembles a large Victorian assembly hall, with plain polychrome brickwork and pointed Gothic windows beneath an open-trussed pine roof at the centre of which is a huge pendant ventilating gas burner. The gilded and coloured proscenium, flanked by pairs of doors, is unlike any other London theatre. Over the doors are four life-size Pre-Raphaelite paintings of *Tragedy*, *Painting*, *Music* and *Comedy* by a highly accomplished, but unknown, artist. The doors and the riser to the stage are covered in beautiful gilded panels and paintings of wild flowers and grasses, which have been attributed to Marianne North, whose stunning paintings can be seen covering the walls of the North Gallery at Kew (see p392).

The stage is a full working version in miniature of a theatre of the period – a simple groove system with wings, borders and painted cloths. The collection of 90 pieces of stock scenery, now restored, is the finest in Britain. Six of the original 21 life-size portrait panels showing costumes from the Savoy Theatre premiere of *Ruddigore* in 1887 have been placed on the walls around the theatre. Originally they swivelled to allow actors to step out and bring the static pictures to life.

After years of uncertainty and decay, the building has been restored beautifully as a venue for theatre and performance art. The basement, once the Kindersaal or children's playroom, is being developed as the Langdon Down Museum of Learning Disability.

Grove House

100 High Street, Hampton, TW12 2ST
Listed: Grade II*

From the outside there is little to suggest that Grove House is anything other than a rather handsome early 18th century house typical of its period, with facings of dark plum brick, flush-framed sash windows and a later early 19th century porch.

The house was built for Lady Mary Downing. It retains a good original timber staircase with twisted balusters, but the pièce de résistance was added much later in 1893, when the house was acquired by a retired army officer, Colonel Charles James Stutfield, who had served in the Mediterranean. He let his imagination run riot by extending the house with a spectacular music room in a full-blown evocation of the Alhambra inspired by Owen Jones's Alhambra Room at the Sydenham Crystal Palace.

Tucked away at the back of the house, it was intended to form part of a wider composition including a long-lost conservatory with a circular pond and canal based on the Court of Lions at the Alhambra.

Inside, the central space and lateral bays are divided by cusped, engrailed arches and pierced screens above which rises a dome decorated with interlaced patterns on embossed paper, and receding *muqarnas*, the small carved corbels stacked in tiers which are such a distinctive hallmark of Islamic architecture. Every surface is encrusted with Moorish decoration, Islamic calligraphy, marble, tilework, coloured glass and rich ornamental plasterwork in a vibrant palette of green, red, blue and gold.

Stutfield died in 1926, at which point the house was sold. Plans to demolish the building for housing were resisted in 1950, and again in 1966, after which it was converted to offices.

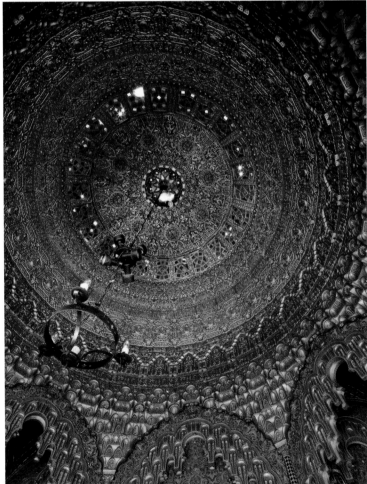

Manor Farm Barn

HARMONDSWORTH, UB7 0AQ
LISTED: GRADE I

In 1424-5, just nine years after the Battle of Agincourt, William Kyppyng made a journey to Kingston to look at timber for a new barn for the manor of Harmondsworth owned by Winchester College. Remarkably, almost 600 years later, the huge barn survives undisturbed in an isolated backwater sandwiched between the M4 motorway and the outskirts of Heathrow Airport.

Referred to by Sir John Betjeman as "the Cathedral of Middlesex", Manor Farm Barn is one of the finest and most complete pre-Reformation buildings in Britain, and one of the country's most precious, but relatively little known, historic buildings.

Built between 1426 and 1427, externally it seems unremarkable. A sweeping unadorned, clay-tiled roof with half-hipped ends and black weatherboarded walls is carried on a mixture of brick and composite ferricrete slabs.

Internally, it is spellbinding: 192ft long, 37ft 6in wide and 37ft high, its 12 huge bays are a magnificent testament to the mediaeval craftsmen who created it with such incredible structural sophistication. Access is through three simple wagon doors to the east front. The massive central timber posts are supported on green Reigate stone plinths which lift the height of the main nave to create an awe-inspiring space of immense power. Owing to its great length, the double-framed structure is highly unconventional, with purlins to provide lateral strengthening. The principal trusses have a single central post between tie-beams, and carved mid-braces at collar level. The sides have strutted aisle ties at wall plate level.

In 2006 the barn was acquired by an offshore company, after which its condition deteriorated, prompting statutory intervention by English Heritage to secure emergency repairs, followed up by the service of a repairs notice and acquisition in 2011.

Jealously guarded by English Heritage and the local Friends of Harmondsworth Barn, it is an astonishing survival and one of the glories of mediaeval England.

Leighton House

12 HOLLAND PARK ROAD, W14 8LZ

LISTED: GRADE 1

Leighton House, the studio-home of the eminent Victorian artist Frederick, Lord Leighton (1830-96), boasts one of the most exotic interiors in London. Triumphantly restored in 2010 by the Royal Borough of Kensington & Chelsea, its jewel-like Arab Hall radiates once more with all the gorgeous extravagance of the East: a romantic vision of the Orient distorted through very Victorian eyes.

The house was built in stages over 30 years, in close collaboration between Leighton and his architect, George Aitchison, the Professor of Architecture at the Royal Academy and president of the RIBA from 1896 to 1899.

Leighton had very definite ideas of the house he wanted. In 1864 he wrote to his father that "architecture and much ornament are not inseparable", but the first phase of the house was a restrained classical affair in red Suffolk brick and Caen stone with little hint of what was to follow. It comprised a north-facing studio and gallery, and, in the interests of propriety, a separate side entrance for his models.

In 1879 a major extension was completed to the west of the house for Leighton's extensive collection of Islamic tiles which he had acquired during various trips to the Near East. Modelled on the palace of Zisa in Palermo, the magnificent Arab Hall is coruscated with hand-painted ceramics from the 14th, 16th and 17th centuries punctuated by Damascene latticework screens. The centrepiece is a fountain and pool set in a floor of elaborate Victorian mosaic surrounded by ottoman seats. But the lustrous Arab Hall was not some self-indulgent exercise in the reuse of architectural antiquities; it was designed for maximum dramatic aesthetic impact and incorporated the work of some of the leading artists of the time. The capitals to the smaller columns are by Sir Joseph Edgar Boehm, the gilded birds on the carved caps of the large columns are the work of Randolph Caldecott, whilst the wonderful gilt mosaic frieze was made in Venice by Walter Crane. The iridescent cobalt-blue tiles to the staircase and corridor are by William de Morgan.

As a gentleman, orientalist, collector and artist, Leighton saw it as part of his mission to educate the masses, so during his trips abroad, the London poor were allowed to trudge through the house in a noble attempt to elevate their aesthetic sensibilities.

In 1889 Aitchison built a winter studio to the east of the house, and in 1927 the architect Halsey Ricardo was commissioned to design the Perrin Galleries which lie beneath it.

On Leighton's death in 1896, attempts were made to offer the house and its contents to the nation, but sadly much of the collection and furniture was sold and dispersed. In 1925 it was acquired by Kensington Borough Council. As part of the recent restoration many of the original paintings have been loaned back, and, after painstaking research, the furniture and furnishings have been spectacularly reproduced to match the originals.

Cabmen's Shelter

WELLINGTON PLACE, NW8 7PD
LISTED: GRADE II

Cabmen's shelters are one of London's delightful curiosities. They owe their existence to the philanthropic efforts of Sir George Armstrong, the editor of the *Globe* newspaper, who established the Cabmen's Shelter Fund in 1875 to provide "good and wholesome refreshment at very moderate prices". Its first president was Lord Shaftesbury.

As cab drivers were required by law not to leave their cabs unattended while parked at cab stands, they had great difficulty obtaining hot meals and drinks other than at public houses, where a minder then had to be paid to guard their vehicles whilst they were inside. All too often the cabmen emerged inebriated. In an effort to inculcate temperance and moral rectitude, the charity therefore resolved to erect and run cab shelters at major cab ranks around the city. Gambling, swearing and alcohol were strictly forbidden.

Between 1875 and 1914, 61 shelters were erected at a cost of £200 each, of which 13 remain. As they were erected on the carriageway, they were required to occupy no more space than a horse and cab. As a result all follow a common pattern with subtle, minor variations. Painted dark green, they resemble Victorian kiosks with vertical timber boarding on a timber frame, ventilators crowning slate or tile covered roofs, and perforated fretwork grilles reading "CSF".

Most accommodate between 10 and 12 people and a small kitchen. This particular example close to Lord's Cricket Ground has an interior decorated with contemporary murals of London taxis. They have been restored with financial assistance from English Heritage, the Heritage of London Trust and private donors.

Debenham House

8 Addison Road, w14 8dj

Listed: Grade I

Close to the Levantine splendours of Leighton House is another extraordinary house on a similarly lavish scale.

No 8 Addison Road was built in 1905-7 for the department store owner Sir Ernest Debenham, by the architect Halsey Ricardo, who put into practice his theory of structural polychromy, where the expression of architecture is primarily dependent on colour; a concept re-adopted 100 years later by many post-modernist architects.

The intention was to build a house immune to atmospheric pollution, so that "the city dirt has only a precarious lodgement on the glazed surfaces", and could be washed off by the rain.

Externally it is a striking composition. The ground and first floors of Doulton Carraraware and green glazed Burmantofts bricks are contained within a giant Florentine framework of pilasters which carry an elaborate modillioned cornice and an attic faced in vivid turquoise bricks. The roof above is clad in green Spanish pantiles punctuated by huge chimney stacks which erupt from each corner to create a distinctive silhouette.

The entrance is through a long loggia lined with wonderful iridescent William de Morgan tiles. Inside it is even more spectacular, designed around a huge central domed hall with a gallery surrounded by pierced marble screens at first floor level. The upper walls, dome and pendentives are swathed in glittering mosaics executed by Gaetano Meo and inspired by San Vitale in Ravenna. Scenes from classical mythology are playfully interspersed with portraits of the Debenham family. Elsewhere, the passages, halls and stairs are covered in nacreous de Morgan tiles in a range of brilliant turquoise, cobalt and purple hues. The library has mahogany bookcases inlaid with mother of pearl and a plaster ceiling by Ernest Gimson, who designed other ornamental plasterwork in the house. The enriched glass is by E S Prior, and the metalwork, including the novel electric light switches, was designed by the Birmingham Guild of Handicrafts.

In 1955 the house became a teacher training college, and later the headquarters of the Richmond Fellowship for Mental Welfare & Rehabilitation.

In 1968 it provided the strange setting of the Joseph Losey film *Secret Ceremony* starring Elizabeth Taylor and Mia Farrow.

Today, once again, it is a private house; a masterpiece of inventive Arts and Crafts decoration by one of the most gifted architects of his age.

The Thematic House

LANSDOWNE WALK, W11 3LN
UNLISTED

Few architectural theorists have the practical skills necessary to translate their intellectual concepts into reality, but at the Thematic House Charles Jencks – architect, landscape designer, theorist and polymath – has done just that. Between 1978 and 1983, with the aid of Terry Farrell, Piers Gough, Michael Graves and other architect friends, the promoter of post-modernism remodelled his conventional 1840s London town house into a remarkable statement of his own world view: that architecture should directly address the question of meaning through the rediscovery of symbolism and metaphor.

The Thematic House is imbued with 22 different levels of meaning around the themes of cosmic time (the seasons and passage of the sun and moon) and cultural time (the rise and fall of civilisations). Everything within the house from the front door to the Cosmic Loo has a deeper meaning and resonance, but all shot through with irreverence, wit and humour.

Windows and doors are abstractions of the human body. The front door leads to the Cosmic Oval with a mural by William Stok depicting the Big Bang (above right) and the creation of the universe, beneath which are portraits of some of the world's great free-thinkers – from Imhotep and Pythagoras via Erasmus and John Donne to Borromini and Thomas Jefferson.

The ground floor rooms are organised around the spiral Solar Stair, an abstract representation of the solar year with 52 steps for the weeks of the year, 7 divisions for the days of the week, 365 grooves, and stainless-steel spheres to the handrails symbolising the sun, earth and moon. Beneath is a spiral mosaic by Eduardo Paolozzi of a black hole which echoes the spiral of the handrail.

Each of the ground floor rooms is dedicated to the cycle of seasons. Winter has a bust of Hephaestus modelled on the features of Paolozzi, and Spring busts of April, May and June sculpted by Jencks's sister are raised on pedestals. Beyond, the Sundial Arcade has a huge remotely-controlled window overlooking the garden. The centrepiece of Summer is a brilliantly-inventive expandable table inspired by the sun. The kitchen on the theme of Indian Summer is littered with visual puns and witty references including "spoonglyphs" – triglyphs made of wooden spoons celebrating the pleasure of food alongside Hindu deities. Autumn is decorated in burnt red with Egyptian ankh symbols of femininity decorating the cupboards.

Upstairs is Jencks's library and office and other thematic rooms including the Four Square Room reminiscent of Mackintosh. Light is drawn down to the landing and dressing rooms by the Moonwell – a shaft of mirrored surfaces designed by Ilinca Cantacuzino.

Jencks stands in the long tradition of single-minded architects from Pugin to Lutyens whose work was underpinned by an underlying intellectual rigour and deeper layers of meaning. Inexpensive materials and artifice have been deployed with imagination and humour to create a total architectural experience which eloquently demonstrates that modernity should not be confused with modernism.

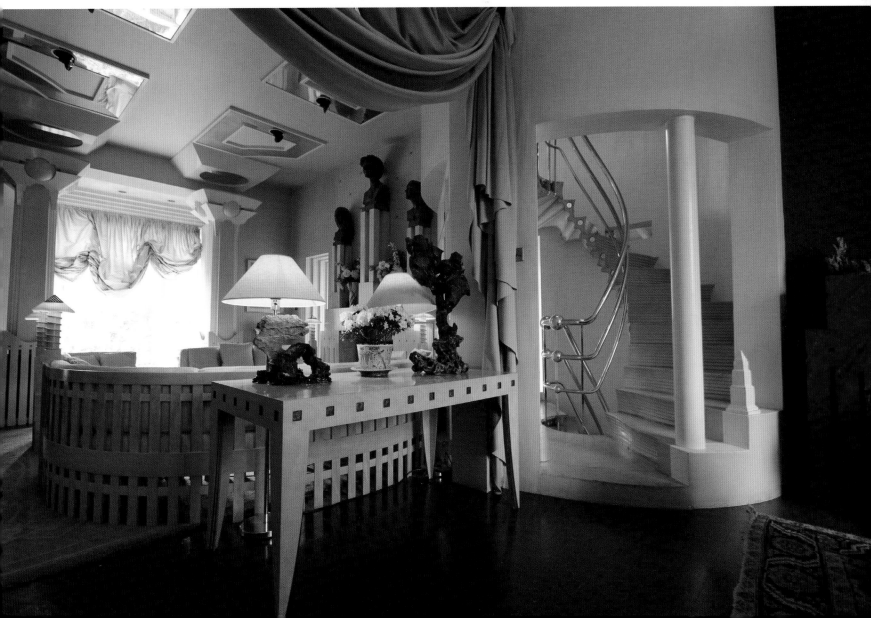

Peter Hone's House

LADBROKE SQUARE, W11 3LX
UNLISTED

Like some latter-day incarnation of Sir John Soane, Peter Hone, connoisseur, collector, antiquarian and antique dealer, has dedicated every inch of his first floor flat to his insatiable appetite for history – the Hone Museum rather than the Soane, he jokes. The interior is an ever-changing tableau of neo-classical statuary, archaeological fragments, garden ornaments and architectural details crammed into every conceivable space.

The front parlour overlooking the gardens of Ladbroke Square is also the "winter bedroom" with a huge canopied bed swathed in drapes from Tyttenhanger Manor. To one side is a colossal alabaster Nelson vase, commissioned to mark the death of Nelson in 1805, and later rediscovered and rescued by Hone from the grounds of the school near Nelson's former home in Merton; its plinth is exquisitely carved with a relief of HMS *Victory* and crocodiles symbolising the Battle of the Nile. Squeezed in behind is a plaster replica of Bernini's throne of St Peter; nearby a Hellenistic bust from 250 BC and a first century head of Midas. Dominating the room is a huge portrait of Thomas Oldknow by Joseph Wright of Derby, with eyes cast downward and clutching his heart, as if overwhelmed by the architectural excess surrounding him. In fact he died of a heart attack before the painting could be completed – hence the pose.

The portrait is flanked by two pairs of beautiful, slender male and female herms, salvaged from a house in the Euston Road, supporting marble shelves piled high with urns, vases, sphinxes and figurines, the walls above lined with architectural fragments of marble, plaster and Coade stone, including a capital from Chiswick House used as a corbel for a bust. Tucked in the corner by the window is a finely modelled terracotta bust of Frederick the Great. Suspended from the ceiling, which is covered with 4,500 hexagonal plaster casts, hangs a pendant light from the old Academy Cinema in Oxford Street designed by Angus McBean, for whom Hone once worked.

A corridor jostling with artefacts and surveyed in one direction by a giant statue of Pallas Athena, goddess of truth, and in the other by a statue of Flora by Canova, leads past Samuel Johnson's death mask to the "summer bedroom" which has a canted bay overlooking the garden. An entire wall is hung with a collection of portrait medallions in *Bois Durci*, a French composite material made with oxblood and sawdust patented in Paris in 1855. Lining the doorcase are more death masks – Voltaire, Wordsworth, Keats, Dante and Cromwell – alongside the hands of Pitt the Younger. In the adjacent bathroom a gold-embossed dinner service once belonging to the previous Duke of Cambridge sits in a Gothic cabinet made by Hone from the remnants of an old gazebo.

Back in the front parlour, lying on the table, the death mask of a woman who drowned in the Seine bears an enigmatic, knowing smile, as if perpetually amused by the company in which she has found herself.

Greek Orthodox Cathedral of Aghia Sophia

MOSCOW ROAD, W2 4LQ

LISTED: GRADE I

Inscribed in marble across the polychrome façade of the Greek Orthodox Cathedral of St Sophia are (in translation) the words "The Greek Community in this island, which is the ruler of the seas, erected this church away from the beloved homeland and dedicated it to the divine wisdom of God, in the reign of the glorious and great Queen Victoria".

St Sophia was designed in an exotic Byzantine style by John Oldrid Scott in 1877 to provide a new spiritual focus for an increasingly wealthy expatriate Greek community of shipping magnates, financiers and merchants, many of whom had settled in west London, and who raised £50,000 for its construction. Consecrated by Antonios Hariatis, the Archbishop of Corfu, on 5 January 1882, the ravishing interior and its huge central dome are coruscated with gilt mosaics, green, black, white and pink marble and Orthodox iconography around a Greek cross plan. It is Scott's masterpiece.

The richly carved, three-tiered iconostasis was designed by Scott with panels of walnut inlaid with mother of pearl and painted by Ludwig Thiersch, who had advised in favour of mosaics for the walls rather than painted frescoes because of the damp London climate. The mosaics, to the design of A G Walker, and later Boris Anrep, a Russian, were from Mercenero and Co. In the narthex is a stone from the earliest Greek church in London, founded in Greek Street, Soho, in 1677.

In 1922 the Holy and Sacred Synod of the Ecumenical Patriarchate resolved that St Sophia should become the Cathedral of the Metropolis of Thyateira with jurisdiction over all Orthodox Christians in western Europe.

During the Second World War, while King George II of Greece and the government in exile were in refuge in London, St Sophia became the cathedral church of the entire Greek nation. Having suffered severe damage in the Blitz, it was repaired painstakingly after the war and remains a deeply spiritual place imbued with all the arcane mystery of the Eastern Church.

Grand Royale
London Hyde Park Hotel

1 Inverness Terrace, W2 3JP
Listed: Grade II

No 1 Inverness Terrace, an elaborate late 19th century Franco-Flemish-style house, stands in marked contrast to the repetitive Italianate stucco terraces of the remainder of the street. Its louche interior has aroused much speculation as to its provenance, the truth of which will probably never be known.

It is alleged that the house was built as a love-nest and private retreat for the actress Lillie Langtry (1853-1929) by the priapic Albert Edward, Prince of Wales. Although there is no actual evidence for this, it remains a remarkably persistent rumour, and it is known that the Jersey Lily lived there.

During their affair, which lasted from 1877 to June 1880, Edward lavished a fortune on his mistress, including building a private retreat at the Red House in Bournemouth (now the Langtry Manor Hotel), so the idea of a London equivalent is not so outlandish. "I've spent enough on you to build a battleship," he once complained, to which she archly replied, "And you've spent enough in me to float one." The connection is reinforced by the presence of an extraordinary private theatre within the building, but this seems not to have been constructed until 1905, long after their affair had ended and he was King.

Even more intriguing is that in the early 1900s the interior was remodelled by the architects of the Ritz – Mewès and Davis – for a new owner, Louis Spitzel. Spitzel was a distinctly dodgy figure: an Australian who accumulated a vast fortune as a jeweller, arms dealer and shadowy agent of the Chinese Empire. On his death in 1906 he left a long train of irate creditors, but a huge legacy for the preparation of patriotic books for distribution to children at British public schools.

The interior created for him shortly before his death is an extraordinary mixture of styles. The entrance hall and ground floor are richly panelled throughout in carved dark oak, behind which, tantalisingly, lies the intriguing private theatre – an intimate circular domed auditorium with mirrored walls and stucco plasterwork, and a separate square room and raised stage with a proscenium arch between the two, now altered for use as a bar.

A huge carved oak Jacobean-style stair leads to the first floor. Hovering above is an allegorical painted ceiling of a well-endowed female figure framed by lively cavorting cherubs lit by stained glass. Behind the landing is an engrailed Moorish arch. Two large first floor dining rooms in a more conventional classical style complete the sequence of public rooms.

The hotel is one of London's most unusual and enigmatic interiors, haunted by memories of long-forgotten financial scandals and sexual misbehaviour.

Chapel of St Sepulchre
St Mary Magdalene Church

ROWINGTON CLOSE, W2 5TF
LISTED: GRADE I

Marooned in a sea of post-war housing, the Church of St Mary Magdalene resembles a huge ship run aground on the banks of the Grand Union Canal, but hidden in the crypt below lies one of London's most magical and secret spaces.

The church was built as a beacon of High Anglicanism amongst densely packed terraces of poor housing by the Rev Dr Richard Temple West as an "outstation" of Butterfield's magnificent polychrome masterpiece, All Saints, Margaret Street, Marylebone, where he was a curate. For the design, West turned to his old friend and member of the congregation, George Edmund Street, who had to contend with a restricted, sloping site. This necessitated levelling the land and the creation of a concrete-vaulted crypt beneath the south aisle. The church was built in stages over 11 years between 1867 and 1878, its slender tower and needle spire soaring over the rooftops in a paean of praise to High Anglicanism.

Inside, the church is an inventive and accomplished essay in High Victorian Gothic style, with banded brick and stone walls, encaustic tiles and arcades with different rhythms and designs punctuated by canopied statues and, on the north side, Stations of the Cross. High up in the gloom of the cradle roof are panels of saints painted by Daniel Bell. The lavishly decorated chancel is dressed with alabaster and mosaic scenes by Salviati.

But what makes the church so unusual is the stunning crypt Chapel of St Sepulchre. This was completed in 1895 by Ninian Comper (his first work in London) as a memorial to Dr West. It is entered by a staircase at the western end, which leads to a large, dark vaulted chamber and sacristies approached through iron grilles and gates. To one side, beneath an exquisite star-spangled, blue-painted groin-vault is a full-blown recreation of a 15th century German chantry chapel dedicated to St Mary Magdalene, the first witness of the Resurrection.

The organ (1899) has beautifully painted late mediaeval figures on the inside of the doors, carved timber screens and stained glass (1898) of the Last Judgement, and Dr West with his patron saint. The walls have quotations from the Sarum Missal. Most spectacular of all is the altar and carved, gilded and painted reredos highlighted in burnished gold with a concealed central tabernacle, after Comper's proposal for a hanging pyx was ruled unacceptable and potentially provocative to Protestants.

The crypt chapel has suffered repeatedly from damp penetration. It was restored by Sebastian Comper in 1967 for the centenary. Further recent works to the chapel have been supported by a £112,000 grant from English Heritage.

In the church above, the Lady Chapel is also dedicated to West with fine stained glass by Henry Holiday made by Heaton, Butler and Bayne. Outside is a poignant war memorial Calvary by Martin Travers (1920s).

Warrington Hotel

93 WARRINGTON CRESCENT, W9 1EH
LISTED: GRADE II

Guarded by a small detachment of K2 telephone kiosks, the Warrington Hotel occupies a prominent corner of the Church Commissioners' Maida Vale estate from which a series of avenues radiates outwards from a central rond-point. Built in 1859 as an hotel, the sedate stucco façades conceal a riotous interior which borders on the promiscuous, adding weight to salacious allegations that the hotel was once a brothel.

Beneath a huge shell niche, mosaic steps flanked by tiled Corinthian columns and octagonal iron lamps lead to the plush interior, which is a theatrical revelation. Stained-glass windows and etched and cut-glass screens divide the bars, the walls lined with arcades of bevelled-edged mirrors separated by twisted mahogany columns. The centrepiece is a sweeping semi-circular marble-topped bar with mahogany panels divided by console brackets. Behind is a magnificent array of bar fittings – glass screens, mirrors and scrolled brackets – culminating in a sinuous overhead canopy decorated with cavorting cherubs.

In 1965 the canopy and walls were painted with some wonderfully erotic Pop Art Nouveau nudes by Colin Beswick, calculated to inflame the thirst of even the most abstemious. So well executed that many believe them to be original, they are an eloquent demonstration that period interiors can be enhanced by high-quality contextual alterations carried out in the original style.

At the rear of the saloon a huge semi-circular niche with Art Nouveau stained glass and lamps, and yet more erotic nudes, add to the louche atmosphere. To one side, beyond a screen of marble pillars, is a grey marble chimneypiece with neo-Jacobean strapwork. The lower flight of the massive staircase has a thick serpentine handrail leading to the upper floors over which sits a stained-glass lantern.

Once the watering hole of jockeys, one of whom is alleged to have won a £100 bet by riding a horse into the bar, the current clientele seem to prefer the more refined pleasures of the first floor restaurant.

Hospital of St John & St Elizabeth Chapel

60 GROVE END ROAD, NW8 9NH
LISTED: GRADE II*

At the heart of the Hospital of St John & St Elizabeth is a Victorian Baroque chapel which once stood in Great Ormond Street in Holborn, but which was dismantled and relocated here between 1898 and 1901.

Inspired by the work of Florence Nightingale in the Crimea, a wave of new institutions opened in mid-19th century London to provide nursing for the sick and needy. One such institution, dedicated to St Elizabeth, was founded in 1856 in Great Ormond Street. It was funded by Sir George Bowyer, the MP for Dundalk and a late convert to Catholicism, whose funeral service was held in the church in 1888. With the completion of the church in 1864, a link was forged with the Knights of St John of Jerusalem, to whom it was dedicated, and the British Association of the Knights of Malta.

The architect was George Goldie, who designed schools, churches and buildings for the Catholic community in England. The design was based on the 16th century church of Il Gesu in Rome with a handsome Portland stone façade, but with the acquisition of the Holborn site by the Hospital for Sick Children, the institution moved to a new purpose-built complex at Grove End Road, St John's Wood.

Goldie's son and partner, Edward, designed the new hospital and arranged for his father's church to be dismantled and re-erected as the centrepiece of the new complex. Much of the original interior was also removed and reused, including the altars and many of the fittings.

The chapel has a central dome, choir stalls and pews carved with the emblem of St John of Jerusalem, and walls divided by purple-red Sicilian jasper pilasters with gilt Corinthian capitals. There are two small side altars; one, the gift of Lord Petrie, from the old chapel at Cowdray, and the other the gift of Cardinal Wiseman from Buckland in Berkshire. Directly beneath the handsome blue and gilt dome is a full-blooded baldacchino with an altar and sarcophagus, the gift of the Grand Master to the English Knights.

The surrounding hospital was designed to a U-shaped plan, with 17-bed wards in the end wings. It was intended for persons of both sexes suffering from illness of "one or another description" and who required long-term care. One ward was set aside for the open-air treatment of 17 female patients suffering from pulmonary tuberculosis.

The chapel continues to offer spiritual solace to all who are suffering at their time of greatest need.

Anglican Chapel
Kensal Green Cemetery of All Souls

Harrow Road, w10 4ra

Listed: Grade I

> For there is good news yet to hear and fine things to be seen;
> Before we go to Paradise by way of Kensal Green.
>
> (G K Chesterton)

In the 50 years from 1801 to 1851 London's population more than doubled from 1 million to 2.5 million, but little provision was made to set aside land for burials. These remained concentrated in the tiny congested burial grounds around inner London's churches. London faced an unprecedented burial crisis and a public health catastrophe. It was not uncommon for rotting bodies to be stacked in heaps awaiting burial. Decaying corpses contaminated the water supply and triggered epidemics of smallpox, typhoid and cholera.

In 1833 Kensal Green was the first of eight new commercial cemeteries to be opened around the capital to address the appalling conditions in the inner London graveyards. Inspired by Père Lachaise Cemetery in Paris, it was founded by the barrister George Frederick Carden and designed by J W Griffith as a place of resort and quiet contemplation, with tree-lined walks lined by mausolea.

Griffith designed the Anglican Chapel in 1836 in a bold Greek Doric style with an interior strongly influenced by Soane. The chapel and its adjacent colonnades are regarded rightly as "among England's most distinguished examples of Greek Revival architecture". Beneath lie huge atmospheric brick-lined catacombs divided into brick vaults, or loculi, stacked with coffins swathed in cobwebs and encrusted with the detritus of almost two centuries of dust and decay.

At the centre of the vaults is the magnificent hydraulic catafalque which glides serenely up and down through hinged doors in the floor of the chapel.

The original hand-cranked screw-jack apparatus was both temperamental and noisy, so in 1843-4 an innovative hydraulic system by Bramah & Robinson was installed, guided by two cast-iron columns either side of the pit.

The catafalque is made of timber reinforced with iron strips and ties and overlaid with brass fittings ornamented with a Greek-key design, all hung with deep black velvet to provide a sumptuous spectacle for mourners as the deceased are conveyed with due reverence on their last journey to eternity.

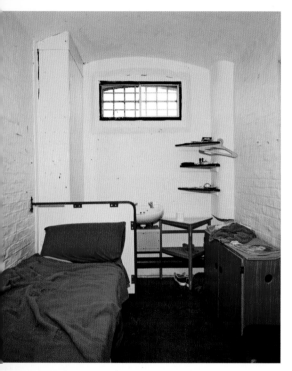

Chapel of St Francis of Assisi
HMP Wormwood Scrubs

W12 OAE

LISTED: GRADE II*

Approached through a portal resembling some great mediaeval gateway, the gatehouse to HMP Wormwood Scrubs is one of London's most unusual architectural and cultural icons. On each of the flanking octagonal towers, terracotta roundels depicting the great prison reformers Elizabeth Fry and John Howard look down in reproach and compassion on those entering below.

The inmates certainly needed the latter, as the prison was designed by Sir Edmund Du Cane, a belligerent former military engineer, who became chairman of the Prison Commission following the 1877 Prison Act. Du Cane was a strict disciplinarian who saw it as "his fate to take up the harsh penal regime … and by effective administration realise its full punitive potential".

To reduce costs the prison was built entirely by convict labour between 1874 and 1891 and to an innovative plan, which departed from the Pentonville model of radiating wings in favour of a "telegraph pole layout" with four parallel cell blocks linked at their centre by covered walkways. This was derived from the pavilion hospitals which had been promoted by Florence Nightingale following her experiences in the Crimean War. Wide blocks orientated from north to south were intended to promote the circulation of fresh air and to ensure that each cell received some sunlight during the day. Communal ablution blocks were introduced as individual toilets and basins in each cell fostered foul air and disease. The model was influential and other examples were built at Bristol, Norwich, Shrewsbury and Nottingham.

The Victorian penal system placed great emphasis on silent contemplation and Bible reading. As a result the chapel at Wormwood Scrubs is the largest and finest prison chapel in England, capable of accommodating 1,000 inmates. Designed by Du Cane in French Romanesque style, the wide nave and narrow aisles ensure maximum security and visibility. Huge arch-braced tie-beams in dark stained oak carry kingposts which support the diagonally boarded roof. A rhythm of seven bay arcades of moulded round arches on thick drum piers surrounds the nave, terminated by an apsidal-ended sanctuary with round-arched panels of saints. The lunette above depicts scenes from the life of Christ, all allegedly painted by prisoners, who were led through the east and west doors via covered walkways from the adjacent cell blocks.

Notable alumni include the spy George Blake, who escaped on 22 October 1966, Oscar Wilde's lover Lord Alfred Douglas, the Labour minister John Stonehouse, who faked his own death, and the rock musicians Keith Richards and Pete Doherty.

W Burrows

1 East Acton Lane, W3 7EG
Listed: Grade II

W Burrows, alas, is no more. It was one of the finest surviving traditional fish and chip shops in London, with a remarkably intact interior from the 1930s. Closed in 1997, consent was granted in 2010 for its dismantling because of its poor structural condition, the cost of repair and the difficulty of finding a beneficial alternative use in an area where the economic base had changed completely.

In the mid-19th century rising working-class incomes triggered a huge expansion of local eateries specialising in inexpensive food – eel, pie and mash shops, chop houses and fish and chip shops. Although Dickens refers to a "fried fish warehouse" as early as 1839 in *Oliver Twist*, the first fish and chip shops are believed to have been established by Joseph Malins in Bow in 1860, and a Mr Lees in Mossley, Lancashire, in 1863. With the concurrent development of the railways, fresh fish could be transported cheaply across the country from ports such as Grimsby, fostering the British culinary tradition of the fish supper. By 1929 there were 35,000 fish and chip shops in Britain.

W Burrows was typical. The family ran a similar shop in Paddington and moved to Acton in the 1930s, trading from a very traditional shopfront with a green and gold glass fascia and tiled stallriser in the style of a generation earlier.

The interior bore a striking similarity to eel, pie and mash shops of the period (see p338) with a marble-topped serving counter opposite booths with marble tabletops and wooden benches supported on ornate cast-iron legs. Copper heating pipes ran along the benches to warm diners.

The walls and other surfaces were lined with green and white tiles, with 75 different hand-painted tiles each depicting different types of fish set in green border panels. The hand-painted tiles were designed and made by Polly Brace, a ceramic artist and designer who co-founded Dunsmore Tiles with Kathleen Pilsbury in Campden Hill in 1925. The fish series was one of their most popular ranges – zoologically accurate, the designs lightly wiped to simulate ripples in water.

At the rear of the shop a single-storey range contained a rare fish-smoking house and stores, above which was a pigeon loft used for the relay of messages in the Second World War.

A condition of the consent for demolition was that the atmospheric interior should be dismantled and donated to the Hop Farm Museum in Kent, where it awaits re-erection.

Shri Swaminarayan Mandir

105-119 Brentfield Road, nw10 8ld
Unlisted

The scientist Charles Steinmetz wrote: "Some day people will learn that material things do not bring happiness." This is why one of the more surreal pleasures of a trip to IKEA in Neasden is the glorious sight of the Shri Swaminarayan Mandir rising serenely above the dreary townscape of the mutilated suburban houses that line the North Circular Road.

The Mandir was the first traditional Hindu temple to be built in Europe, and the largest outside India. Completed in 1995, it is one of the seven wonders of modern Britain and a magnificent testament to Indian craftsmanship: 2,828 tons of Bulgarian limestone and 2,000 tons of Carrara marble were despatched to India, where a team of over 1,500 sculptors and masons carved the stone for over two years. The 26,300 components were then shipped back and reassembled in London in a sort of giant 3D jigsaw puzzle. Funds were raised entirely by the Hindu community, including children collecting and recycling aluminium cans. It was opened in August 1995 by the spiritual guru and head of the organisation Pujya Pramukh Swami Maharaj, who has written:

"A mandir is a centre for realising God.

A mandir is where the mind becomes Still.

A mandir is a place of paramount Peace.

A mandir inspires a higher way of Life.

A mandir teaches us to respect one another."

Designed by the architect C B Sompura, the £12m Mandir is the focal point of a wider complex including a *haveli* – a multi-functional cultural centre – and an ashram for resident *sadhus* (monks). Raised high on a stone platform, seven tiered shikharas crowned by golden spires adorn the serrated roofline, complemented by five ribbed domes.

Within is a series of seven shrines housing sacred *murtis* (depictions of Hindu deities) which are attended each day by *sadhus*. Each surface is carved profusely with sacred figurative sculpture expressing spiritual symbolism through posture, hand gestures and facial expressions. Sinuous ribbons of beautifully carved stone link the arches to convey a sense of weightlessness and levitation.

The adjacent *haveli* of English oak and Burmese teak (opposite below left) is carved with stylised animal heads, flowers, garlands and iconography in a cornucopia of patterns taken from the traditional courtyard houses of Gujarat. Within lies a vast prayer hall unobstructed by intermediate columns which can accommodate 3,000 people.

The Mandir is a rich and exotic addition to London's architectural heritage and the living embodiment of Britain's special relationship with India.

"Paddock" Underground Bunker

BROOK ROAD, NW2 7DZ

UNLISTED

Forty feet below ground in the suburbs of north-west London lies Churchill's secret bunker, a place deemed so secret that even in his memoirs he referred to it only as "near Hampstead".

From 1937 onwards the British government invested extensively in air-raid precautions. A crucial part of the strategy was contingency planning for the evacuation and dispersal of government functions should central London become unusable, or, in the event of invasion, overrun. Three war rooms were built in north-west London – at Neasden for the Cabinet and Chiefs of Staff, codenamed Paddock; at Oxgate Lane, Cricklewood, for the Admiralty, referred to as the I P building; and in a basement next to the Kodak building in Harrow for the RAF, known as Station Z.

Massive excavations for Paddock started early in 1939. Tons of soil were removed covertly in bread vans to avoid the unwanted curiosity of local residents. Paddock was designed to withstand a direct hit from a 500lb bomb and could accommodate over 200 people. Located on the edge of the Post Office Research Station site, it was completed in June 1940 at a cost of £250,000, with a large map room and adjacent space for the Cabinet and Prime Minister, and a complex of generators, ventilation plant and hardened radio transmitters and receivers. Living and sleeping accommodation was made available in Neville's Court, an inter-war block of apartments nearby, where Churchill was allocated a double flat.

However Churchill resolutely refused to contemplate leaving Whitehall and branded Paddock a "useless piece of folly". "The accommodation at Paddock is quite unsuited to the conditions which have arisen. The War Cabinet cannot work and live there for weeks on end ... Paddock should be treated as a last-resort Citadel," he wrote on 22 October 1940.

As a result it was only ever used twice – on 3 October 1940 and 10 March 1941. When it closed finally in 1944, the Post Office Research Station used it as a test centre for battlefield acoustics. It was in the research centre above in 1943-4 that Tommy Flowers designed and built Colossus, the world's first programmable electronic computer, for top-secret use at Bletchley Park.

The site is now occupied by a housing development built by the Stadium Housing Association. A discreet steel door is the only clue to what lies beneath.

It is curious to reflect that had circumstances been different the British Empire might have made its last stand amid the suburban splendours of Neasden.

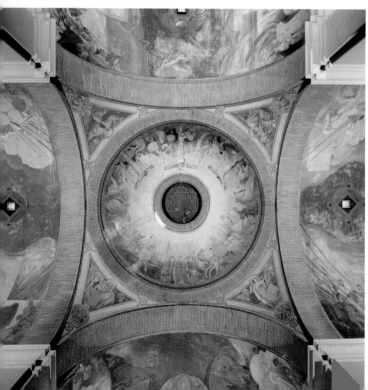

Church of St Jude-on-the-Hill

CENTRAL SQUARE, NW11 7AH
LISTED: GRADE I

Prominent in views across a great arc of north-west London, the Church of St Jude-on-the-Hill is one of the most distinguished churches of the 20th century. Its tall tower and tapering lead-clad spire provide a symbolic spiritual focus to the heart of Hampstead Garden Suburb.

The Garden Suburb, the brainchild of Dame Henrietta Barnett, was laid out by Sir Raymond Unwin from 1904 as a model community intended to bring together all classes in a stimulating, idyllic environment – the rich and the poor, the old and the young, the learned and the ignorant, even the wicked and the naughty – and transform them through the spirit of Christian charity and friendship into a harmonious whole.

St Jude's was the culmination of Dame Henrietta's desire for the highest point in the Suburb to have houses for worship and learning. In 1906 Sir Edwin Lutyens was appointed as consultant architect to assist Unwin with the layout of the area. At St Jude's he produced a remarkable composition which ranks amongst his finest works – an ingenious hybrid of Gothic, Byzantine and Quattrocentro styles. Imbued with spiritual symbolism, the intention was to provide a tangible architectural expression of the transfiguring power of spiritual aspiration at the very centre of the community. At the cutting of the first sod in October 1909, Dame Henrietta said: "That is our hope, that the outside ... will aid those who ... have not yet the privilege of knowing God to seek higher things ... and to comprehend ... what is meant by the Beauty of Holiness".

These ideas were taken up enthusiastically by the first vicar – the charismatic Reverend Basil Bourchier, who commissioned Walter Percival Starmer, a little-known war artist he had met on the Western Front in 1918, to prepare a scheme of internal painting, initially for the Lady Chapel and later for the entire church.

The Lady Chapel, dedicated as a war memorial in 1921, is a celebration of women of the Bible, with eminent heroines from Florence Nightingale to Edith Cavell interspersed with mediaeval female saints. Eighteen months later, at the Royal Academy, Starmer exhibited his designs for the rest of the church on the theme of the life of Christ, which he then executed in phases until 1930 when he finished in the choir and the apse.

Starmer's murals, executed over a period of nine years, 1921-30, are the most complete set of church paintings to survive from the inter-war period, and a window on the social and religious concerns of the time.

Elsewhere in the church is a poignant memorial to Michael Rennie by Starmer, the son of the third vicar, who died from exhaustion rescuing children from the SS *Benares*, which was torpedoed in the Atlantic in September 1940 – "To the faithful Death is the Gate to Life". A replica of an original bronze war memorial to the horses of the First World War can also be seen. On the east wall outside the church is a magnificent carved stone Calvary designed by Lutyens which closes the vista from Middleway.

St Lawrence Whitchurch and Chandos Mausoleum

WHITCHURCH LANE, LITTLE STANMORE, HA8 6RB
LISTED: GRADE I

Engulfed in the sea of inter-war suburbs between Edgware and Stanmore, externally St Lawrence Whitchurch appears to be both conventional and unassuming – a plain brick box with corner Tuscan pilasters and an older 15th century tower – but the interior is a complete revelation. Every surface is a blaze of colour, painted with pictures of the Virtues, Evangelists and biblical scenes of Christian salvation with all the theatrical flourish associated with the continental Baroque. It is totally unlike any other parish church in the country.

The reason for this is that the church was rebuilt in 1715 by John James for James Brydges, the 1st Duke of Chandos (1674-1744). Brydges was the corrupt Paymaster General to Marlborough's army who amassed a huge fortune siphoning off public funds to gratify his own lavish tastes. In 1709 he acquired the Canons estate and appointed a succession of architects to design what Daniel Defoe described as "the most magnificent house in England!". St Lawrence was reconstructed as a surrogate private chapel for the duke, which accounts for its astonishing interior.

Inside, the drama of the theatrical design is enhanced by a shallow elliptical barrel vault terminated by a retro-choir. This is framed by a proscenium arch in the form of a segmental pediment carried on Corinthian columns carved by Grinling Gibbons. At the centre is the organ in a fine case, also by Gibbons. Here the duke's organist, George Frideric Handel (1685-1759), played. Handel lived at Canons as composer in residence for over a year in 1717-18, where he composed 11 Chandos anthems, a Te Deum and two masques – *Acis and Galatea* and *Haman and Mordecai*.

The paintings are by various artists: the ceiling by Louis Laguerre, the east and west ends by Antonio Bellucci and the grisaille paintings on the north wall from about 1736 by Francesco Sleter, who worked nearby at Moor Park, Rickmansworth. At the west end a staircase leads to a gallery containing the duke's private box with a semi-dome above painted by Bellucci depicting the Transfiguration after Raphael. Either side are separate compartments for his bodyguard and servants. The original box pews in the nave retain small pieces of chain showing the original location of chained prayer books, and 18th century graffiti carved by bored men and boys.

In the north transept is the Antechamber, built by the duke as his monument room, with 18th century paintings and family hatchments. Beyond is the jaw-dropping Chandos Mausoleum, built in 1735 after the death of his second wife.

The mausoleum, designed by James Gibbs, has walls of *trompe-l'oeil* columns and figures by Gaetano Brunetti approached through a fine wrought-iron gate. Carved in marble by Gibbons, the 1st duke stands in the centre bewigged and dressed in Roman costume and flanked by his two wives, who kneel at his feet. On the south wall are two later monuments – to Mary, wife of the Marquess of Carnarvon by Sir Henry Cheere (1738), and to Margaret, Marchioness of Carnarvon (c1760) inscribed with characteristic hyperbole: "But reader commiserate not her fate … but the unhappy husband in losing in the prime of life the virtuous partner of his bed and heart – best of women! Most unfortunate of men!"

Close to the church door in the churchyard is one of the oldest known outdoor graves in England, from 1596. Nearby is that of the iconic blues singer Long John Baldry (2005). The gravestone erected in 1868 to William Powell – inscribed "The Harmonious Blacksmith" – is reputed to mark the resting place of the man who inspired Handel's eponymous piece. Powell was a parish clerk and apprentice blacksmith who died in 1780, and the connection is spurious.

Bentley Priory

THE COMMON, STANMORE, HA7 3HH
LISTED: GRADE II*

Bentley Priory is world-famous as the headquarters of Fighter Command during the Battle of Britain, but the house itself is of considerable interest in its own right.

In 1755 the land was acquired by James Duberly, an army contractor, who built a modest country villa on the remains of the original 12th century Augustinian priory. The estate was sold to John James Hamilton, the 1st Marquis of Abercorn, in 1788, who employed Sir John Soane to enlarge and remodel the house in three phases over a 10-year period, including a library, breakfast room and circular tribune to the east of the house.

The result was so successful that, given its proximity to the capital, the marquis was overwhelmed by an endless succession of house guests as it became one of the leading salons of its time. Pitt, Wellington and Canning all visited, as did Sir William and Lady Emma Hamilton, Sarah Siddons and John Kemble. Sir Walter Scott wrote "Marmion" in the summerhouse on the lake during a series of visits in 1807. Lady Blessington called it "the most singular place on Earth".

In 1846 Queen Adelaide, the widow of William IV, took a lease on the Priory and died in the house from dropsy in 1849. After her death, in 1863 the estate was bought by the eminent Victorian engineer Sir John Kelk, who added the distinctive Italianate clock tower, a library and gallery, a cedar garden, and one of the most magnificent conservatories in England, sadly demolished in 1939.

After a period as an hotel, and later a girls' school, the estate was split up and sold. The house and 40 acres were acquired in 1926 by the Air Ministry. Ten years later it became the headquarters of Fighter Command.

Prior to the Second World War, the house was adapted to create operational offices for the RAF. The exterior was camouflaged and a new Operations Room built in a bunker 42ft beneath the garden. From his office in the house, Air Chief Marshal Sir Hugh Dowding controlled a strategic overview of the Battle of Britain, co-ordinating the activities of the four group sector stations, which in turn controlled the response from individual fighter stations (see p440). In June 1944 the D-Day landings were monitored from the underground Operations Room by King George VI, Churchill and Eisenhower.

Dowding's office and the officers' mess remain preserved with their original furniture, together with a rare Battle of Britain embroidered lace panel, a bust of Goering and trophies taken from the Luftwaffe at the end of the war.

On 21 April 1979 the house was damaged extensively by fire, following which some of the interiors were carefully recreated. Bentley Priory remains a house with a fascinating multi-layered past which lay at the very epicentre of world history during the momentous events of the Second World War.

Following the closure of the site in 2008, the Battle of Britain Trust has been created to manage the historic rooms and collections in the house. The remainder of the house and site is being developed sensitively for housing.

Harrow School

HIGH STREET, HARROW, HA1 3HP

LISTED: GRADE I AND II*

Harrow School was founded by a local yeoman farmer, John Lyon, under a royal charter of Elizabeth I in 1572. On his death 20 years later, Lyon left money for the maintenance of the road to London and for a new school building, which was completed in 1615. Widely regarded today as one of the best schools in the world, before 1845 Harrow had a harsh reputation. Anthony Trollope recalled bitterly, "I was never spared, and was not even allowed to run to and fro between our house and the school without daily purgatory". Later, as a teenager, he was an outcast: "I had not only no friends, but was despised by all my companions." By the late 17th century the custom of boarding boys in houses dispersed around the neighbourhood was established, a practice which continues to this day.

Under the headship of Dr Charles Vaughan, a pupil of the reformer Thomas Arnold at Rugby, between 1845 and 1859 the school was transformed, and the numbers expanded to accommodate demand.

The Old Schools lie to the west of the High Street in a characteristic Tudor building with crowstepped gables and oriel windows. But appearances are deceptive. Externally Lyon's original building, designed by Sly, was enlarged and refaced by C R Cockerell in 1819-21, but the interior retains an astounding 17th century schoolroom, the Fourth Form Room, which is lined with fielded panelling covered with the names of generations of past pupils as incised graffiti, including Byron and Sheridan. At the north end is a simple hooded throne for the headmaster. Opposite is an usher's chair. The long sides of the room are lined with forms, or benches, for the boys, interrupted only by a large stone fireplace of 1730. Above lies the Governor's Room with panelling from 1661-2.

The Speech Room of 1874-7 was a tercentenary project designed by William Burges – a huge, idiosyncratic D-shaped space on a classical plan, but with rampant Gothic detailing which Burges planned to embellish with Moorish decoration *à la* Cardiff Castle, but unfortunately he died before its completion. The stained glass is by J C Bell.

The War Memorial building (1921-6, by Sir Herbert Baker) created a formal approach to the Old Schools and reconfigured the area with broad steps and terraces added in 1929. The War Memorial is an austere domed and vaulted crypt with a simple stone catafalque to mark the sons of Harrow that fell in the First World War. Inside is a vaulted hall and stone stair enriched with timber and bronze panels inscribed with a poignantly long roll-call of names of those who fell across the Empire between the First and Second World Wars. The hall and staircase contain a fine range of busts including Peel by Noble (1850), Palmerston by Johnson (1870), and Churchill by Clare Sheridan (1941).

The architectural climax of Baker's building is totally unexpected – the Alexander Fitch Room (opposite below) is lined with superb Elizabethan fittings from Brooke House, Hackney, complete with a stone fireplace, fluted pilasters and a huge plank table in pride of place at the centre of the room.

Amongst the many alumni are seven British prime ministers including, most notably, Winston Churchill, as well as Sir Robert Peel, Lord Palmerston and Stanley Baldwin. Other distinguished former pupils include Admiral Rodney, Jawaharlal Nehru, Lord Shaftesbury, Field Marshal Alexander and not least Lieutenant Teignmouth Melville, who died trying to save the colours after the disaster at Isandhlwana during the Zulu War, one of 18 Old Harrovians who have received the Victoria Cross.

Zoroastrian Centre

440 Alexandra Road, Harrow, HA2 9TL
Listed: Grade II*

Frequently conservation involves the creative adaptation of old buildings to new uses. Sometimes this requires compromise, and the partial loss of elements of special interest, but equally new uses can enhance a building by accentuating its inherent architectural or spatial qualities.

The former Grosvenor cinema in Rayners Lane is just such a case. Designed by F E Bromige, it opened with a performance of *The Country Doctor* starring Jean Hersholt on 12 October 1936. Two years later it became the Odeon. In 1990, after various changes of use, it was converted to a bar before falling vacant and vulnerable. For several years it was one of London's most worrying buildings at risk. However in 2000 the Zoroastrian Trust Funds of Europe came to the rescue and the cinema was adapted and restored with great skill and sensitivity as a place of worship and the European centre for the Zoroastrian community.

The building is one of the finest Art Deco cinemas in the country. Above the entrance canopy, curving sinuously upwards is a huge concrete prow in the shape of a stylised elephant's trunk, its curved head standing proud of the bowed parapet.

The little-known interior is a *tour de force* of 1930s streamlined design. An oval-shaped foyer with steps and railings leads to what was once a sunken central tea room, over which hovers a futuristic curvilinear plaster ceiling aglow with concealed lighting.

The auditorium, now the Zartoshty Brothers Hall, retains its original fluted gallery front and inward-curving walls, with deep carved ribs shooting across the ceiling to draw the eye to the proscenium arch.

Zoroastrianism is one of the world's oldest religions, and one of the first to postulate belief in a single, omnipresent and invisible God. It was founded in Persia in the 6th century BC, based on the teachings of the prophet Zarathustra. Following persecution, its adherents, the Parsees, migrated to India, where they came to dominate commercial and industrial life in and around Bombay.

Their scripture, the Zend Avesta, describes the eternal conflict between the forces of good and evil in a destructive universe. The god of light, Ahura Mazda, is symbolised by fire. The focus of religious life is the fire temple; in India these are often distinctive Art Deco style buildings, which makes the former Grosvenor cinema an ideal spiritual home for Parsees in Europe.

No 11 Group Operations Room

RAF Uxbridge, UB10 0RN

Listed: Grade I

In the summer of 1940, hour upon hour, day after day, the fate of Britain and the entire free world was determined by the tactical decisions taken in this bunker. It was from here that a handful of RAF pilots turned the tide of history in the skies over London in one of the epic battles of the 20th century, inflicting a decisive strategic defeat on the Luftwaffe which altered the whole direction of the Second World War.

In 1939 Britain had the most sophisticated layered air-defence system in the world. Three years earlier a new strategic headquarters had been created for Fighter Command at RAF Bentley Priory (p432), with four group sector stations around the country. No 11 Group Operations Room at RAF Uxbridge was responsible for the air defence of London and south-east England.

Construction of the bunker began in August 1937 and was completed ten days before the outbreak of the Second World War. Located 60ft underground, it was designed to withstand a direct hit from a 500lb bomb.

During the Battle of Britain overall control was exercised from Bentley Priory by Air Chief Marshal Sir Hugh Dowding. From there information on air threats was received from the Royal Observer Corps and radar stations around the country, sifted, assessed and passed to the four group operations centres to co-ordinate action from individual sector airfields.

On 16 August 1940 Churchill visited the bunker to watch the battle in progress. He was profoundly moved. As he left with tears streaming down his face he remarked to General Ismay: "Never in the field of human conflict has so much been owed by so many to so few," a phrase which he used four days later in his legendary speech to the House of Commons. King George VI and Queen Elizabeth visited on 6 September. Churchill returned again at the climax of the battle on 15 September – now Battle of Britain Day – as the last remaining RAF squadrons were sent into battle. "How many reserves have we?" Churchill asked, to which Air Vice Marshal Keith Park replied, "There are none."

Later in the war, General de Gaulle, Lord Mountbatten and Anthony Eden all visited. Air support for the Dieppe Raid in August 1942 and for the Normandy Landings on 6 June 1944 was co-ordinated from here.

In 1975 the bunker was refurbished by 9 Signals Unit. The map table was restored and the sector signal boards returned to their appearance on 15 September 1940. Today it is a museum which can be visited by groups by prior arrangement.

The events controlled from this unprepossessing bunker on the outskirts of London were one of the decisive tipping points in the history of the 20th century. To this day the site remains extremely moving – hallowed ground infused with an intangible aura of national destiny.

Derek Kendall, Photographer

With over 40 years' experience Derek Kendall is one of the most talented and respected architectural and fine art photographers of his time. Benefiting from his intimate knowledge of London's built heritage and his exceptional eye for detail Derek's pictures have graced the pages of over 60 authoritative publications. His exhibitions include The City of London Churches at St Paul's Cathedral and The West End Theatres at the Victoria & Albert Museum.

Derek writes...

The images in this book are especially presented to all who call themselves "Londoners" but they will appeal to all who have a curious nature and have perhaps toyed with the hope that the front door to that familiar place, passed almost daily, would open, even if just a little, to allow a peek inside. The photographs capture that moment when someone visits for the first time – when their eyes are acclimatising and widening to peer into dark rooms, with more and more details being revealed. The photographic process I use mimics human vision by capturing ranges of exposures of the same scene to overlay into one frame. These layers of colour and detail are then selectively painted onto a new canvas to overcome the inherent capture limitations of the electro-mechanical camera. Many of the images are 170 degree views of the rooms and spaces, which required up to 40 exposures, giving coverage of height and width and depth of exposure. The resulting picture is in effect a scan of the room – a replication of the way we humans move our field of vision in an unfamiliar space.

This collection of photographs comes with a personal thank you to all the "Londoners" from across the globe who opened their doors and let me share their space.

"Next time you walk one of London's streets just stop, pause and be curious, look and listen. When travelling a familiar route make a detour down a different street. Experience the moment because everything changes."

Index

Acknowledgements and Credits

A book of this magnitude and complexity could not have been completed without the skill, dedication, hard work and enthusiasm of a small team of people over several years.

Particular thanks are due to the staff at Atlantic Publishing, in particular Greg Hill, Murray Mahon and Christine Hoy, who have been the ideal publishing team. The design, form and quality of the book are a lasting testament to their vision, skill and expertise, and also their forbearance as I disappeared to remote parts of the world at crucial moments in the publishing schedule.

Various people need to be singled out for their outstanding and selfless contribution to the project. There would not be a book were it not for the skill and professionalism of Derek Kendall, latterly the senior photographer at English Heritage, who worked tirelessly for over 18 months to visit over 120 buildings at all hours in pursuit of the pictures seen here. English Heritage and the team owe him an outstanding debt of gratitude. Richard Dumville's brilliant negotiating and organisational skills proved invaluable in liaising with building owners to secure privileged access to over 180 buildings and in subsequently keeping track of over 5,000 photographs. In her own imperturbable fashion, Sue Woods transformed 150,000 words of unintelligible scrawl into an immaculate typescript and cheerfully tolerated my own ineptitude in all IT and word processing matters. June Warrington provided invaluable picture research, advice, guidance and enthusiasm throughout the entire project, and I am very grateful to her for reading and commenting on the final manuscript.

Other English Heritage staff who were unfailingly helpful and who provided support include Edward Impey, John Cattell, John Hudson, Paul Backhouse, Steve Cole, James O Davies, Charles Walker, Anna Eavis and the English Heritage Archives Services Team including Alyson Rogers, Nigel Wilkins, Lucinda Walker, Amanda Rowan and Emma Whinton-Brown.

As always, thanks are due to Jane Davies, whose perceptive comments and suggestions, and abiding love of London, have done much to enrich the book. Finally, our cat Hector requires recognition, if not thanks, for making a number of interesting editorial interventions by sitting on the keyboard at crucial moments and periodically lacerating my arms when his observations were not followed.

A very large number of people provided help with access and information about particular buildings including:-
Mark Antoniou, 10 Downing Street; Mick Pedroli, Dennis Severs House; Charles Arkwright, Two Temple Place; Ivo Dawnay, Tessa Wild, National Trust; Edmund Bird, Mike Ashworth, Transport for London; Marisa Crocetta, Algerian Coffee Shop; Andrew Wallington-Smith, Worshipful Society of Apothecaries of London; Diane Waldron & Lesley Healy, Honourable Artillery Company; Rosey Jeffery, Bank of England; Paul Keenan, Harper Downie Ltd; Jeremy Castle, Treasury Holdings; Maria Hibbert, The Beefsteak Club; George Wade, All Design; Mr & Mrs Bluston; Neil Handley, British Optical Association; Teacher P K Lom Pabhassaro, Buddhapadipa Temple; James Jenkins, Cabmen's Shelter Fund; Charles Henty, Central Criminal Court; Father Henry Everett & Lesley Chakravorty, St Mary Magdalene Church; Charles Jencks, The Thematic House; John Major & Valerie Mills, The Dulwich Estate; Mark Wenlock, Chelsfield Partners; Joanna Ismail, The Clermont Club; David White (Somerset Herald), College of Arms; Dr Jim Walsh & Martha Lee, South Place Ethical Society; Lucy Ayton, London Film Museum Experience; Annabel Hunt, Criterion Restaurant; Peter Keasley, Crossness Engine House; Christopher Moran, Crosby Hall; John Allen, The Worshipful Company of Cutlers; Kayode Akinola, Goldman Sachs London; David Wykes, Dr Williams's Library; Penny Fussell, The Drapers' Company; Tony Binns, Dulwich College; Ziggy Gaji, Urdang Academy; Patricia Dilley, Foreign and Commonwealth Office; Graham Sparks, JP Morgan Chase; Stephen Traube & Andrew Smith, Former Middlesex House of Detention; James MacDonald, General Demolition Co Ltd; Amber Greenwood, Luchford APM; Karen Haigh, United Grand Lodge of England; Mustapha, Gala Bingo; Paulette Bersch, Geo F Trumper; Mr Mirza, Georgian Orthodox Cathedral Church of the Nativity of our Lord; Greer Allison, Argent Group PLC; Belinda Metcalfe, Kudos; Richard McRow and Melanie Eddy, The Goldsmiths' Company; Gerard Menan, Gordon's Wine Bar; Ekta Pathela, Shaftesbury Hotels London; Jack Ashby, Grant Museum of Zoology; Father Theonus, Greek Orthodox Cathedral of Aghia Sophia; Jon Rogers, PWR Events Limited; The Revd Anna Macham, King's College London, Guy's Campus; Kirsty Shanahan, Harrow School; Dan Tolhurst, Arsenal Football Club; Reece Williams and Marie-Claire Holthuizen, Home House; Jenny Guest and Tom Howat, The House of St Barnabas; Sean Fernley, Institute of Chartered Accountants in England & Wales; David Smith & Wendy Greenhalgh, Institute of Civil Engineers; Sally MacDonald & Tony Slade, University College London; Christian Dettlaff, Wesley's Chapel; Oliver Pearcey & Dick Fillery, Kew Bridge Steam Museum; The Revd Tim Ditchfield, King's College London; Justin Hobson, Country Life Picture Library; Hugh Merrell, Caroline Fiennes & Rob Lloyd, The Law Society; Rodney Hillis, Leighton House; Daniel Robbins, Leighton House; Emmanuel Tremolani, Les Trois Garçons; Murray Campbell & Guy Holborn, The Honourable Society of Lincoln's Inn; Valary Murphy, Sutton Council; Tom Foxton, Lloyd's of London; John Coombes, Lloyds TSB; Louise Bloomfield, Lloyd's Register Group Services Limited; Davide Giordano, Zaha Hadid Architects; Ayaz Zuberi, The London Central Mosque Trust Ltd. & Islamic Cultural Centre; Dr Jules Wright, The Wapping Project; Ben Brown, Maggs Bros Ltd; Professor Angela McFarlane & Gina Fullerlove, Royal Botanic Gardens, Kew; Dr John Callow, The Marx Memorial Library; Fiona Pouchard, Masonic Temple ANDAZ Liverpool Street Hotel; Ian Garwood, The Honourable Society of the Middle Temple; Frank Pickard; Charlotte Henwood, Ministry of Defence; Simon Roberts, National Liberal Club; Tobi Isenberg, Guoman Hotels; Gabrielle Allen, Guy's and St Thomas' Charity; Sue Mussett, Queen Mary University of London; Kevin Flude, The Old Operating Theatre & Herb Garret; Jackie McQuarrie & Ian Golding, Oxford and Cambridge Club; John Ryan, Oxford House in Bethnal Green; Katy Bajina, Network Housing Group Limited; Daada Luogon, Paget Memorial Mission Hall; Terry Eiss & Briony Potts, David Prior & Mari Takayanagi, Alexandra Wedgwood, Amanda Leck

& Ian Westworth, Palace of Westminster; Steve Moore and Carla Connolly, Queen Mary's University of London; Peter Hone; Tonya Nelson, Petrie Museum of Egyptian Archaeology; Eddy Fawdry, Pollock's Toy Museum; Nick Bodger, City of London; Tanvir Hasan, Donald Insall Associates Ltd; Hugh Fowler, CG Restaurants; Michael McKerchar, The Reform Club; Jayne Wills & Bill Mannix, The Rivoli Ballroom; Charlotte Gray, Royal Automobile Club; Davina Pyndiah, MOJ Estates Directorate; Annemarie Hiscott & Susannah Deller, The Royal Foundation of St. Katharine; Kate Bell, Purple PR; Sarah Whitham, Starwood Hotels & Resorts; Phil McCann, Rogge global partners Sion Hall; Jane Rick, Spencer House; Andrea Ttofa, Great Ormond Street Hospital Children's Charity; Reverend Paul Reece & Stuart Cawthorne, St Lawrence, Little Stanmore; Caroline Drayton, St Pancras Renaissance Hotel London; Jo Wisdom & Simon Carter, St Paul's Cathedral; Nick Smith, Strawberry Hill; Ben Wilson, The Supreme Court; Clare Stewart, De Vere Venues; Sue Collier, The Sherlock Holmes Pub & Restaurant; Adam Kirkaldy, Rex Restaurant Associates; Gemma Colgan, The Foundling Museum; Graham Jasper, Camden Council Highway Engineering; Barry Lang, Jones Lang Lasalle Ltd; William Martyn, W Martyn; Laurence, Ronald & James Sitch, W Sitch & Company Ltd; Susan Morgan, The United Welsh Church in Central London; Chris Silcock, Westminster School; Kathryn and Alan Hughes, Whitechapel Bell Foundry; Frances Mayhew, Becky Ruffell & Oona Patterson, Wilton's; Paurush Jila, Zoroastrian Trust Funds of Europe.

The majority of photographs in London Hidden Interiors were taken by Derek Kendall, until recently one of English Heritage's most senior staff photographers, numerous images drawn from the existing archive needed to be refreshed because of renovations or refurbishment and Derek and other of his fellow EH staff photographers, James O Davies and Nigel Corrie provided the very latest images to make this book as up to date as possible. Richard Dumville, Charles Walker and Philip Davies all provided images from their personal collections.

Additional photographs have been provided as follows and are used with permission of the copyright owners:
P375 575 Wandsworth Road: NTPL/Cristian Barnett
P181 Aldwych Underground Station: Ian Bell/Transport for London
P226 Armoury House: Honourable Artillery Company
P304 Blizard Institute of Cell & Molecular Science: Morley von Sternberg
P404 Charles Jencks Thematic House: Charles Jencks
P30 Commonwealth Institute: Chelsfield Partners
P25 Fleet Sewer: Steve Duncan
P27 Gants Hill Underground Station: Thomas Riggs/Transport for London
P18 German Gymnasium: John Sturrock
P246 Goldsmiths' Hall: Richard Valencia
P325 Highbury Square (former Highbury Stadium): Arsenal FC
P108 Home House: Home House
P137 Jeremy Bentham Auto-icon: UCL
P386 Kew Bridge Steam Museum: Dick Fillery
P44 Lambeth Palace: Country Life Picture Library
P94 Lancaster House: Mark Fiennes/NATO
P320 Les Trois Garcons: Les Trois Garcons
P258 Lloyds of London: Lloyds of London
P342 London Aquatics Centre: Hufton + Crow
P396 Manor Farm Barn: Boris Baggs
P392 Marianne North Gallery: Andrew McRobb © RBGKew
P130 Middlesex Hospital Chapel: Frank Pickard
P24 Nursery Rhyme Tiles: Nick David, 2011
P126 Sanderson Hotel: Sanderson, London
P90 Spencer House: Mark Fiennes/Bridgeman Art Library/Richard Davies
P364 Spirit Collection Darwin Centre, Natural History Museum: Natural History Museum
P142 St Christopher's Chapel, Hospital for Sick Children:
Jacqueline Banerjee www.victorianweb.org
P426 St Jude on the Hill: Pat Payne/EH
P10 St Pancras Renaissance Hotel: St Pancras Renaissance Hotel
P388 Strawberry Hill: Kilian O'Sullivan
P48 Supreme Court: Tim Imrie/UK Supreme Court
P381 Tomb of Sir Richard Burton: Alexa Bailey
P26 Tower Bridge Bascule Chamber: Joe Lord, Docklands & East London Advertiser
P18 Walthamstow Dog Track: Yui Mok/PA Archive/Press Association Images

Finally the Publishers would like to thank the production team: Cliff Salter, John Dunne, Maureen Hill, Alison Gauntlett, Sarah Rickayzen, Vicki Harris, Marie Clayton, Jill Dorman, Wendy Toole and Melanie Cox.

Select Bibliography

Atwell, David: Cathedrals of the Movies, Architectural Press 1980

Baedeker's London and its Environs, London 1898

Baring-Gould, William S: Sherlock Holmes: A Biography, Rupert Hart-Davis 1962

Barlow, Kate: The Abode of Love - A Memoir, Mainstream Publishing 2006

Barker, Felix and Jackson, Peter: Pleasures of London, London Topographical Society Monograph No167 2008

Beard, Geoffrey: The Work of Robert Adam, Bartholomew 1978

Bell W G: Unknown London, London 1919

Besant, W: London in the Nineteenth Century, London 1909

Bird, Peter: The First Food Empire: A History of J Lyons & Co: Phillimore 2000

Brandwood, Geoff, Davison, Andrew and Slaughter, Michael: Licensed to Sell: The History and Heritage of the Public House, English Heritage 2004

Briggs, A: Marx in London, London 1982

Briggs, A: Victorian Cities, London 1963

Brodie, Fawn: The Devil Drives, Eyre & Spottiswoode 1967

Burke, Thomas: Nights in London: A London Autobiography, London 1915

Cannadine, David: The Decline and Fall of the British Aristocracy, New Haven 1990

Chancellor E Beresford: A History of the Squares of London, Kegan Paul 1907

Chancellor E Beresford: The Private Palaces of London, Kegan Paul 1907

Chandler, Arthur R: Christ's Chapel of Alleyn's College of God's Gift at Dulwich, Heritage Consultancy 2000

Clout H: The Times London History Atlas, London 1991

Clunn Harold: London Rebuilt, John Murray 1927

Clunn, Chris: Eels, Pie and Mash, Museum of London 1995

Colvin, Howard: Biographical Dictionary of British Architects 1600-1840, John Murray 1978

Cooke, Sir Robert: The Palace of Westminster: Houses of Parliament, Burton Skira 1987

Cooper Nicholas: The Opulent Eye, Architectural Press 1976

Cornforth, John: London Interiors, Aurum Press 2000

Cornforth, John: English Interiors 1790-1848: The Quest for Comfort, Barrie and Jenkins 1978

Croft, Taylor: The Cloven Hoof: A Study of Contemporary London Vices, London 1932

Crossley, Joan: Sacred Spaces: The Hospital Chapels of London, MOLAS 2005

Cunningham, Colin: Victorian and Edwardian Town Halls, Routledge and Kegan Paul 1981

Curl, James Stevens: Kensal Green Cemetery, Phillimore 2001

Davies Philip: Lost London: 1870-1945, TransAtlantic Press 2009

Davies Philip: Panoramas of Lost London: Work, Wealth, Poverty and Change, TransAtlantic Press 2011

Davies Philip: Troughs and Drinking Fountains, Chatto & Windus 1989

Dean, Ptolemy: Sir John Soane and London, Lund Humphries 2006

Desmond, Shaw: London Nights of Long Ago, London 1927

Draper-Stumm, Tara and Kendall, Derek: London's Shops – The World's Emporia, English Heritage 2002

Edwards, Jane: London Interiors Taschen 2000

Emmerson, Andrew and Beard, Tony: London's Secret Tubes, Capital Transport 2004

English Heritage: Behind Bars: The Hidden Architecture of England's Prisons, English Heritage 1999

English Heritage: London Suburbs, Merrell Holberton 1989

English Heritage: London's Town Halls, English Heritage 1999

English Heritage: Picture Palaces, English Heritage 1999

English Heritage: Scene/Unseen: London's West End Theatres, English Heritage 2003

English Heritage: Survey of London, English Heritage, 1900 - 2011

Fabian, Robert: London After Dark, London 1954

Freeman, John: London Revealed, Little Brown 1989

Friedman, Joe: Inside London, Phaidon 1988

Friedman, Joseph: Spencer House: Chronicle of a Great London Mansion Zwemmer 1993

Georgian Group: Banking on Change, Georgian Group 1992

Girouard, Mark: Victorian Pubs, Studio Vista 1975

Glasstone, Victor: Victorian and Edwardian Theatres, London 1975

Graves: Charles: The Price of Pleasure, London 1935

Gray, A.S: Edwardian Architecture, Duckworth 1985

Green, Edwin: Banking: An Illustrated History, Phaidon 1992

Hare Simon M: Goldsmith's Hall in the City of London, London 1996

Hare, Kenneth: London's Latin Quarter, London 1926

Haydon, Peter and Coe, Chris: The London Pub New Holland 2003

Hitchcock, Henry-Russell: Architecture Nineteenth and Twentieth Centuries, Penguin 1958

Honri, Peter: John Wilton's Music Hall, The Handsomest Room in Town, Ian Henry 1985

Howard, Diana: London Theatres and Music Halls 1850-1960, London 1970

Inwood Stephen: A History of London, Macmillan 1988

Jencks, Charles: Symbolic Architecture, Academy 1985

Kadish, Solomon: The Synagogues of Britain and Ireland, Yale 2011

Keene, Derek, Burns, Arthur and Saint, Andrew: St Paul's: The Cathedral Church of London 604-2004, Yale 2004

Kent, W: The Lost Treasures of London, London 1947

Kilburn, Mike: London's Theatres, New Holland 2011

Knight, Caroline: London's Country Houses, Phillimore 2000

Lawrence, David: Underground Architecture, Capital Transport 1994

Lea, Richard and Miele, Chris with Higgott, Gordon: Danson House: The Anatomy of a Georgian Villa, English Heritage 2011

Lejeune, Anthony: The Gentlemen's Clubs of London, Bracken Books 1987

Library and Museum of Freemasonry: The Hall in the Garden, 2006

Matthews, D Hugh: Castle Street Meeting House – A History, John Penry 1990

Melling, John Kennedy: Discovering London's Guilds and Liveries, Shire 2003

Miele, Chris: The Supreme Court of the United Kingdom, Merrell 2010

Montefiore, Simon Sebag: Young Stalin, Weidenfeld & Nicholson 2007

Nairn, Ian: Nairn's London, Penguin 1966

Olsen D J: Town Planning in London: The Eighteenth and Nineteenth Centuries, New Haven 1964

Pearce, David: London's Mansions: The Palatial Houses of the Nobility, Batsford 1986

Pevsner N: The Buildings of England: London Volumes 1-6, Yale 1991-2002

Piggott, Jan: Dulwich College: A History 1616-2008, Dulwich College 2008

Port, M H: Imperial London, Yale 1995

Powell, Kenneth: New London Architecture, Merrell, 2001

Powell, Kenneth: New London Architecture 2, Merrell 2007

Riding. C and Riding, R (Ed): The Houses of Parliament: History, Art, Architecture, Merrell 2000

Robinson, John Martin: The Wyatts, Oxford 1979

Scarlet, Iain: A Puff of Smoke, London 1987

Schumann-Bacia, Eva: John Soane and the Bank of England, Longman 1991

Seldon, Anthony: The Foreign Office Harper Collins 2000

Service Alastair: London 1900, Granada 1979

Sion College: A Brief History of the Site and Building, Sion 2000

St Lawrence Whitchurch: St Lawrence Whitchurch, Little Stanmore Pitkin Publishing 2010

Starrett, Vincent: The Private Life of Sherlock Holmes, Macmillan New York 1933

Stow, John: A Survey of London, Chatto & Windus 1876

Summerson John: Georgian London, Barrie & Jenkins 1988

Sykes, Christopher Simon: Private Palaces: Life in the Great London Houses, Chatto & Windus 1985

Trench, Richard and Hillman, Ellis: London Under London: A Subterranean Guide John Murray 1985

The Houses of Parliament: A Guide to the Palace of Westminster, HMSO 1994

Turner, Michael: Eltham Palace, English Heritage 2011

Venables, Sally and Williams, Steve: Still Open: A Guide to Traditional London Shops, Black Dog Publishing 2006

Walford Edward: Old and New London Volumes I-VI, Cassell & Co 1899

Walker, Alan: The Centenary Book of St Jude on the Hill, Alan Walker 2011

Watkin, David: Morality and Architecture Revisited, John Murray 2001

Watson, Nigel: Lloyd's Register: 250 Years of Service, Lloyd's Register 2010

Weinreb Ben & Hibbert Christopher: The London Encyclopaedia, Macmillan 1983

White Jerry: London in the 20th Century, Vintage Books 2008

Worshipful Company of Cutlers: The Worshipful Company of Cutlers, Jarrold 2009

Worshipful Society of Apothecaries: The Worshipful Society of Apothecaries, 1992

Yorke, James: Lancaster House: London's Greatest Town House, Merrell 2001